SECURING SQL SERVER
Protecting Your Database from Attackers

DENNY CHERRY

THOMAS LAROCK, Technical Editor

ELSEVIER

AMSTERDAM • BOSTON • HEIDELBERG • LONDON
NEW YORK • OXFORD • PARIS • SAN DIEGO
SAN FRANCISCO • SINGAPORE • SYDNEY • TOKYO
Syngress is an imprint of Elsevier

Acquiring Editor:	Angelina Ward
Development Editor:	Heather Scherer
Project Manager:	Kirubhagaran Palani
Designer:	Kristen Davis

Syngress is an imprint of Elsevier
30 Corporate Drive, Suite 400, Burlington, MA 01803, USA

Library of Congress Cataloging-in-Publication Data
Cherry, Denny.
Securing SQL server: protecting your database from attackers/Denny Cherry.
   p. cm.
Summary: "There is a lot at stake for administrators taking care of servers, since they house sensitive data like credit cards, social security numbers, medical records, and much more. In Securing SQL Server you will learn about the potential attack vectors that can be used to break into your SQL Server database, and how to protect yourself from these attacks. Written by a Microsoft SQL Server MVP, you will learn how to properly secure your database, from both internal and external threats. Best practices and specific tricks employed by the author will also be revealed. Learn expert techniques to protect your SQL database environment"– Provided by publisher.

Includes bibliographical references and index.
ISBN 978-1-59749-625-4 (pbk.)
1. SQL server. 2. Client/server computing. 3. Database security. 4. Computer security. I. Title.
QA76.73.S67C478 2011
005.8–dc22
2010049453

British Library Cataloguing-in-Publication Data
A catalogue record for this book is available from the British Library.

ISBN: 978-1-59749-625-4

For information on all Syngress publications
visit our website at www.syngress.com

Printed in the United States of America

11 12 13 14   10 9 8 7 6 5 4 3 2 1

SECURING SQL SERVER

Dedication

This book is dedicated to my lovely wife who is gracious enough to allow me to spend every waking moment working on this, and to spend countless nights, weekends and entire weeks traveling in support of the SQL Server community.

Samson wanted something in here about him being really handsome, but I don't think that's going to make it into the final copy.

Oh, and Tim is short, really short, like garden gnome short.

CONTENTS

Acknowledgments

I'd like to thank everyone who was involved in putting this book, my first solo project, together (if I forgot you on this list, sorry). This includes my editors Angelina, and Heather, my friends/coworkers/piers/whatever Thomas, Mark, Aaron, Rod and Sergey who all helped me out greatly in putting this book together.

Author Bio

Denny Cherry has over a decade of experience managing SQL Server, including some of the largest in the world. Denny's areas of technical expertise include system architecture, performance tuning, replication and troubleshooting. Denny currently holds several all the Microsoft Certifications related to SQL Server for versions 2000 through 2008 as well as being a Microsoft MVP. Denny is a longtime member of PASS and Quest Software's Association of SQL Server Experts and has written numerous technical articles on SQL Server management and how SQL Server integrates with Enterprise Storage, in addition to working on several books including this his first solo book project.

INTRODUCTION

As you move through this book you may notice that this book doesn't gently flow from one topic to another like a lot of technical books. This is intentional as many of the subjects covered in this book are going to be related, but separate fields of study. As you move through the various chapters in this book you'll be able to secure a portion of your infrastructure. If you think about each chapter of the book as an independent project that you can take to your management the way that the book is structured may make a little more sense. My goal for this book, is that after reading it you'll have the most secure database that you can have within your environment.

Our book starts from the outside looking in, with the most outside thing that can be controlled being your network design and firewalls. In larger shops this will be outside the realm of the database professional, but in smaller shops there may be a single person who is the developer, DBA, systems administrator.

There are a lot of database encryption options available to the DBA. Usually many, many more than most people realize. As we move through this chapter we'll start by looking at how to encrypt the data within the database itself, then move to having the SQL Server automatically encrypt all the data, having the MPIO driver encrypt all the data, and having the HBA encrypt all the data. Not only will we look at how to do each one, but what the upsides and the downsides of each of these techniques are.

One of the most common problems at smaller database shops are password policies, and using week passwords in production. In Chapter 3 we'll go over using some ways to ensure you are using a strong password, and some best practices to give yourself some extra layers of protection.

In chapter 4 we'll look at securing the instance itself, including minimizing the attack surface, and securing the parts of the database which we have to leave open for client connections.

Chapter 5 is really geared towards the smaller companies who have to have their databases accessible from the public Internet (hopefully if this is you, you'll be going through chapter 1 as well). In this chapter we are going to look at some extra precautions that you can take to protect yourself to make it as hard as possible for someone to break into your database.

In Chapter 6 we are going to look at one of the most common techniques for breaking into a Microsoft SQL Server, the SQL Injection attack. We'll look at why this attack vector is so successful, how to protect yourself, and how to clean up after an attack.

The next chapter is Chapter 7 where we are going to talk about what is probably the least favorite subject of everyone in an Information Technology role, backups. No matter how secure your database is, if your backups aren't secure then nothing is secure.

Probably the next least popular topic is Chapter 8, auditing. You need to know when something is happening within your database, and who is doing it.

In Chapter 9 we look at the various operating system level rights that people within the organization should have.

The appendix at the end of this book is a set of checklists which you can use to help pass your various audits. While they aren't a sure fire way to ensure that you pass your audits, they are a set of bullet points that you can use to work with your auditors to ensure that you can get to passing quickly and easily.

SECURING THE NETWORK

INFORMATION IN THIS CHAPTER

- Securing the Network
- Public IP Addresses versus Private IP Addresses
- Accessing SQL Server from Home
- Physical Security
- Social Engineering
- Finding the Instances
- Testing the Network Security

Securing the Network

You may think that talking about the network is a strange way to start off an SQL Server book, but the network, specifically the perimeter of your network, is the way that external threats will be coming to attack your SQL Server. A poorly defended network will therefore give an attacker an easier time to attack your network than if the network were properly secured. In larger companies the network design and lockdown would be under the control of the network administration and network security departments. However, in smaller companies, you may not have either a network security department or a network administration department. You may not even have a full time database administrator (DBA) or systems administrator. In a typical larger company, developers do not have to worry about the network design and setup as this is handled by the network operations team. However, in smaller companies the software developer may be asked to design or even configure the network along with the web servers or application servers.

No matter your position within the company, it is always a good idea to have a working understanding of the other technologies in play within IT. This will allow for decisions to be made in a more thorough manner by looking at the entire infrastructure instead of examining how the process needs to be completed with just one piece of technology or another.

Network Firewalls

At your network parameter will be your network's firewall. This will probably be a network device in its own right or a software component within your network's main router to the Internet. This firewall is designed to block and allow traffic based on a set of rules that have been loaded into its configuration. Some routers do not have a firewall software package loaded into them. In the case of network devices that don't have a built-in firewall, you'll want to use the Access Control List (ACL) of the device to control what port connections are allowed through the network router. With regard to blocking access through a device, an ACL can be just as effective as a full firewall. However, a full firewall will give you additional protections that the ACL cannot, such as providing you with Distributed Denial of Service (DDoS) protection. DDoS protection is used to keep a network up and running in the event that the network comes under a DDoS attack. A DDoS attack occurs when a group of computers, usually zombie computers owned by unsuspecting people being controlled by a hacker, send large numbers of requests to a specific website or network in an attempt to bring the network offline. DDoS protection is handled by specific network devices that are configured to look for patterns in the network traffic that is coming into the network, and block network traffic from reaching the destination if the network traffic appears to be part of a DDoS attack.

Typically, your firewall would sit between the public Internet and your border router. A border router is the device that sits at the edge, or border, of a network between the company's network and the Internet Service Providers (ISP) network. This allows the firewall to protect not only the internal network from the Internet, but also the border router from the Internet. A typical network diagram is shown in Figure 1.1 and will be the network design that is referenced throughout this chapter. In this sample network design, the Internet cloud is shown in the upper left. Connected to that is the firewall device that protects the network. Connected to the firewall is the network router that allows network traffic to flow from the public network, which uses an IP Address network range of 204.245.12.1-204.245.12.254, to the internal network, which uses an IP Address network range of 192.168.0.1-192.168.0. 254. Because the firewall sits on the front side of the network, you'll be granting access through the firewall to the public IP Addresses that your company was issued, in this case 204.245.12.0. If you placed the router on the internal side, then you would grant rights to the internal 192.168.0.1 network.

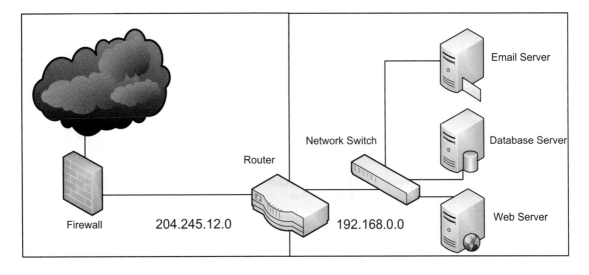

Figure 1.1 Basic network diagram.

When you first fire up the hardware firewall, typically all access through the firewall is allowed. It is up to you to shut down the network access that you want blocked. In a typical network firewall the configuration will be written into a file, although some newer devices may present you with a web interface that you can use to configure them. In either case, the configuration of the network firewall will be read line by line from the configuration and processed in that order, opening and closing ports in the firewall. Like access to objects within an SQL Server, the firewall is configured via a series of GRANTs and DENYs. While in SQL Server DENY always overrides a GRANT, typically within a firewall you will want to instruct the firewall to close all ports and then open only the needed ports (keeping in mind that every network administrator has a different technique for writing firewall rule sets).

Typically the first line that you would see in your configuration of your firewall or ACL would be similar to "extended permit ip any any." This would then grant all access from all networks, in this case the public Internet, to the 204.245.12.0 network no matter what TCP port was used. We would then want to follow this with a line similar to "permit tcp 204.245.12.0 255.255.255.0 any." This line then allows all computers within our public IP space access to everything on the public Internet on any TCP network port. You can see these firewall rules from a sample configuration file in the following sample code.

```
access-list Firewall line 56 extended permit tcp any 204.245.12.
    17 255.255.255.0 eq www
access-list Firewall line 64 extended permit tcp any 204.245.12.
    17 255.255.255.0 eq https
access-list Firewall line 72 extended permit tcp any host 204.
    245.12.18 eq smtp
access-list Firewall line 74 extended permit tcp any host 204.
    245.12.18 eq pop3
access-list Firewall line 74 extended permit tcp any host 204.
    245.12.20 eq 1433
access-list Firewall line 104 extended deny ip any any
```

Example 1.1: Sample firewall rules allowing access from the Internet to various ports on various servers.

When a user or a server accesses the Internet, the firewall will see them as coming from an IP Address on the 204.245.12.0 network. This is because the router will use Network Address Translation (NAT) so that the computers on your internal network can use private IPs to access the public Internet. Because of this NAT setup, all the computers that access the network will usually report as coming from the same public IP Address. You can verify this by using several computers in your network and browsing to the website www.whatismyip.com. All the computers in your office will more than likely report back the same public IP Address.

FAQ
Network Address Translation

NAT is a very important concept in Networking. NAT is used to allow mapping from a public IP Address to a private IP Address so that the computers do not need to have a public IP Address.

NAT is often used with Network Masquerading (also known as IP Masquerading). Network Masquerading is where a series of computers accesses the public network from a single public IP Address. Communications are established from the private IP Network to the public Internet and are controlled via a stateful translation table as the network packets flow through the router that is performing the Network Masquerading. This allows the router to ensure that the proper network packets are sent to the connect private IP Address. Because of the stateful translation table, any communication requests that originate from the public network side would be rejected by the router as the router would have no way of knowing which private IP Address the network traffic should be sent to.

From a proper naming point of view, NAT and Network Masquerading are two totally separate concepts. However, from a normal conversation point of view and for practical purposes, they are both referred to as Network Address Translation, or NAT.

Now that the router is configured to block everyone on the Internet from accessing the public IP Addresses, the next step is to allow our customers to access our web server so that they can access our website and purchase the product that is being offered. In order to do this, a decision needs to be made as to which network topology design will be used. The three most common topology design options are: (1) web server on the public internet network, (2) web server on the internal side of the network, and (3) web server in the Demilitarized Zone.

Web Server on the Public Internet Network

You can connect the web server to a network switch between the firewall and the router, and then configure the server with a public IP Address, as shown in Figure 1.2.

Web Server on the Internal side of the Network

You can connect the web server to the network switch on the internal side of the network and configure NAT to allow people to connect to a public IP Address and have the router send that traffic to the internal IP Address of the web server, as shown in Figure 1.1. By comparing Figure 1.1 and Figure 1.2 you can see that the web server has been moved from the outside network to the internal network.

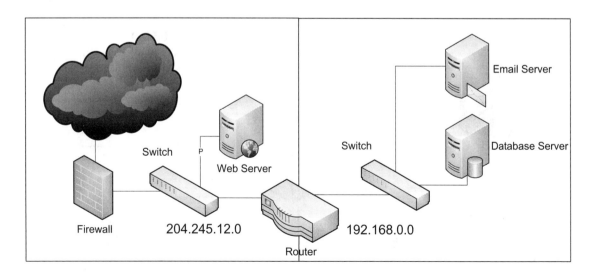

Figure 1.2 Network diagram with web server on the public Internet network.

Web Server in the Demilitarized Zone

You can create a DMZ (Demilitarized Zone) network that will contain the web server in a separate network from your internal network and that is separate from your public network, and then use NAT to allow Internet users to access the server within the DMZ network as shown in Figure 1.3.

No matter which of these three network designs you use, the users from the Internet will access your public website via a public IP Address. In this example the IP Address 204.245.12.2 will be used as the public IP Address of the web server. If you were to use option #1 shown above, you would simply enter this Network Address into the Windows Network Control panel (or if you were using Linux or Unix the appropriate file for your specific distribution, typically /etc/network/interfaces or something similar). If you were to use option #2, you would use an IP Address from the 192.168.0.0 network for the web server, then configure the NAT on the router to redirect traffic from the 204.245.12.2 public IP Address to the private IP Address that you chose. If you were to use option #3, you would use an IP Address from the 192.168.2.0 subnet for the web server, then configure NAT on the router to direct traffic from the 204.245.12.2 IP Address to the correct 192.168.2.0 subnet.

After you have selected the network design to use you will need to configure the firewall to allow access to the web server. You will want to restrict the ports that the firewall allows access through to just the specific ports that are used by a web server,

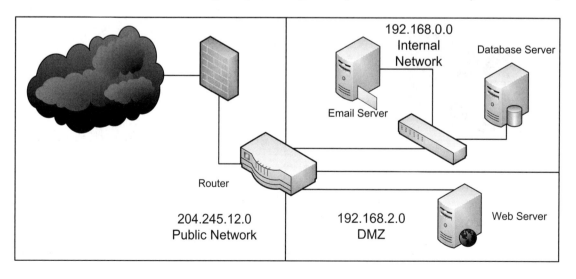

Figure 1.3 Network diagram with a Demilitarized Zone (DMZ) for customer facing websites.

Table 1.1 The IP Addresses Used in the Three Network Design Options

	Public IP Address	Private IP Address	Computer's IP Address
Web server on the public Internet network	204.245.12.2	None	204.245.12.2
Web server on the internal side of the network	204.245.12.2	192.168.0.2	192.168.0.2
Web server in the Demilitarized Zone	204.245.12.2	192.168.2.2	192.168.2.2

in this case ports 80 for normal HTTP traffic, and port 443 for encrypted HTTPS traffic. This would be done by using a line similar to "permit tcp any host 204.245.12.2 eq www". This line tells the firewall to allow traffic on ports 80 from any Internet IP Address to 204.245.12.2. The IP addresses shown in the examples in this chapter are shown in Table 1.1.

If you didn't block the network traffic, then anyone on the public Internet would have access to all the TCP ports on the server. This includes the web server, but also the file shares if this is a Windows server, the database if there is a database installed on the server, and any other software that is running on the server. Attackers would exploit a configuration such as this and attempt to break into the server by attacking known weaknesses in those services. These weaknesses could include known bugs in the Windows File Share protocol, or a brute force attack against the database server. Once the attackers had broken into the server, they could install just about any software that they wished to on the server, capturing your customer information, configuring your web server to install malware on your customers' computers, install software to turn your server into a zombie bot, have it send out SPAM or launch a DDoS attack against another website, and so on.

Server Firewalls

In addition to the network firewalls described within this chapter, the firewall on the Windows Operating System should also be enabled and configured to allow just the needed network connections. By installing and configuring the Windows firewall to block all unexpected network connections, if any unauthorized software is installed on the server that software won't be able to be contacted. Ideally, any outbound network connections that aren't expected should also be blocked so that any software installed can't phone home. While legitimate software phoning home isn't necessarily a problem, unauthorized software shouldn't be allowed to phone home as it may be passing confidential data to the controller or the server may be part of a bot-net.

FAQ
Phoning Home

Phoning home is a phrase that is used to describe when an application makes network requests back to the person or company that has created the software. Both legitimate and illegitimate software can be configured to phone home, and sometimes for legitimate reasons. Legitimate software such as Windows will phone home in order to check for updates or to upload crash information looking for updates that could fix the problem.

Illegitimate software will usually try and phone home often, especially if the application is designed to be part of a bot-net. It would need to contact a computer under the control of the person who controls the bot-net. Once the application has made contact to the control computer, it would be able to receive commands to do anything that the bot-net operator wanted, including capturing data and uploading it to the bot-net operator.

Windows Firewall Inbound Rules

The most secure Windows firewall configuration option is to allow the needed inbound network connections such as TCP (Transmission Control Protocal) connections to the SQL (Structured Query Language) Server, UDP (User Datagram Protocol) connections to the SQL Server Browser, and SMB (Server Message Block) connections to the server's network file shares. Most SQL Servers wouldn't be running any other network software that would need to be contacted from outside the SQL Server's Windows Operating System. It is also usually a good idea to allow ICMP (Internet Control Message Protocol) packets through the firewall so that things like ping will work against the server, as this is a good way to see if the server has completed rebooting.

Windows Firewall Outbound Rules

A few outbound firewall rules must be in place for the operating system that is running the SQL Server to function correctly. These include:

- DNS lookups to Active Directory DNS servers
- Full access to Active Directory domain controllers (Not all port access is needed, but Active Directory requires a wide range of ports to be opened depending on the services running on each domain controller. These ports are specified in Table 1.2.)
- Web access to the server running WSUS (Windows Server Update Service) or other patching servers
- Network access to storage array if needed
- Network file share access to company file servers (for installing software)
- Access to other database servers on the company network as needed

Not all the ports shown in Table 1.2 will need to be allowed from every SQL Server to every domain controller. The ports that do need to be opened will depend on the domain configuration and the roles that the SQL Server will be performing. For example, if an SQL Server is also functioning as a domain controller (which is not recommended), then more ports will

Table 1.2 The TCP and UDP Ports Used for Active Directory Authentication

Application	Protocol	Port Range
Active Directory 2003 and below	TCP	1025–5000
Active Directory 2008 and up	TCP	49152–65535
Active Directory with 2003 and 2008 domain controllers	TCP	1025–5000 and 49152–65535
LDAP	TCP and UDP	389
LDAP (SSL)	TCP	636
Global Catalog	TCP	3268
Kerberos	TCP and UDP	88
DNS	TCP and UDP	53
SMB over IP	TCP	445
WINS	UDP	137
WINS Replication	TCP and UDP	42
DHCP	UDP	67
SMB Network Shares	TCP	445
Active Directory Web Services	TCP	9389

need to be opened in order to allow for Active Directory replication and authentication.

Direct Internet Access

One of the most common database server configuration mistakes, usually made by small companies and sometimes by larger companies as well, is to make the SQL Server available on the public Internet. While people set up their SQL Server in this configuration for a number of reasons, the most common reason, especially with smaller companies, is to make access from home when troubleshooting easier.

Tip
Easy isn't best...

When it comes to security, especially network security, the mantra that I firmly believe in, is that if it is easy, it probably isn't secure.

When you have a computer connected directly to the public Internet, the computer is left open to attack. There are numerous bots scanning the public Internet looking for unprotected computers that can be broken into. These bots look for unprotected services such as Microsoft SQL Server. The reason for this is that services such as Microsoft SQL Server have an inherent weakness; there is an account that is always running on the SQL Server and is available for use on nearly all SQL Servers out there. That is the systems administrator (sa) account. The database administrator uses the sa account as a way to log into the SQL Server in the event that the Windows Domain Authentication isn't available for some reason. The sa account is also used internally by the SQL Server Service. The username is always the same, it always has full rights to everything on the database, and it can turn features of the database on and off, if you know how to do it. And most passwords on the database servers that can be accessed from the Internet have passwords that can be guessed fairly easily, especially if the version of SQL Server is SQL Server 2000 or older as those versions used a blank password by default for the sa account.

Simple Decisions, Turn into Major Problems

This brings me back to a forum post that I posted answers on a while back. A company's SQL Server was connected directly to the Internet, and the SQL port was wide open to the world on the public Internet. The forum post was made because the poster was complaining that people kept trying to break into the SQL Server instance.

The first option that people threw out was to close the SQL Port. The poster didn't like this answer because the application that the poster had written needed direct access to the SQL Server. At this point a variety of options were given to the poster such as to convert the direct SQL Access to using web methods, setting some sort of authentication process in place that would open the firewall when someone was using the application. The poster didn't like any of these options because it would cause a new version to have to be written.

Unfortunately for this forum poster, and many other people like him, there is no good solution to his problem without making application changes. Because of poor application design decisions that were made far in the past, the database server was required to be left wide open to the public, allowing attackers to attempt to break into the application's database with no way to correct this configuration without a major application redesign.

The best practice is to not install the SQL Server on a server that is directly accessible from the Internet. If, however, you need to install the SQL Server on the same computer (and there are some valid reasons for doing so), then the best practice is to not allow any direct access to the SQL Server ports from the Internet. If you have to allow direct access from the Internet to the SQL Server's TCP port, then only do so from the smallest set of network connections possible. In other words, don't allow all of the IP Addresses in the world to connect; instead restrict access to the TCP port so that only the static IP from your office has access. Then if you need to manage the SQL Server, connect to a machine in your office over remote desktop (preferably after using a Virtual Private Network (VPN) to connect to your office so that the office's computers aren't available directly on the public Internet) and then connect to the SQL Server from the machine at your office.

Some applications are configured to connect directly to the database from the user's home computer. These are the toughest situations to deal with, as increasing security will require that your users upgrade your software, which some may not want to do. However, this is one case where it is in your best interest to force the issue and require that they upgrade. It is also in their best interest that they upgrade because as long as the SQL Server's port is publicly available their data is the data at risk.

If your application currently requires that your Microsoft SQL Server be on the public Internet, a major architecture change will be needed. You will need to turn your software package from a two-tier application (the software installed on their computer is one tier, and the SQL Server is the second) to a three-tier application, with the third tier being a web server that they will connect to and issue commands against. That web server will then connect to the database and run the actual database query. This is done by building web methods that are placed on the web server and that the client can then connect to over HTTP or HTTPS; for security purposes HTTPS would be the better option. HTTPS would be a better option than HTTP for this because the HTTPS connection would be encrypted, which would prevent a third party from being able to use a network monitoring application to view the data being sent from the client application to the web server.

Although these rules will make the management of the SQL Server a little more complex, the database will be much, much more secure, and the more secure that your database is, the lower the chance that your database will be compromised or lost.

Public IP Addresses versus Private IP Addresses

All IPs are not created equal: Some are routable on the public Internet, and some are not. The IP Addresses that are available for use on the public Internet are issued by Internet Corporate for Assigned Names and Numbers (ICANN), which has strict rules for how many can be used, based on the requirements of the person requesting the IPs. When requesting IP Addresses from your network provider, you have to justify the number of IP Addresses that you are requesting. The typical requirement is that 50% of the IP Addresses need to be in use within 6 months, and 80% of the IP Addresses need to be in use within 12 months. This policy is designed to prevent companies and network providers from requesting much larger blocks than are actually needed, as well as to prevent the available number of IP Addresses from being depleted. Private IPs, such as the 192.168.0.0, subnet can be used any way for any device, as long as those devices are not directly connected to the Internet. All routers on the Internet know to ignore network requests from these private IPs. A list of all the private IP Address subnets is shown in Table 1.3 later in this chapter.

Depending on the size of your internal network, you have a few ranges of IP Addresses to select from, as you can see in

Note
ICANN

ICANN is a private nonprofit company that was established in 1988 for the purpose of managing the root DNS servers and issuing IP Addresses to companies that request them. While ICANN doesn't manage specific DNS servers, the worldwide DNS infrastructure, or the domain registrars that are used to register websites, they do provide an accreditation system for domain registrars, and ICANN draws up contracts for the registrars that run the Internet's root DNS servers.

With regard to IP Addresses, ICANN serves as the authoritative source for IP Addresses. Because IP Addresses cannot be duplicated on the Internet, a single source needs to be in charge of assigning IP Addresses, or network traffic will not be routed properly. ICANN doesn't issue IP Addresses directly to companies or network providers. There are regional IP Address registries to which ICANN issues large blocks of public IP Addresses, and these regional registries then issue the IP Addresses to requesting companies and network providers.

Normally a company would not need to contact ICANN or a regional registry directly to request IP Addresses. Typically a company would receive the public IP Addresses that they needed from their ISP (Internet Service Provider) who would receive them from their ISP, unless the company's ISP was a large enough ISP to request them directly from ICANN's regional registries.

Table 1.3. You can use part of these ranges for your internal network, or the entire range, depending on how many devices will be on your network. In order for a machine with a private IP Address to access the Internet, you have to put a NAT router between the private IP network and the public Internet. This allows the machines with the private IPs to access the Internet via the configured public IP on the router.

Table 1.3 Private IP Address Ranges

IPv4 Subnet	Number of IP Addresses Available	Network Size	Subnet Mask
192.168.0.0-192.168.255.255	65,536	192.168.0.0/16	255.255.0.0
172.16.0.0-172.31.255.255	1,048,576	172.16.0.0/12	255.240.0.0
10.0.0.0-10.255.255.255	16,777,216	10.0.0.0/8	255.0.0.0

Note
Choose Carefully

When selecting the private IP subnet range to use for your network, it is important to plan ahead. While it isn't impossible to change the network subnet that is being used from a smaller 192.168.0.0 network to a larger 10.0.0.0 network, it isn't an easy change to make. If there is a chance that you'll need a larger network, then start with a larger network.

Although it is easy enough to put a router between a network that is 192.168.0.0 and a network that is 10.0.0.0, which would allow you to extend a network, this would require additional routers to be purchased to go between these networks. A much easier solution would be to select a large enough network from the beginning.

Now the 192.168.0.0 network size looks at first glance as if it would be a very large network. After all, the 192.168.0.0 private IP subnet allows for over 65,000 IP Addresses, which is quite a few. But there are lots of devices on today's networks, not just the workstations. Any virtual machines need IP Addresses, all the servers need IP Addresses, all the networking devices need IP Addresses, and any network attached printers need IP Addresses. If the company has a wireless network, any device that connects will need an IP Address. If there is a VPN connection to allow users to connect from home, IP Addresses will be needed for those devices as well. A company that has 100 employees can quickly need 500 or more IP Addresses to get all the devices on the company network.

When configuring your SQL Server, or any server on your network, you'll want to assign a private IP Address to the machine and then use NAT to map a public IP Address to the private IP Address. This NAT technique, combined with the firewalling techniques above, will keep your internal servers secure as only the needed services will be exposed to the public Internet.

FAQ
Public IPs for Everyone?

A common question that is asked is, "If you are going to firewall off everything on the network from the public Internet anyway, why not simply use a public IP for every computer on the network?" The first reason not to is that only a limited number of IP Addresses are available. The current IP addressing schema that is used (and shown in Table 1.3) is the fourth version of the IP addressing standard and is called IPv4. IPv4 has approximately 4.3 billion IP Addresses available in it (including the private IP Addresses shown above). As more and more devices become Internet connected and more and more people began using the Internet, the demand for these public IP Addresses started to increase immensely. The first solution was to assign the IP Addresses that are shown in Table 1.3 as private IP Addresses, which slowed the use of public IP Addresses. However, as IP Addresses are still being issued, eventually they will run out. When we will run out depends on who you ask, with estimates ranging from 2011 through 2020. Because of this

FAQ—*Cont'd*

shortage, the IPv6 protocol has been released, and many ISPs are now beginning to support IPv6 IP Addresses. However, the uptake of IPv6 has been very slow to proceed as a global network configuration change such as moving from IPv4 to IPv6 takes a very long time to complete and billions of dollars to implement.

Due to the slow implementation of IPv6 across the Internet, some ISPs and their customers have begun supporting both IPv4 and IPv6. This way when new Internet users begin being put onto the public Internet using only IPv6 IP Addresses, these customers will still be able to access the company websites without the traffic having to be routed through an IPv6 to IPv4 NAT. This dual support is being done on a case-by-case basis at each company's discretion. However, for new implementations it would be recommended to support both IPv4 and IPv6 at the network interface to the ISP.

Accessing SQL Server from Home

The most common reason for not following the advice laid out in this chapter is to make it easier for the database administrator or developer to connect to the SQL Server remotely, so that problems can be addressed as quickly and easily as possible. Being able to respond to issues quickly is an admirable goal; however, keep in mind that if you can connect to the SQL Server from anywhere, then so can someone who isn't supposed to be able to.

The only secure way to connect from outside a network to inside the network is to use a Virtual Private Network (VPN) connection. This allows you to create a secure encrypted tunnel between your home computer to your office or data center. Your home computer is then issued an IP Address on the office network, and you are able to communicate with the office computers over the secured link instead of connecting to the machines directly over the public Internet. Even if you have multiple offices or an office and a data center, you can configure your network so that you can connect to one location and then access the other sites over secure connections between your facilities.

The office-to-office or office-to-data center connections are usually made in the same way, with a persistent site-to-site VPN connection. This site-to-site VPN connection is very similar to the one that you use from your home computer to the office, except that it is a persistent, always on connection that connects as soon as the devices on both sides of the VPN connection are booted up. This allows you to easily and cheaply expand your network across multiple sites without the expense of purchasing a dedicated

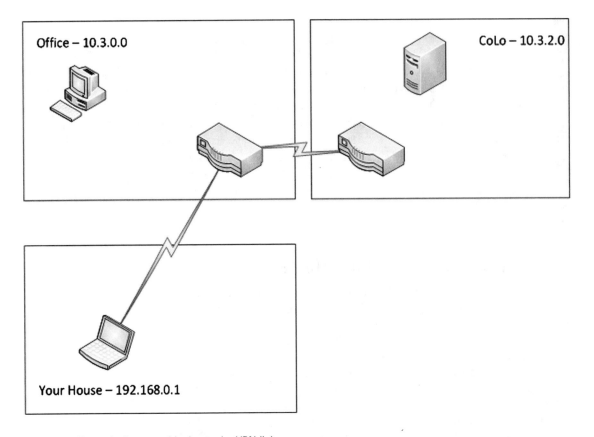

Figure 1.4 Network diagram with site-to-site VPN links.

network line between the sites. This network connection design may be better explained with the diagram shown in Figure 1.4.

Figure 1.4 shows two facilities: the office that uses the subnet 10.3.0.0, and the CoLo that has our servers in it, which uses the subnet 10.3.2.0. Our house uses the default IP range, which our home router uses and is probably 192.168.0.1. There is then a site-to-site VPN connection between the routers at the CoLo and the office that allows those two networks to talk to each other securely. When a connection is needed to an office computer, or a server located at the CoLo, you can simply VPN (Virtual Private Network) into the office network. This VPN connection effectively puts the remote machine on the office network. From the office network, the network routers allow access to the office machines and the servers at the CoLo over a secure, encrypted connection. This secure VPN connection allows users to quickly and easily manage the servers in their environment without exposing the

FAQ
What is Better, Site-to-Site VPNs or Leased Lines?

As the amount of network traffic increases between sites, a site-to-site VPN may no longer provide an acceptable level of performance. This performance dropoff is explained by the CPU (Central Processing Unit) load that the increased network traffic would place on the CPU of the routers that maintain the VPN connection. Eventually the cost of purchasing larger and more expensive routers will increase beyond the cost of a leased line between the sites. There are no hard set numbers as to when the change from a site-to-site VPN to a leased line should be made. This is because network connection costs vary from city to city (often from street to street within the same city) and router costs change depending on your company's purchasing power.

servers to the public Internet, allowing the user not only to manage the servers, but to manage them safely.

Physical Security

So far we have focused on threats that come in over the Internet or that are coming from users within the network. There is, however, a more serious threat that is fortunately less likely to be exploited. This threat is a physical breach within the data center. A physical breach can actually take a couple of different forms.

1. An unauthorized person gets into the data center and is able to physically access servers.
2. An unauthorized person gets into the office, and connects his or her own computer to an open network port or company WiFi accessing company resources over the company network.
3. An unauthorized person gets into the office and uses an employees workstation or laptop that was left unattended, allowing them access to whatever resources the employee's login grants them.

Keep Your Hands Off My Box

An unauthorized person getting into the data center and accessing company servers is pretty much the worst case scenario. If a server is left with the console logged in for some reason, this person would have access to whatever rights the account that was logged in would have. What makes this even worse is that the server is probably logged in as a domain administrator. The unauthorized person could easily enough plug a USB (Universal Serial Bus) drive into the server, which would by default launch whatever is in the autoexec.ini file on the thumb drive. A smart intruder would configure a data-logging application that would then spread itself to all the servers and workstations within the company network.

Due to the danger of unauthorized people in the data center, server room, network closet, or the like, the room's physical security should be given special treatment. All doors to the data center should be locked at all times, with access given only to those people who require access to the room and the physical servers. If the servers are left sitting out, then anyone who makes his or her way into the office has access to them.

When securing the data center, it is important to remember to include the cleaning crew, upper management, human resources, and building security on the list of people that do not normally need access to the room. The cleaning crew is probably the most important to keep removed from that list. While getting hired as a company's systems administrator can be quite difficult, getting hired as a cleaning person is quite a bit easier. Cleaning is usually outsourced to another company that probably doesn't have the tightest hiring practices. This is usually the weakest point in a company's security against a potential attacker. The cleaning crew is a great way into a building: They are there all night, they are typically alone, and they generally have keys to every room and office within the company.

Open Network Ports

Having unused network ports at desks connected to network switches sounds like a pretty basic thing. It makes it much more convenient when you need to move a new computer to a new desk. However, because these network ports at the desks are connected to a switch, if DHCP (Dynamic Host Configuration Protocol) is enabled on the network (which it probably is), then if someone were to make his or her way into the office and connect a laptop to the port, the stranger suddenly would have the ability to scan the network looking for SQL Servers (or other servers) that can be broken into.

Keeping the desk ports connected to the network switches isn't necessarily a problem, provided that the ports on the network switch have been disabled. Switch ports can be disabled on any managed switch such as a Cisco Catalyst, Foundry, or Juniper switch among others. Unmanaged network switches, such as lower end switches, do not support this functionality. Keeping the network ports disabled on the network switch has the same net effect as unplugging the network cables. The upside of keeping the desk ports connected and having the ports disabled on the network switch is that a systems administrator or network administrator can enable the port from anywhere, as long as the ports are well documented, so that new ports can be quickly and easily enabled.

Unlocked Workstations

When users leave their desks, they should always lock their workstations. Employees who have been at the company for a while are probably used to locking their workstations when they step away from them. However, younger or newer employees may not be aware that this should be done for both the company's and their own security.

On the side of the company's security, if an unauthorized person were to sit at an employee's desk, he or she would have access to all the company resources to which that employee has access. This includes the employee's e-mail, chat programs, customer service applications, sales systems, and reports. Whatever company data the intruder accessed there would be in no way identify what was accessed by the employee and what was accessed by the intruder, for all the access would be done under the name of a valid employee account.

With regard to the employee's personal security, if an unauthorized person were to sit at the employee's desk, he or she would have access to all the personal websites on which the employee has saved his or her password. This includes bank websites, iTunes, Zune Pass, forums, and so on—not to mention that if an unauthorized person were to access company data that the employee was not authorized to view, it could end up costing the employee his or her job.

Automatically Locking Computers

One of the most common domain settings to set is to have all employee computers lock automatically when the computer screen is idle. When computers are within a Windows Active Directory domain, this setting can be controlled through a group policy setting. This setting can be found by editing the group policy setting and navigating to:
1. User Configuration
2. Administrative Templates
3. Control Panel
4. Display
Within the Display folder there are four settings that are of interest. These policies affect all computers that are running

Windows 2000 Service Pack 1 and higher, including both the server and client versions of the operating system.

1. Screen Saver
2. Screen Saver executable name
3. Password protect the Screen Saver
4. Screen Saver timeout

The "Screen Saver" setting controls whether the screen saver is enabled or disabled. When this policy setting is set to "Not Configured," the user logged in can decide whether or not the screen saver is enabled. When this setting is Enabled, the screen saver will always be enabled. When this setting is disabled, the screen saver will always be disabled.

The "Screen Saver executable name" setting sets the name of the screen saver that will be used. When this policy setting is set to "Not Configured," the user can select which screen saver to use. When this setting is enabled and the "Screen Saver executable name" is set to a valid screen saver, that screen saver will be used on the user's desktop, and the user will not be able to change the setting. When this setting is disabled, the user can select any screen saver. If the screen saver that is specified does not exist, then the setting is ignored and the user can select any screen saver. If the "Screen Saver" setting is disabled, then the "Screen Saver executable name" is disabled.

The "Password protect the Screen Saver" setting determines whether the screen saver requires a password to disable it. When the setting is set to "Not Configured," the user can select if the screen saver should be password protected. When the setting is "Enabled," then the screen saver will always require a password to turn the screen saver off. When the setting is "Disabled," then the screen saver will never require a password to turn the screen saver off.

The "Screen Saver timeout" setting determines how long the computer will wait before activating the screen saver. When this setting is set to "Not Configured," the user can configure the timeout. When this setting is set to "Enabled," a number of seconds is specified, from 1 second to 86,400 seconds (24 hours). If the setting is set to 0 seconds, then the screen saver will never be started. When the setting is "Disabled," it has the same effect as being set to "Not Configured." This setting is ignored if the "Screen Saver" setting is disabled, or if the screen saver specified in the "Screen Saver executable name" setting is not a valid screen saver on the computer.

If all four settings are configured, there is another setting that can be of interest, which is located within the same folder. This is the "Hide Screen Saver tab." When this setting is set to "Enabled," the Screen Saver tab will not be shown within the Display control panel icon. When the setting is set to "Not Configured" or "Disabled," then the tab will be shown as normal.

Social Engineering

Social engineering is a way for an attacker to gain access to a company network or computer by getting a current employee to give the access. This is typically done by calling a user and pretending to be a help desk employee. Once the employee believes the attacker is an employee, the attacker asks for the employee's username and password to "fix" something. The attacker may also ask for other items to obtain more information about the internal network such as the VPN site, webmail server, internal application, and server names. Once attackers are able to get into the network using the employee's information, they are probably done with the employee; however, they may move up to the supervisor to get more information.

Story Time
The Most Famous Social Engineer of All Time

The most famous Social Engineer of all time would probably have to be Kevin Mitnick. Kevin first used social engineering at the age of 12 when he got a bus driver to tell him where to get a bus transfer punch that would allow him to ride the Los Angeles city bus system for free. Throughout Kevin's criminal escapades he often used social engineering to get usernames and passwords, as well as modem phone numbers for corporate systems (today he would ask for the VPN server name instead).

By getting people's usernames, passwords, and phone numbers, it is confirmed that Kevin broke into DEC's (Digital Equipment Corporation) computer systems to view the VMS (Virtual Memory System) source code as well as gaining full administrative rights to an IBM minicomputer at the Computer Learning Center (CLC) in Los Angeles. The purpose of break-in to the minicomputer at the CLC in Los Angeles was probably the most interesting case as it was to win a bet. Kevin is also known to have broken into Motorola, NEC, Nokia, Sun Microsystems, and Fujitsu Siemens computer systems.

In addition to these confirmed acts, Kevin is rumored to have stolen computer manuals from the Pacific Bell telephone switching center in Los Angeles, reading the e-mail of computer security personal at MCI and Digital; wiretapped the California State Department of Motor Vehicles (DMV); and hacked into Santa Cruz Operation (SCO), Pacific Bell, the FBI, the Pentagon, Novell, the University of Southern California, and the Los Angeles Unified School District (LAUSD).

Kevin has served five years in prison, four and half years during pretrial confinement, and eight months of solitary confinement postconviction. Kevin claims that the solitary confinement was imposed because law enforcement was able to convince a judge that he would be able to "start a nuclear war by whistling into a pay phone." During his parole Kevin was prohibited to access the Internet or to use any other communications technology other than a landline telephone.

Two books have been written specifically about Kevin Mitnick's case: John Markoff and Tsutomu Shimomura's *Takedown*, and Jonathan Littman's *The Fugitive Game*. In 2000, the movie *Takedown*, which was based on the book of that title was released. A documentary titled *Freedom Downtime* was a fan-based documentary created in response to the big-budget documentary *Takedown*.

Finding the Instances

Before you secure Microsoft SQL Server instances, the trick may be to find all the servers. This can be done in a few different ways. The simplest way is to query the network for all responding Microsoft SQL Servers. This is most easily done using the osql command line application (when using SQL Server 2000 or older) or the sqlcmd command line application (when using SQL Server 2005 or newer). With either application, using the −L switch will query the local network for available SQL Server instances as shown in Example 1.2. This technique will send out a broadcast request to all the servers on the local network. All the machines with the SQL Server service browser running will respond with all the installed instances on the machine, as long as those instances have not been configured to be hidden. More information on hiding the instances is presented in Chapter 2 within the section "Encrypting Data on the Wire."

```
sqlcmd -L
```

Example 1.2: Using the sqlcmd application to query the network for available SQL Server instances.

Using Windows PowerShell, the network can also be queried for all the available instances. The PowerShell example shown in Example 1.3 uses the same technique as the sqlcmd example shown in Example 1.2, as well as the SQL Server Management Studio connection dialog.

```
[System.Data.Sql.SqlDataSourceEnumerator]::Instance.
   GetDataSources()
```

Example 1.3: PowerShell command to query for instances using the .NET API call to query for SQL Server Instances.

Note
These Lists Won't Always be Accurate

When using sqlcmd with the −L switch shown in Example 1.2 or the PowerShell example shown in Example 1.3, the lists can be incomplete for a number of reasons. Among the reasons are the following: the instance is set as hidden; the firewall is blocking access to the instance; the instance is not listening on port 1433; the instance is a named instance and the SQL Browser service is not running; the network does not pass the broadcast request to the SQL Server if the SQL Server is hosted on a different subnet; the person requesting the list does not have access to the SQL Instance; or the SQL Server's OS.

Another technique that can be used involves using Server Management Objects (SMOs). The SMO can be easily used through Windows PowerShell as shown in Example 1.4. The downside to using SMO is that like the code shown in Example 1.2 and Example 1.3, the services will be shown only if the services are not marked as hidden and if the SQL Browser service is running.

```
[System.Reflection.Assembly]::LoadWithPartialName
  ("Microsoft.SqlServer.Smo") | out-null
[Microsoft.SqlServer.Management.Smo.SmoApplication]::
  EnumAvailableSqlServers() | ft
```

Example 1.4: Using SMOs (Server Management Objects) to list available SQL Servers.

The PowerShell code shown in Examples 1.2, 1.3, and 1.4 rely on the .NET framework or SMO in order to query for the available SQL Servers. As these code samples use the "proper methods" for finding the services, services that are hidden, or if the SQL Browser is disabled on the server (as the SQL browser is what does the responding), are not returned by these commands. The PowerShell code shown in Example 1.5, on the other hand, connects to Active Directory and downloads a list of all computers on the domain, and then it queries each of those computers, one by one, looking for any services that are named using the Microsoft SQL Server database engine naming standard. The sample code in Example 1.5 searches for both named and default instances within a single command.

```
$objDomain = New-Object System.DirectoryServices.
  DirectoryEntry
$objSearcher = New-Object System.DirectoryServices.
  DirectorySearcher
$objSearcher.SearchRoot = $objDomain
$objSearcher.Filter = ("computer")
$objSearcher.PropertiesToLoad.Add("name")
$Computers = $objSearcher.FindAll()
foreach ($machine_name in $Computers | sort computername)
{
  $sql_servers = get-wmiobject -class win32_service -computer
  $machine_name
  $sql_servers | where { $_.name -like 'MSSQL$' -or $_.name -eq
  'MSSQLSERVER'} | select name
}
```

Example 1.5: Using Windows PowerShell to query WMI (Windows Management Instrumentation) on each computer within a Windows Active Directory domain to see if those computers have any SQL Server Services installed.

The catch with the code shown in Example 1.5 is that it requires that the user running the code be a local administrator on each machine within the domain (typically this will require being a member of the "Domain Admins" Windows domain group). This elevated right is required as querying the list of services from a remote computer requires an elevated permission set. This sample code, however, will be the most accurate as the OS is being queried for a list of services, instead of asking the SQL Browser what services it is configured to tell you exist. If you wish to search for SQL Server Reporting Services instances, the Windows PowerShell code shown in Example 1.5 can be modified to search for the Reporting Services name by adding another "or" to the where clause.

Testing the Network Security

Once the network has been secured, it is time to begin testing the network security. There are a few different ways that it can be tested. The first is the easiest and cheapest: Have an employee go home and attempt to break into the network or the servers using a known username and password (such as her own, or one that was set up specifically for this testing) and have her see how much damage she can do. This employee should attempt to break into web servers, routers, and anything else that is Internet facing using brute force password attacks. This includes attacking the company's VPN server to ensure that its security is strong enough, as the VPN system in an inherent weak point because VPN servers are designed to allow users full access to the network.

Once the systems and the network have been configured to resist this first round of testing, it's time to pay for some testing.

A variety of companies will perform network attacks against a company's network. The number of tests and the type of tests performed by each of the testing companies will vary based on the strengths of the testing company's programmers.

By running automated penetration testing against the company network on a regular basis, the company and its customers can be sure that the data the company stores within its databases is secure from outside attack. Many of the automated penetration testing companies will provide a logo that can be placed on the company website showing when the last test was completed without a successful attack so that the company's customers are able to see just how secure and up-to-date the testing is.

These penetration testing companies will check a variety of things from the front end, including attempting an SQL Injection attack against the web forms, seeing that the strongest level of encryption is being used, and ensuring that services that shouldn't be available from the Internet are not available (such as Windows file shares, SQL Servers, Oracle, MySQL, LDAP, etc.).

There are a wide variety of penetration tests that can be performed. Different testing companies will call these tests different things, but the basic idea is the same no matter the name.

Testing against an outside attack from an unknown attacker can be done with a black box test, also known as a blind test. A black box test gives the tester no knowledge of the company, network infrastructure, system source code, and so forth. With the black box test, only the most basic information is given, such as the URL for the company website. The attacking company must see what they can discover through the attack process.

On the other end of the testing spectrum is the white box test, also known as a full disclosure test. With a white box test, the testing company is given full knowledge of the company, the network infrastructure (both Internet facing and Internal), application source code, IP Address settings, and so on. A white box test allows the testing company to simulate an internal attack where the attacker is an insider (typically an employee) or someone to whom an employee has leaked company information.

Between the two extremes of black box testing and white box testing is grey box testing, also known as "partial disclosure" testing. With grey box testing the testing company is given a subset of the information about the company's network infrastructure. This type of attack is probably a more realistic external attack test when an employee has divulged company information to an outside party. Most employees have very limited knowledge of the company network, with the exception of the network administration and systems administration teams (and then usually neither one will know everything). Thus most of the time the attacking person would only have been told a subset of information about the network design, IP Addresses, and the like.

Some auditing processes require that this sort of automated testing be performed on a regular basis. In the United States, any company that takes credit card data from customers (including when the customer pays for services, even if the credit card data isn't stored) needs to be able to pass some sort of PCI (Payment Card Industry) audit (read more about PCI audits and see the PCI audit checklist in Appendix A). Different countries will have different laws and regulations that will need to be followed; possibly there are multiple, different sets of laws and regulations, depending on the states and countries in which a company's customers live.

Summary

In this chapter we have gone over the network design options that are available to you. This will have shown you where the network design problems in your network are and how to shore up these design problems. The ultimate goal here is to secure the data and the database so that your customer data isn't available to prying eyes, while managing the SQL Server is still as easy as possible. Without knowing where the database instances are, there is no way to know that you are correctly securing them.

References

"2600 Live Mitnick interview." *2600*, January 1, 2003: no pages. *2600 Live Mitnick interview*,. Web. September 27, 2010.

Markoff, John. "A Most-Wanted Cyberthief Is Caught in His Own Web." *New York Times*, February 16, 1995: 0. Print.

Track Down. Dir. Joe Chappelle. Perf. Skeet Ulrich, Russell Wong, Angela Featherstone. Dimension, 2000. Film.

2

DATABASE ENCRYPTION

Database Encryption

A key way to protect the data within your database is to use database encryption. However, no one encryption solution is correct for every database. The encryption requirements of your application will dictate which encryption solution you select. One thing to remember about database encryption is that the more data you encrypt and the stronger the encryption, the more CPU power will be required in order to encrypt and decrypt the data that is needed. So, be sure to balance the encryption requirements with the increased system load.

Hashing versus Encryption

There are two techniques for protecting your data: hashing and encryption. Encryption is done using one of several different algorithms that give you a value that can be decrypted when using the correct decryption key. Each of the different encryption options provides you with a different strength of encryption. As you use a stronger level of encryption, you will be using more CPU load on the Microsoft SQL Server. Microsoft SQL Server only supports a subset of the available encryption algorithms; however, it does support some of the more popular algorithms, from weakest to strongest, which are DES, TRIPLE_DES, TRIPLE_DES_3KEY, RC2, RC4, RC4_128, DESX, AES_128, AES_192, and AES_256. The full list of available algorithms hasn't changed since Microsoft SQL Server 2005 and the newest version as of the writing of this book, which is Microsoft SQL Server 2008 R2. The list gives you a variety of options that will provide an encryption option for just about everyone.

Note
Algorithm Selection

Something to keep in mind when selecting the Data Encryption Standard (DES) algorithm is that the DES algorithm was incorrectly named when it was put into the product in Microsoft SQL Server 2005. Data that is encrypted with the DESX algorithm isn't actually being encrypted with the DESX algorithm. The Microsoft SQL Server engine is actually using the TRIPLE DES algorithm with a 192-bit key. Eventually the DES algorithm within the Microsoft SQL Server engine will be removed, so future work using the DES algorithm should be avoided.

Triple DES

Triple DES or 3DES are the common names for the Triple Data Encryption Algorithm cipher. This cipher uses the Data Encryption Standard (DES) algorithm three times for each block of data that is to be encrypted. Triple DES actually uses three encryption operations to encrypt or decrypt the data three times for each 64-bit block of data that is to be encrypted or decrypted. The encryption and decryption processes can be expressed as shown.

```
Encryption
Encryptedvalue = Ek3(Dk2(Ek1(PlainValue)))
Decryption
PlainValue = Dk3(Ek2(Dk1(Encryptedvalue)))
```

Expressions showing the encryption and decryption processes done using the 3DES algorithm. Processes marked with an E are encryption processes, while processes marked with a D are decryption processes.

As shown in the code block above, three keys are used, shown as k1, k2, and k3. Three keying options are used by the 3DES algorithm, which are defined by how many independent key bits are used. The strongest keying option has each of the three keys with different values of 56 bits, each giving a total of 168 bits represented within SQL Server as the TRIPLE_DES_3KEY algorithm or the DESX algorithm. The second keying option is a little weaker as keys k1 and k3 use the same key values and k2 uses a different value giving you 112 key bits, which is represented within SQL Server as the TRIPLE_DES algorithm. There is a weaker TRIPLE_DES algorithm, which is backwards compatible with the DES algorithm. In this case the TRIPLE_DES algorithm uses the same key values for all the possible keys.

RC Algorithms

Microsoft SQL Server supports two of the four common RC algorithms, RC2 and RC4. RC2 uses a 40-bit key size, making it a much weakened algorithm such as RC4, which supports key sizes from 40 bits to 2048 bits depending on the needs of the application. In the case of Microsoft SQL Server, you can select from 40 bit and 128 bit configurations. There are some weaknesses in the RC4 algorithm, which have caused Microsoft to deprecate the RC4 algorithms in a future release of SQL Server. As such, new database applications should use another encryption algorithm. RC4 is probably the most widely used encryption algorithm, serving as the encryption algorithm that secures SSL (Secure Socket Layer) encryption for both SSH (Secure Shell) and HTTPS communications.

AES

Three different sizes of cyphers can be used with Advanced Encryption Standard (AES) algorithm. These cyphers can be 128, 192, and 256 bits in size, which are represented by AES_128, AES_192, and AES_256, respectively, within Microsoft SQL Server. The variable key sizes are then used to combine data that are 128-bit blocks. Attackers have had some success in breaking the AES encryption algorithm when using the lower end AES encryption. To date, the higher end versions of AES have remained stable.

Hashing

Now on the flip side, you have hashing algorithms. Hashing algorithms provide you with a one-way technique that you can use to mask your data, with a minimal chance that someone could reverse the hashed value back to the original value. And with hashed techniques, every time you hash the original value you get the same hashed value. Microsoft SQL Server has supported the same hashing values from Microsoft SQL Server 2005 to Microsoft SQL Server 2008 R2. You can use MD2, MD4, MD5, SHA, or SHA1 to create hashes of your data. As long as you use the same hashing algorithm each time you hash a value, then you will always get the same hashed value back. For example, if you use the MD5 hash algorithm to hash the value "SampleValue," you will always give the value of "0x777E628ACB1D264A8CE4BC6942 7B3855" back.

Hashing is done, regardless of the algorithm used, via the HASHBYTES system function. The HASHBYTES function accepts two values: the algorithm to use and the value to get the hash for. The catch when using the HASHBYTES system function is that it does not support all data types that Microsoft SQL Server supports. The biggest problem with this lack of support is that the HASHBYTES function doesn't support character strings longer than 8000 bytes. When using ASCII strings with the CHAR or VARCHAR data types, the HASHBYTES system function will accept up to 8000 characters. When using Unicode strings with the NCHAR or NVARCHAR data types, the HASHBYTES system function will accept up to 4000 characters. When passing in binary data using the VARBINARY data type, the HASHBYTES function will accept up to 8000 bytes of binary data.

There are two ways that a hashed value can be used to find the original value. The first is rather simple: Simply create a database that stores all of the potential values. Then take the hashed value and compare it to the values in the database looking for matches. There are in fact websites such as http://tools.benramsey.com/md5/ that handle this lookup for you across several databases available on the Internet. The second attack method against MD5 is called a collision attack. A collision attack is when you find two different values that can be hashed to the same hash value, effectively allowing the check of the values to pass. Mathematically, you could express the attack as hash(value1) = hash (value2).

Note
MD5 is Not Totally Secure

In 1996, collisions were first identified in hashed data against the MD5 algorithm causing the long-term usefulness of MD5 to be reduced. In 2005, researches were able to create pairs of documents and X.509 certificates that, when hashed, produced the same hash value. Later that year the creator of MD5, Ron Rivest, wrote "MD5 and SHA1 are both clearly broken (in terms of collision-resistance)." Then in 2008, researchers announced that they were able to use MD5 and create a fake Certificate Authority certificate, which was created by RapidSSL and would allow them to create certificates for websites. Although these attacks do bring into question the long-term usability of the MD5 and SHA1 algorithms, these are the strongest hashing algorithms that Microsoft SQL Server supports natively. The other algorithms,

Note—*Cont'd*

which are weaker in nature than MD5 and SHA1, are considered to be severely compromised and shouldn't be truly trusted to provide a hash which cannot be broken. As of Microsoft SQL Server 2008, R2 MD5 and SHA1 are the most secure hashing algorithms that are available. However, Microsoft has stated on the Connect website (http://connect.microsoft.com/SQLServer/feedback/details/585006/) that in the next version the SHA2 hashing algorithm will be supported within SQL Server. The only way to support this more secure hashing algorithm in Microsoft SQL Server 2005 through 2008 R2 would be to use a .NET CLR assembly.

Encrypting Data within Tables

When it comes to encrypting data within your database table, there are a few different options. Where you encrypt the data within your application stack is just as important a question as is the technique you use to encrypt the data. Your choices for where to encrypt your data will typically be at the client side (in your fat client or within your web app) or within the database. Each option has pros and cons that have to be properly weighed before you make the decision.

When you handle the encryption within the database, you have the benefit of minimal to no changes to the front-end client (this assumes that you control all your database access via stored procedures). However, the downside here is that all the CPU load of the encryption is handled on the database server. Because all the encryption is handled on the database server, this can cause a bottleneck on the database server as the encryption and decryption of data will increase the CPU load of the database server. The other main disadvantage of encrypting the data with the SQL Server is that you have to store the decryption mechanism within the database. Granted the SQL Server will help mitigate these risks with object-level permissions and strong encryption of the certificates, but given enough time, any encryption scheme is crackable. The stronger the encryption that is used, the longer it would take an attacker to break the encryption with the strongest encryption levels, taking many years of CPU power to break the encryption.

On the other hand, you can handle all the encryption in the application tier (either the fat client or the web app). This gives you the benefit of spreading the entire encryption load across all the computers that run the application, but it gives you the downside of a load of application changes. Now while this does place a lot of extra work on the development team to implement these changes, the workload is spread across the application tier. When using a fat client on the user's desktop, this work is done on the client computer; when using a web application, this work is done on the web servers. In a web application environment, this increased CPU load on the web servers can be mitigated by adding more web servers to the web farm or by moving the encryption functions to another web farm that is only used to encrypt the data.

No matter where within your application you encrypt your data, and no matter what encryption technique you use your data storage requirements will typically increase by 10% to 20%. This is because encrypted data is larger due to the nature of encryption as well as any padding data that is put within the data.

Tip
Data Encryption Laws

Depending on where you live, where your company base is, and where your customers are located, you may have to deal with a variety of local, state, and federal (or national) laws that reference data protection. Most of these laws are very vague about how the data encryption needs to be implemented (which is considered to be a good thing by some), but some laws such as the state law in Massachusetts have some very serious consequences if your data is leaked. In the case of the law in Massachusetts, you will incur penalties if you have customer data that isn't encrypted—even if the data isn't breached and even if neither the company nor the data are within the borders of the state of Massachusetts. The Massachusetts state law is designed to protect the citizens of the state no matter where the company that the citizen does business with is located. Be sure to check with the laws in all the jurisdictions that you do business and in which your customers reside. Each state in the United States maintains a website that will have a list of all the available laws governing them. If you cannot locate the laws for your state, your company's legal department should be able to get a copy of these laws. When designing an encryption plan for company data, be sure to include the company's legal counsel in these planning meetings as the company's legal counsel will be the one responsible for defending the company in court in the event of a data breech or other legal action; as such, they should be involved in the planning phase.

Encrypting within Microsoft SQL Server

When planning to encrypt data within Microsoft SQL Server, there is a clear dividing line that you have to keep in mind. Any version of Microsoft SQL Server, which is Microsoft SQL Server 2000 or older, does not include any usable techniques for encrypting functions natively. However, there are third-party DLLs (Dynamic-Link Library) which can be used to encrypt and decrypt data. When using Microsoft SQL Server 2000 or older, the only hashing functions that you can use is pwdencrypt. It is highly recommended, however, that you not use this function, for the algorithms used by this function have changed from version to version of Microsoft SQL Server, and this function has been deprecated in the newer versions of Microsoft SQL Server. If you must use this undocumented system function, it accepts a single parameter and returns a varbinary (255) value.

```
SELECT pwdencrypt('test')
```

Showing how to use the undocumented system function pwdencrypt.

Starting with Microsoft SQL Server 2005, you can use native hashing and encryption functions. When encrypting data within the Microsoft SQL Server, you can encrypt the data using one of three functions: EncryptByCert(), EncryptByKey(), and Encrypt-ByPassPhrase().

When using the EncryptByCert() function, you are using a certificate that is created within the database in order to encrypt the data. Encrypting data with a certificate allows you to easily move the certificate from one platform to another or to use a certificate purchased from a third party such as VeriSign and GoDaddy.

When using the EncryptByKey() function, you use a symmetric key to encrypt the data. The symmetric key can be created using a password, a certificate, or another symmetric key. When you create the symmetric key, you specify the encryption algorithm that you want to use in order to encrypt the data.

When using the EncryptByPassPhrase() function, you specify a password when calling the EncryptByPassPhrase function. This passphrase is used to create a symmetric key, which is then used in the same manner as the EncryptByKey function is used.

As of the summer of 2010, none of the encryption functions shown in this section can be used with SQL Azure. SQL Azure does not support creating certificates, nor does it support using any of the encryption functions. The encryption functions will return an error saying that they are not supported in that version of SQL Server. The CREATE CERTIFICATE statement will return the same error message.

Encrypting within the Application Tier

The most common (and usually the more scalable) place to encrypt data is within the application tier. Putting the encryption within the application tier probably requires the most changes to the application. However, it is the most scalable place to handle the encryption as the encryption workload is placed on all the

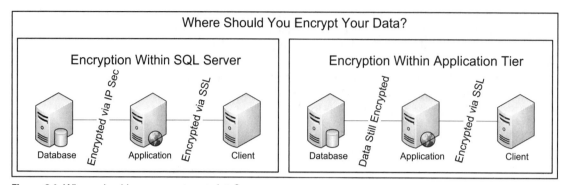

Figure 2.1 Where should you encrypt your data?

web servers or the user's desktops (when using a fat client). The advantage of handling the decryption within the application tier is that the data is transmitted between the database server and the application tier in an encrypted form without having to configure and manage IP Sec within the network like it is when encrypting the data within the Microsoft SQL Server. These different techniques can be seen in Figure 2.1.

To encrypt data within your application tier, you'll need to use the native encryption functions. For the purposes of this book all sample code will be written in VB.NET and C#. These same techniques can be used using other programming languages, but the syntaxes will be different.

Within .NET this is done using the System.IO. Cryptography namespace. The Cryptography namespace gives you access to a variety of hashing and encryption functions. The specific functions that are available to you will depend on the version of .NET framework that you are using; however, the basic technique will be the same no matter which hashing or encryption function you use. The sample code in Examples 2.1 and 2.2 shows how to use these encryption functions in C# and VB.Net, and in Example 2.3 and 2.4 how to use the hashing functions in C# and VB.Net.

```
using System;
using System.IO;
using System.Security.Cryptography;
using System.Text;
namespace ConsoleApplication1
{
    class Program
    {
        static void Main(string[] args)
        {
            Console.WriteLine(EncryptData("Test"));
```

```csharp
Console.WriteLine (DecryptData(EncryptData("Test")));
Console.ReadLine();
}
static string EncryptData(string plainText)
{
    //Setting the Passphrase, salting value, and vector
        which will be used to encrypt the values. These must be
        the same in your encryption and decryption functions.
    string passPhrase = "YourStrongPassword!";
    string SaltValue = "Your$altValue";
    int passwordIterations = 2;
    string initVector = "d83jd72hsOwk3ldf";
    //Convert the text values into byte arrays
    byte[] initVectorBytes = Encoding.ASCII.GetBytes
        (initVector);
    byte[] saltValueBytes = Encoding.ASCII.GetBytes
        (SaltValue);
    byte[] plainTextBytes = Encoding.UTF8.GetBytes
        (plainText);
    //Create the password which will be used to encrypt the
        value based on the Passphrase, salt value, SHA1 hash,
        and Password Iterations specified.
    PasswordDeriveBytes password = new PasswordDerive-
        Bytes(passPhrase, saltValueBytes, "SHA1",
        passwordIterations);
    //Create an array to hold the pseudo-random bytes for the
        encryption key.
    byte[] keyBytes = password.GetBytes(32);
    //Create an object to use for encryption.
    RijndaelManaged symmetricKey = new RijndaelManaged();
    //Set the encryption object for Ciopher Block Chaining.
    symmetricKey.Mode = CipherMode.CBC;
    //Generate the encryptor from the key bytes and the
        vector bytes.
    ICryptoTransform encryptor = symmetricKey.Create
        Encryptor(keyBytes, initVectorBytes);
    //Create a memory stream object to hold the encrypted
        data.
    MemoryStream memoryStream = new MemoryStream();
    //Create cryptographic steam to do the encryption.
    CryptoStream cryptoStream = new CryptoStream(memory-
        Stream, encryptor, CryptoStreamMode.Write);
    //Begin the encryption.
    cryptoStream.Write(plainTextBytes, 0, plainText
        Bytes.Length);
    //Finish the encryption.
    cryptoStream.FlushFinalBlock();
    //Convert the encrypted value into a new byte array.
    byte[] cipherTextBytes = memoryStream.ToArray();
```

```
        //Close the streams.
        memoryStream.Close();
        cryptoStream.Close();
        //Convert the encrypted value to a string value and
            return to the calling code.
        return Convert.ToBase64String(cipherTextBytes);
}
static string DecryptData(string EncryptedValue)
{
    //Setting the Passphrase, salting value, and vector
        which will be used to encrypt the values. These must be
        the same in your encryption and decryption functions.
    string passPhrase = "YourStrongPassword!";
    string SaltValue = "Your$altValue";
    int passwordIterations = 2;
    string initVector = "d83jd72hsOwk3ldf";
    //Convert the text values into byte arrays
    byte[] initVectorBytes = Encoding.ASCII.GetBytes
        (initVector);
    byte[] saltValueBytes = Encoding.ASCII.GetBytes
        (SaltValue);
    byte[] cipherTextBytes = Convert.FromBase64String
        (EncryptedValue);
    //Create the password which will be used to decrypt the
        value based on the Passphrase, salt value, SHA1 hash,
        and Password Iterations specified.
    PasswordDeriveBytes password = new PasswordDerive
        Bytes(passPhrase, saltValueBytes, "SHA1",
        passwordIterations);
    //Create an array to hold the pseudo-random bytes for the
        encryption key.
    byte[] keyBytes = password.GetBytes(32);
    //Create an object to use for encryption.
    RijndaelManaged symmetricKey = new RijndaelManaged();
    //Set the encryption object for Ciopher Block Chaining.
    symmetricKey.Mode = CipherMode.CBC;
    //Generate the decryptor from the key bytes and the
        vector bytes.
    ICryptoTransform decryptor = symmetricKey.Create
        Decryptor(keyBytes, initVectorBytes);
    //Create a memory stream object to hold the decrypted
        data.
    MemoryStream memoryStream = new MemoryStream(cipher
        TextBytes);
    //Create cryptographic steam to do the decryption.
    CryptoStream cryptoStream = new CryptoStream(memory-
        Stream, decryptor, CryptoStreamMode.Read);
    //Create a byte array based on the size of the memory-
        stream object
```

```
byte[] plainTextBytes = new byte[cipherTextBytes.
   Length];
//Decrypt the data
int decryptedByteCount = cryptoStream.Read(plain-
   TextBytes, 0, plainTextBytes.Length);
//close the streams
memoryStream.Close();
cryptoStream.Close();
//Convert the decrypted value to a string value and
   return to the calling code
return Encoding.UTF8.GetString(plainTextBytes, 0,
   decryptedByteCount);
    }
  }
}
```

Example 2.1: C# code showing how to encrypt and decrypt data within the application layer.

```
Imports System.Text
Imports System.Security.Cryptography
Imports System.IO
Module Module1
  Sub Main()
    Console.WriteLine(EncryptData("Test"))
    Console.WriteLine(HashData("Test"))
    Console.ReadLine()
  End Sub
  Function EncryptData(ByVal plainText As String)
    'Setting the Passphrase, salting value, and vector which
       will be used to encrypt the values. These must be the same
       in your encryption and decryption functions.
    Dim PassPhrase As String = "YourStrongPassword!"
    Dim SaltValue As String = "Your$altValue"
    Dim PasswordIterations As Integer = 2
    Dim initVector = "d83jd72hs0wk3ldf"
    'Convert the text values into byte arrays
    Dim initVectorBytes() As Byte = Encoding.ASCII.GetBytes
       (initVector)
    Dim SaltValueBytes() As Byte = Encoding.ASCII.GetBytes
       (saltValue)
    Dim plainTextBytes() As Byte = Encoding.UTF8.GetBytes
       (plainText)
    'Create the password which will be used to encrypt the value
       based on the Passphrase, salt value, SHA1 hash, and
       Password Iterations specified.
    Dim password As PasswordDeriveBytes = New PasswordDer-
       iveBytes(PassPhrase, SaltValueBytes, "SHA1",
       PasswordIterations)
```

```
'Create an array to hold the pseudo-random bytes for the
    encryption key.
Dim KeyBytes As Byte() = password.GetBytes(32)
'Create an object to use for encryption.
Dim SymmetricKey As RijndaelManaged = New RijndaelManaged
    ()
'Set the encryption object for Ciopher Block Chaining.
SymmetricKey.Mode = CipherMode.CBC
'Generate the encryptor from the key bytes and the vector
    bytes.
Dim Encryptor As ICryptoTransform = SymmetricKey.
    CreateEncryptor(KeyBytes, initVectorBytes)
'Create a memory stream object to hold the encrypted data.
Dim memoryStream As MemoryStream = New MemoryStream()
'Create cryptographic steam to do the encryption.
Dim CryptoStream As CryptoStream = New CryptoStream
    (memoryStream, Encryptor, CryptoStreamMode.Write)
'Begin the encryption.
CryptoStream.Write(plainTextBytes, 0,
    plainTextBytes.Length)
'Finish the encryption.
CryptoStream.FlushFinalBlock()
'Convert the encrypted value into a new byte array.
Dim CipherTextBytes As Byte() = memoryStream.ToArray()
'Close the streams.
memoryStream.Close()
CryptoStream.Close()
'Convert the encrypted value to a string value and return to
    the calling code.
Return Convert.ToBase64String(CipherTextBytes)
End Function
Function DecryptData(ByVal EncryptedValue As String)
    'Setting the Passphrase, salting value, and vector which
        will be used to encrypt the values. These must be the same
        in your encryption and decryption functions.
    Dim PassPhrase As String = "YourStrongPassword!"
    Dim SaltValue As String = "Your$altValue"
    Dim PasswordIterations As Integer = 2
    Dim initVector = "d83jd72hsOwk3ldf"
    'Convert the text values into byte arrays
    Dim initVectorBytes() As Byte = Encoding.ASCII.GetBytes
        (initVector)
    Dim SaltValueBytes() As Byte = Encoding.ASCII.GetBytes
        (SaltValue)
    Dim CipherTextBytes() As Byte = Convert.FromBase64String
        (EncryptedValue)
'Create the password which will be used to decrypt the value
    based on the Passphrase, salt value, SHA1 hash, and
    Password Iterations specified.
```

```
        Dim Password As PasswordDeriveBytes = New Password
            DeriveBytes(PassPhrase, SaltValueBytes, "SHA1",
            PasswordIterations)
        'Create an array to hold the pseudo-random bytes for the
            encryption key.
        Dim KeyBytes As Byte() = Password.GetBytes(32)
        'Create an object to use for encryption.
        Dim SymmetricKey As RijndaelManaged = New RijndaelManaged()
        'Set the encryption object for Ciopher Block Chaining.
        SymmetricKey.Mode = CipherMode.CBC
        'Generate the decryptor from the key bytes and the vector
            bytes.
        Dim Decrypter As ICryptoTransform = SymmetricKey.
            CreateDecryptor(KeyBytes, initVectorBytes)
        'Create a memory stream object to hold the decrypted data.
        Dim memoryStream As MemoryStream = New MemoryStream
            (CipherTextBytes)
        'Create cryptographic steam to do the decryption.
        Dim CryptoStream As CryptoStream = New CryptoStream
            (memoryStream, Decrypter, CryptoStreamMode.Read)
        'Create a byte array based on the size of the memorystream
            object
        Dim PlainTextBytes() As Byte = memoryStream.ToArray
        'Decrypt the data
        Dim decryptedByteCount As Integer = CryptoStream.Read
            (PlainTextBytes, 0, PlainTextBytes.Length)
        'close the streams
        memoryStream.Close()
        CryptoStream.Close()
        'Convert the decrypted value to a string value and return to
            the calling code
        Return Encoding.UTF8.GetString(PlainTextBytes, 0,
            decryptedByteCount)
    End Function
End Module
```

Example 2.2: VB.Net code showing how to encrypt and decrypt data within the application layer.

```
using System;
using System.IO;
using System.Security.Cryptography;
using System.Text;
namespace ConsoleApplication1
{
    class Program
    {
        static void Main(string[] args)
        {
```

```
Console.WriteLine (DecryptData(EncryptData
  ("Test")));
Console.ReadLine();
}
static string HashData(string plainText)
{
  UnicodeEncoding UnicodeString = new UnicodeEncoding
    ();
  //Convert the string into a byte array
  Byte[] PlainTextByte = UnicodeString.GetBytes
    (plainText);
  //Initalize the MD5 provider
  MD5CryptoServiceProvider MD5 = new MD5CryptoService-
    Provider() ;
  //Computer the hash and store it as a byte array
  byte[] HashBytes = MD5.ComputeHash(PlainTextByte);
  //Convert the byte array and return as a string value
  return Convert.ToBase64String(HashBytes);
}
  }
}
```

Example 2.3: C# code showing how to hash data within the application layer.

```
Imports System.Text
Imports System.Security.Cryptography
Imports System.IO
Module Module1
  Sub Main()
    Console.WriteLine(HashData("Test"))
    Console.ReadLine()
  End Sub
  Function HashData(ByVal PlainText As String)
    Dim UnicodeString As New UnicodeEncoding()
    'Convert the string into a byte array
    Dim PlainTextByte As Byte() = UnicodeString.GetBytes
      (PlainText)
    'Initalize the MD5 provider
    Dim MD5 As New MD5CryptoServiceProvider()
    'Computer the hash and store it as a byte array
    Dim HashedByte As Byte() = MD5.ComputeHash(PlainTextByte)
    'Convert the byte array and return as a string value
    Return Convert.ToBase64String(HashedByte)
  End Function
End Module
```

Example 2.4: VB.Net code showing how to hash data within the application layer.

Encrypting Data at Rest

Microsoft SQL Server 2008 introduced the Transparent Data Encryption feature of SQL Server. This feature allows the SQL Server to encrypt the data as it is written to the hard drive of the server, and the SQL Server decrypts the data as it is read from the hard drive into memory. The advantage of this system is that you are able to encrypt all data with no change to the data whatsoever. This feature also protects all your data when it is backed up as the backup is also encrypted. This encryption is done by encrypting the blocks of data instead of the data stored within the blocks. The difference between the two concepts is that when the data is encrypted, only the data within the table is encrypted, while TDE will encrypt the meta data about the tables, the white space in the data pages, and so forth.

The downside to using Transparent Data Encryption is that if someone is able to access the SQL Server through normal means, or by using something like an SQL Injection, they will still be able to download the data from your SQL Server by simply querying the data.

Transparent Data Encryption will also increase the CPU load on the SQL Server because each data page being read from or written to the disk must be encrypted. On very high load systems this can turn into a great increase in CPU resources. Turning on Transparent Data Encryption is extremely easy. From within SQL Server Management Studio simply right click on the database and select properties. Then select the options tab and scroll to the bottom of the option list. Locate the Encryption Enabled option and change it from False to True as shown in Figure 2.2 and click OK. This will enable the Transparent Data Encryption setting for this database.

When you enable Transparent Data Encryption as data is being written, the data within the page will be encrypted. As the SQL Server has free cycles available, it will read the unencrypted blocks from the disk, encrypt them, and then write the encrypted blocks to the disk. As data is written to the transaction log, it is also encrypted by the Transparent Data Encryption.

When you enable Transparent Database Encryption for any database within the instance, Transparent Database Encryption will also be enabled for the tempdb database for that instance. This will cause a performance impact to other databases within your instance that use the tempdb database for storing temporary data.

If you wish to enable Transparent Database Encryption with T/SQL, you'll need to perform a few steps as shown in Figure 2.3. First, you'll need to create a master key within the master database using the CREATE MASTER KEY command. Second, you'll

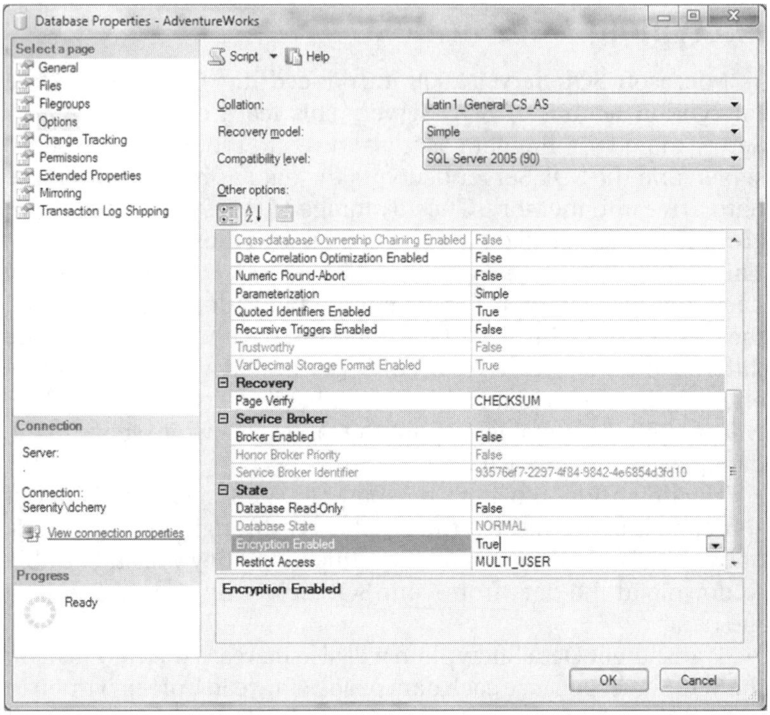

Figure 2.2 Enabling Transparent Data Encryption on a database.

need to create a certificate within the master database using the CREATE CERTIFICATE command.

After this switch to the database, you wish to encrypt and create the database encryption key by using the CREATE DATABASE ENCRYPTION KEY command. When you use the CREATE

```
SQLQuery1.sql - (I...nity\dcherry (53))*
    USE master;
    GO
    CREATE MASTER KEY ENCRYPTION BY PASSWORD = 'YourPassw0rdGoe$Here';
    go
    CREATE CERTIFICATE MyCertificate WITH SUBJECT = 'My TDE Certificate';
    go
    USE AdventureWorks;
    GO
    CREATE DATABASE ENCRYPTION KEY
    WITH ALGORITHM = AES_128
    ENCRYPTION BY SERVER CERTIFICATE MyCertificate;
    GO
    ALTER DATABASE AdventureWorks
    SET ENCRYPTION ON;
    GO
```

Figure 2.3 Enabling Transparent Data Encryption with T/SQL.

DATABASE ENCRYPTION KEY command, you can select the algorithm you wish to use. Specify the certificate that you created in the prior step. Then lastly use the ALTER DATABASE command to enable Transparent Database Encryption within the database.

Transparent Data Encryption makes use of a database encryption key that is stored within the database's boot record so that it can be used for recovery when the database is first started. The database encryption key is a symmetric key, which is secured by a certificate stored in the master database of the instance. If you use a third party Enterprise Key Manager, such as the RSA Tokenization Server or the Cisco Key Management Center, then the database encryption key is an asymmetric key that is protected by the Enterprise Key Manager.

FAQ
Certificate Expiration

When you look at the sample code in Figure 2.3, you will notice that there is no expiration date created on the certificate. By default, SQL Server creates a certificate with an expiration date one year in the future. A question quickly comes up as to what happens after one year when the certificate expires as there is no way to renew the internal certificates that are used for Transparent Data Encryption.

The short answer is that nothing happens. The Transparent Data Encryption engine ignores the expiration date of the certificate so that when the certificate is created and the user forgets to set the expiration date far enough into the future, the SQL Server doesn't have any problems using this certificate. While this sounds like it might be a security problem, it doesn't present one because this is the only check that that SQL Server skips when validating the Transparent Data Encryption certificate.

When you enable Transparent Data Encryption, you should be sure to back up the encryption keys immediately and store them securely. If you do not back up these keys and the database needs to be restored, you won't be able to read the backup because you will not have the key to the encrypted backup. If the key is downloaded by someone other than your company, that person would then be able to read your database backups, or attach the database to any server.

If you use database mirroring along with Transparent Data Encryption, then both the primary and the mirror will be encrypted. As the log data is moved between the instances, it will be encrypted for transport to preserve the security of the data within the transaction log as well as to protect the data from network sniffing.

If you use full-text indexing with Transparent Data Encryption, the data within the full text index will be encrypted by the Transparent Data Encryption process. This will not happen immediately, however. It is very possible that new data written to the full-text index could be written to the disk in an unencrypted form; therefore, Microsoft recommends not indexing sensitive data when using Transparent Data Encryption.

When using Transparent Data Encryption along with database backup encryption, you'll notice a much lower amount of compression when you back up the database. This is because encrypted data cannot be compressed as the amount of unique data within the database greatly decreases when you compress the database.

If you replicate data from a database that has been encrypted by the Transparent Data Encryption, the replicated database will not be fully protected unless you enable Transparent Data Encryption on the subscriber and distributor as well as the publisher.

If you use FILESTREAM within a database encrypted with Transparent Data Encryption, all data written via the FILESTREAM will not be encrypted. This is because the FILESTREAM data is not written to the actual database files. Only the data within the actual database files (mdf, ndf, ldf) is encrypted with TDE. The FILE-STREAM files cannot be encrypted by the SQL Server engine because a user can access the FILESTREAM files directly via the Windows network share, so if the files that the FILESTREAM created were encrypted, the user would not be able to access the files. If you wanted to secure the data stored within the FILE-STREAM, you would need to use a file system-based encryption process, as long as it is supported by the SQL Server Engine. The native Encrypting File Stream (EFS) encryption process that Windows 2000 and newer support is a supported encryption process for data stored by the SQL Server FILESTREAM.

The big catch with Transparent Data Encryption is that it is an Enterprise Edition and up feature. This means that in SQL Server 2008 the Enterprise Edition is required. With SQL Server 2008 R2 you can use either the Enterprise Edition or the Data Center Edition.

Encrypting Data on the Wire

If your worry is that someone will sniff the network traffic coming into and out of your SQL Server, then you will want to encrypt the data as it flows over the network between the SQL Server and the client computers. This is typically done by either enabling SSL for the SQL Server connection or using IP Sec to secure all network communication (or a subset of the network communication) between the client computer (end users' computer, web server, application server, etc.) and the database engine.

The upside to using SSL is that you manage the connection encryption between the SQL Server and the clients from within the SQL Server. This encryption is also more limited as only the SQL Server traffic is encrypted, while with IP Sec you have the option to encrypt all or some of the network traffic between the SQL Server and the client computer. The advantage of IP Sec is that there are Network Cards that can offload the IP Sec work from the CPU of the SQL Server to a processor on the network card. These IP Sec network cards will require a different configuration than the one shown later in this chapter.

When using Microsoft SQL Server Reporting Services, encryption over the wire is very important between the end user and the SQL Server Reporting Services server. When encryption is not used, the user's username and password are passed in plain text from the client application (usually a web browser) to the server, and any data that is returned is also returned in plain text. If the reports that are being viewed contain confidential information, this information could be viewed by an unauthorized person. When SQL Reporting Services is being used within an internal company network, this can be done by using SSL (which will be discussed in Chapter 5 within the section titled "Reporting Services") or IP Sec (which is discussed later in this section of this chapter). If the SQL Server Reporting Services instance is accessed directly over the public Internet (or another untrusted network), then SSL should be used, as the IP Sec policies may not be in place on both sides of the connection.

SQL Server Over SSL

Before you can configure SQL Server over SSL, you'll need to acquire an SSL certificate from a trusted Certificate Authority. If you have an internal Enterprise Certificate Authority, you can get one from there; if not you'll want to get one from a recognized Certificate Authority such as Verisign or GoDaddy, among others. After you have acquired the certificate, you'll need to import it into the SQL Server. If you are using an SQL Server Cluster, then you'll need to export the certificate from the server that you first requested the certificate be created for, and to import it into the other servers in the cluster. When you request the certificate, you'll need to specify the name that your users will connect to the SQL Server as the subject of the certificate.

Microsoft SQL Server has some rather specific requirements when it comes to the certificate. The certificate must be stored in either the local computer certificate store or the current user certificate store (when logged in as the account that runs the SQL Server). The certificate must be valid when the valid from and valid to values are compared against the local system time. The certificate must be a server authentication certificate that requires the Enhanced Key Usage property of the certificate to specify Server Authentication (1.3.6.1.5.5.7.3.1). The certificate must also be created using the KeySpec option of AT_KEYEX-CHANGE; optionally the key usage property will include key encipherment. SQL Server 2008 R2 supports the use of wildcard certificates, while prior versions will require a specific name within the subject of the certificate.

Although you can use self-signed certificates to encrypt data connections between the client computers and the SQL Server, it is not recommended as this opens the server up to man-in-the-middle attacks where the user connects to another process; that process decrypts the connect and then forwards the connection along to the final destination while reading and processing all the traffic, exposing all your data you are attempting to protect to the third-party process.

Before you can tell the SQL Server that you want to encrypt the connection, you need to request and install a certificate from your Certificate Authority. In the case of these examples, we will be using a local Enterprise Certificate Authority.

To request a certificate, open Microsoft Management Console (MMC) on your Windows 2008 R2 Server (other operating systems may have slightly different instructions than are shown here) by clicking Start > Run and typing MMC and clicking OK. This will open an empty MMC console. When the empty MMC console has opened, click on the File drop down menu and select "Add/Remove Snap-in." From the list on the left select "Certificates" and click the Add button to move the snap-in to the right. You'll then get the certificate snap-in properties, which asks if you want to manage certificates for your user account, a service account, or the computer account. Select the computer account and click next, then select the local computer and click Finish. Once you have closed the certificate snap-in properties wizard, click OK to close the Add or Remove snap-in page. At this point within the MMC console you should see the Certificates snap-in with a variety of folders beneath "Certificates (Local Computer)." Navigate to Personal > Certificates to view the list of certificates that are installed on the computer. By default there shouldn't be any certificates listed here.

To request a certificate from your Certificate Authority (CA), right click on Certificates (under Personal) and select "All Tasks" from the Context menu; then select "Request New Certificate." This will open the Certificate Enrollment wizard. Click next on the wizard to see the list of certificate templates. Check the box next to the "Computer" template and click the double down arrows next to Details on the right, then select properties. This will pull up the Certificate Properties window.

On the General tab set the friendly name to the DNS name of the SQL Server. In the case of our sample server, the domain name is ati.corp, and the server name is sql2008r2, so the friendly name is sql2008r2.ati.corp. On the subject tab, in the subject name section change the type dropdown to Common name and set the value to the same value as the friendly name, in this case sql2008r2.ati.corp. Click the add button to move the value to the column on the right, and then click OK. Back on the Certificate Enrollment page click the Enroll button to request the certificate. After the Certificate Enrollment window has closed, you should now see the certificate listed in the MMC console.

SQL Server 7 and 2000

In the older versions of Microsoft SQL Server, there is no User Interface (UI) to tell the SQL Server which certificate to use. By default the SQL Server will use the certificate that has the same name as the SQL Server. If you have multiple certificates or you wish to use a certificate that doesn't have the same name as the server, then you can force the SQL Server on which certificate to use by setting a registry key. This key can be found at HKEY_LOCAL_MACHINE\SOFTWARE\Microsoft\MSSQLServer\MSSQL Server\SuperSocketNetLib. Create a binary value called "Certificate" and place the thumbprint of the certificate as the value of the key. The thumbprint of the certificate can be found by viewing the certificate in the MMC console and looking at the Details tab as shown in Figure 2.4.

Configuring Microsoft SQL Server 2000 to use encryption is very easy to do. Open the SQL Server Network Utility by clicking on Start > Programs > Microsoft SQL Server, then Server Network Utility. When the Server Network Utility opens, simply select the instance you wish to configure and check the box that says "Force protocol encryption" as shown in Figure 2.5. Then click OK and restart the Microsoft SQL Server Services.

If the SQL Service doesn't start after making these changes, check the ERRORLOG and application log. If the SQL Server can't find the correct certificate, specify the certificate to use in the registry as shown above. The same applies if the SQL Service does

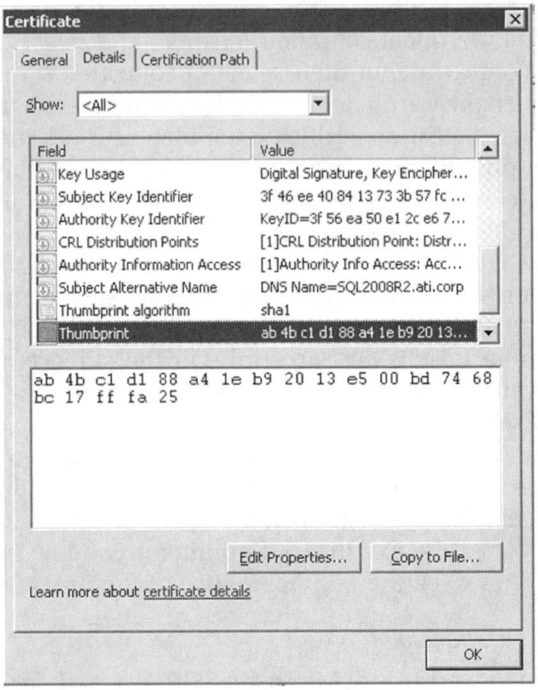

Figure 2.4 The thumbprint value of our sample certificate.

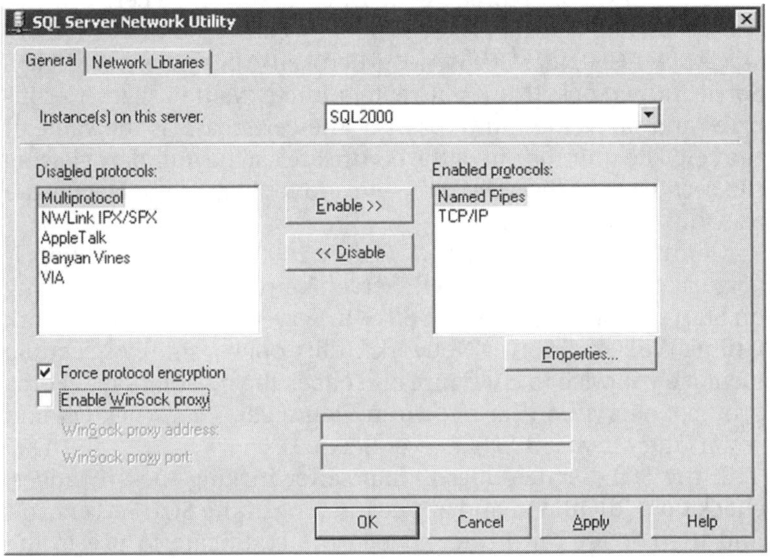

Figure 2.5 SQL Server Network Utility configured for encryption.

start but you get messages back from the SQL Server saying that the name that you are connecting to does not match the certificate.

SQL Server 2005 and Up

After you have imported the certificate into the SQL Server open the SQL Server Configuration Manager by clicking Start > Programs > Microsoft SQL Server 200n > Configuration Tools. Expand the "SQL Server Network Configuration" menu (if you have installed the 32-bit build of SQL Server on a 64-bit server, then you'll need to expand the "SQL Server Network Configuration (32-bit)" menu) and right click on "Protocols for {Instance Name}" and select properties. On the certificate tab select the certificate you wish to use to encrypt the network traffic. After selecting the certificate, switch back to the Flags tab. On the Flags tab you can force enable encryption or you can hide the instance. The screenshot shown in Figure 2.6 shows an instance configured to force encryption, while remaining visible to users on the network.

When you force encryption on an instance, the SQL Server will reject all connections that do not support encryption. If you do not force encryption, the SQL Server will accept both encrypted and nonencrypted connections, allowing you to set specific

Figure 2.6 Forcing Database Encryption for all connections to an SQL Server Instance.

applications to use encryption via the applications connection string. This is done by putting the "FORCE ENCRYPTION=true" flag within the applications connection string. After you change the encryption settings you'll need to restart the SQL Instance in order for the settings to take effect.

Note
Authentication Encryption

It is a common misconception that no network traffic between the SQL Server and client computer is encrypted. In all versions of Microsoft SQL Server starting with Microsoft SQL Server 2005, the authentication information passed between the SQL client and SQL Server is encrypted so that the passwords are protected when sent over the wire. For versions older than Microsoft SQL Server 2005, the username and password are sent in clear text. When using Microsoft SQL Server 2000, if you have Service Pack 3 installed on both the client and the server, then the authentication information will also be sent in an encrypted form.

When connecting to versions of SQL Server older than SQL Server 2000 Service Pack 3 using Multiprotocol Net-Library, your authentication information is transmitted in an encrypted form. This is made possible because the Multiprotocol Net-Library has its own native encryption, which is implemented by calling the Windows RPC Encryption API. This is an independent encryption configuration that the SSL encryption talked about in this chapter and in Chapter 3. When using TCP/IP or Named Pipes to connect to the same instance, the authentication is not encrypted as these protocols do not support encryption using drivers older than the Microsoft SQL Server 2005 Native client. Because Multiprotocol Net-Library cannot be used to connect to named instances, no encryption of authentication information is supported on SQL Server 2000 named instances, unless SSL encryption has been configured on the named instance. This is not a problem for versions of Microsoft SQL Server 7.0 and older because these versions of Microsoft SQL Server do not support named instances.

Hiding the Instance

Microsoft SQL Server instance can be easily found by querying the network and using a specific feature within the SQL Server Native Client. When using the sqlcmd command line tool, this feature is exposed by using the -L switch. When using SQL Server Management Studio, this feature can be exposed by selecting the "<Browse for more…>" option from the Connection dialog box and selecting the "Network Servers" tab in the window that pops up. This feature can also be called via a custom .NET application. No matter which technique is used, the same result occurs, showing a list of all the SQL Server Instances that are available on the network.

It is possible to hide an instance of the database engine from reporting that it is there by changing the "Hide Instance" setting within the SQL Server Service's protocol properties, shown disabled (set to "no") in Figure 2.6. To hide the instance, change this setting from "no" to "yes" and restart the instance for the setting to take effect. After the setting is enabled and the instance has been restarted, the instance will not respond to queries by the Native drive querying for instance. Users will still be able to connect to the instance as before; however, they must know the name of the server name and the name of the instance, when not using the default instance.

IP Sec

IP Sec is the process by which all network communication between two computers is encrypted. IP Sec can be configured either on the local machine or on the domain via group policies. In the example local configuration will be shown, but the screens look very similar for a group policy configuration.

To configure IP Sec, open the Local Security Policy application by clicking on Start > Programs > Administrative Tools > Local Security Policy. Right click on the "IP Security Policies on Local Computer" option on the menu on the left and select "Create IP Security Policy." This will bring up the IP Security Policy Wizard.

On the first screen of the wizard, type a name and description of the policy. On the second screen you are asked to activate the default response rule. This default response rule tells the computer how to respond to requests for security when no other rule applies. The default response rule only applies when running against Windows Server 2003 and Windows XP. The third screen of the wizard asks you for the initial authentication method to use when negotiating the connection. You can select from Kerberos, a certificate from a CA, or a preshared key. If your SQL Server or any member of the communication is not a member of the domain (the SQL Server or web server is within a DMZ, for example), then you cannot select Kerberos as the Kerberos settings must come from a Windows domain. After this you have completed the wizard and the computer is configured for IP Sec communication. Once the wizard has been closed, you can see the rule listed in the list on the right-hand side of the window as shown in Figure 2.7.

Once the blank policy has been created you need to tell the policy what IP Subnets this policy applies to and what it should do if it can't set up a secure connection. To do this, right click on the policy and select "Properties" from the context menu. On the rules tab of the Policy Properties click the "Add" button to bring up the Security Rule Wizard. When the wizard opens, click next on the informational screen. The next screen of the wizard allows

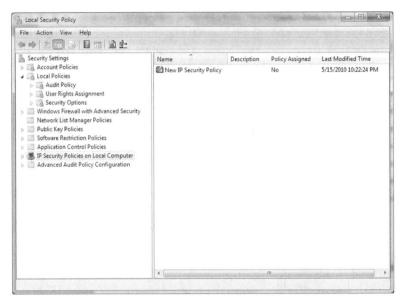

Figure 2.7 Local Security Policy with a newly created IP Sec Policy.

you to specify a tunnel endpoint. A tunnel endpoint allows you to specify a tunneling endpoint at the remote site, which will then pass the traffic unencrypted to the destination computer. For the purposes of this book we'll assume that you are not specifying a tunnel. After you click next you'll be asked to specify the network type that this rule will apply to. Most people will want to select "All network connections" and click next. If you have the server configured as a VPN Endpoint or have dial-in via modem configured on this server (for a third-party vendor to have access, for example) and if you do not want to encrypt these connections, you would then want to select the "Local area network (LAN)" option. If you only want to encrypt VPN or dial-in connections, you would select the "Remote access" option. The next screen shows the list of IP Address subnets to which this rule will apply. If this is the first rule you have created, the IP filter list will be empty; to add an entry, click the Add button, which will bring up the IP Filter List editor. When the IP Filter List editor opens, click the Add button, which will open another wizard. Click next on the information screen and enter a description if you would desire and unselect the Mirrored checkbox if desired and click next. On the next screen select the source address you wish to use. The source address is the IP Address, which is the source of the connection. If you are trying to encrypt all traffic coming to this machine, select the "Any IP Address" option. If you are trying to encrypt all traffic from a specific subnet, then select the

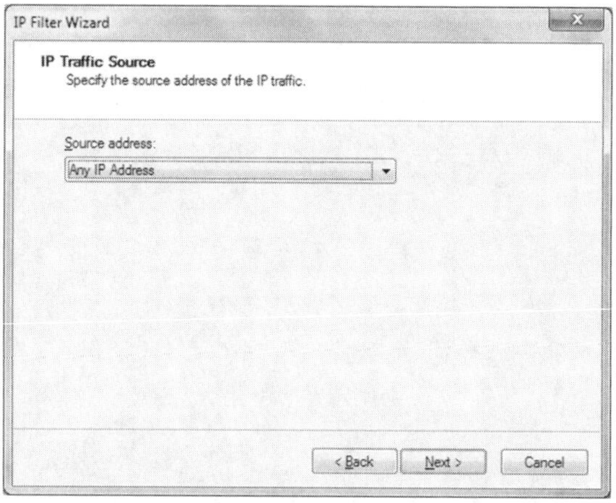

Figure 2.8 IP Traffic Source Screen of the IP Sec Policy Wizard.

"A specific IP Address or Subnet" option and fill out the IP Address or subnet field with the correct information. For the purposes of this book we'll assume you wish to encrypt all traffic to the server so you will have selected the "Any IP Address" option as shown in Figure 2.8.

After you have set the source address information and clicked the next button, you'll be prompted for the destination address information. If you only want to encrypt the traffic to the SQL Server but not network traffic from the SQL Server to other machines, you'll want to select the "My IP Address" option. If you want to encrypt access to and from the server, then select the "Any IP Address" option. As with the source address screen we looked at on the prior screen, this screen has several other options that can be used depending on your requirements. For the purposes of this book we will assume that you have selected the "Any IP Address" option as you want to encrypt all network traffic in and out of the SQL Server. After setting your Destination IP Address information click next, which will allow you to configure which protocol should be encrypted. Assuming that you only wish to encrypt the connections to and from the SQL Server Service, select the TCP option from the protocol drop down as shown in Figure 2.9 and then click Next.

On the next screen you'll be asked which TCP ports you want to encrypt the network traffic between. As we only want to encrypt the traffic to and from a Microsoft SQL Server we select "From any port" and "To this port" and enter TCP port 1433 (or whichever TCP your SQL Server is configured for) in the text box under the "To this port" field as shown in Figure 2.10. Configuring the filter in this way will only encrypt the traffic to or from the SQL

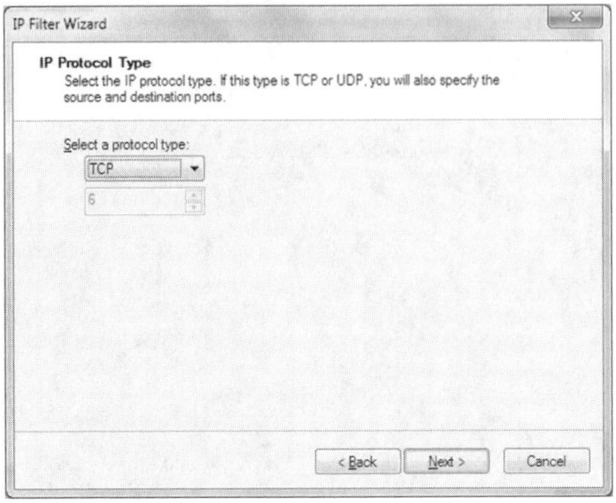

Figure 2.9 IP Protocol Type Screen of the IP Sec Wizard.

Server service. This will leave the network traffic such as to and from Active Directory to be secured through the normal mechanisms and not through IP Sec.

After setting the TCP Port numbers, click next and then finish, which will complete the wizard. If you need to add additional connections to encrypt (such as if there are multiple SQL Server instances installed on the machine that you wish to encrypt traffic to), click the Add button again to run through the wizard and add additional configurations. Once you have completed all your IP Address filters to this filter list, click the OK button.

Back on the IP Filter List screen select the IP Filter List that you wish to apply to this IP Sec policy and click the Next button. The

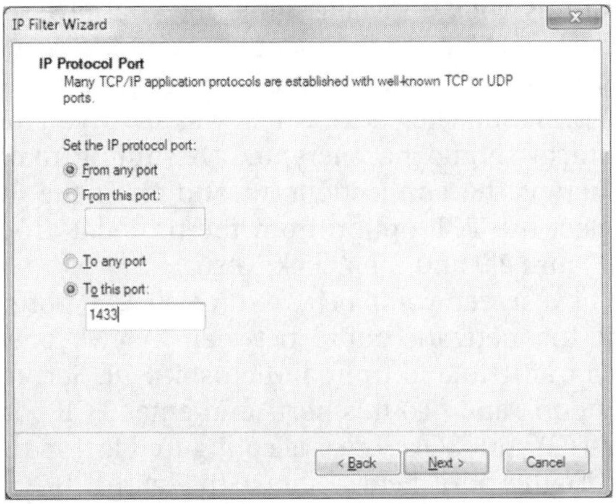

Figure 2.10 IP Protocol Port selection screen of the IP Sec Wizard.

next screen in the wizard asks you for the filter action. By clicking Add you will tell the wizard how to handle the network traffic, what do you want to encrypt, what protocol should be used to encrypt the data, what traffic can't be encrypted, and so on. After clicking on the Add button, click next on the first screen of the wizard to pass the information screen. On the next screen name your filter and provide a description, then click the next button. On the next screen you'll be asked what to do with the network traffic: Permit it, Block it, or Negotiate Security. You will want to select the Negotiate Security option and click Next. On the next screen you can specify what to do with communications from computers that don't support IP Sec. The default is to not allow unsecured connections. If you change the option from the default to "Allow unsecured communication if a secure connection cannot be established," then users who do not have IP Sec configured correctly or that do not support IP Sec may put your SQL Servers data at risk. After making your selections click the next button.

On the next screen you are telling the policy what to do with the data. Three options are shown on this page of the wizard: "Integrity and encryption," "Integrity only," and "Custom." The "Custom" option allows you to select the algorithms that are used for the Integrity and Encryption options as well as how often new keys are generated. If you use Integrity only, then the information is validated upon transmission using the MD5 or SHA1 algorithms. What this means is that the data is hashed using the selected algorithm before it is transmitted. This hash is then transmitted along with the data, and the receiving computer hashes the data and compares the hashes. If they are different, the data has been modified in some way and is discarded. When you enable Encryption you can select from the DES or 3DES algorithms to decide what level of encryption should be used. This encryption setting is in addition to the Data Integrity option. When selecting the Data integrity and encryption option (from the customer editor), you can opt to disable the Integrity option if you prefer. You can also set the triggers, which will cause a new encryption key to be generated. You can trigger new key generation by either the amount of data that has been transferred, or based on the amount of time that the current key has been active, or both. Generally accepted high security settings for IP Sec are shown in the screenshot in Figure 2.11.

If you have customized the settings, click the OK button. After setting the settings on the IP Traffic Security page, click the "Next" and then "Finish" buttons to close this wizard. This will take you back to the "Filter Action" page of the prior wizard.

Figure 2.11 Generally accepted high security settings for IP Sec.

Select the "Filter Action" that you just created from the list and click "Next."

On the next screen select the initial security method for this rule. The default selection of Active Directory default should be the correct selection for most companies to use. If you prefer to use a certificate or preshared key, you can change the option here before clicking next. If your computer is not a member of a domain, you'll need to select an option other than Active Directory as you can't use Active Directory without both computers being a member of the same Active Directory forest. Complete the wizard using the "Next" and "Finish" buttons. Click OK to close the IP Sec policy properties window.

At this point the policy has been created, but it has not been assigned. To assign the policy, simply right click on the policy and select "Assign" from the context menu. This tells the computer that this policy is now active and should be followed. In order for IP Sec to encrypt the data between the SQL Server and the workstations, you'll need to now create a corresponding policy on the workstations that need to connect to the SQL Server.

Encrypting Data with MPIO Drivers

Multi-path Input Output (MPIO) drivers are only used when your SQL Server is connected to a Storage Array via either fiber

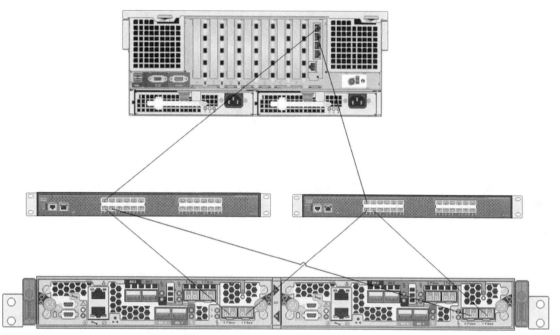

Figure 2.12 A redundant storage network diagram.

channel or Internet Small Computer System Interface (commonly referred to as iSCSI). When you connect a server to a storage array, you typically do so over multiple cables (also called paths). This allows you to connect the server to multiple controllers on the array and have multiple Host Bus Adapters (HBAs) on the server so that you have a redundant connection in the event of an HBA, cable, or Storage Controller failure. The most common way of making these connections is with two switches so that each HBA is connected to each storage controller. A sample diagram of these connections is shown in Figure 2.12.

Not all MPIO drivers are created equally. Some MPIO drivers, such as EMC's PowerPath include encryption features which allow the MPIO driver to encrypt and decrypt all the traffic between the server and the storage array. This is done by taking the write requests and encrypting the data portion of the write request (the data within the block, but leaving the block address un-encrypted) so that when the data is written to the disk it is in an encrypted form. EMC was able to bundle this encryption into the PowerPath MPIO driver because of its purchase of RSA a few years ago.

FAQ
Options Besides PowerPath?

As of this writing in the summer of 2010, the only MPIO driver that can be used to encrypt data between the server and the storage array is EMC's PowerPath. You can use EMC's PowerPath even if you don't have an EMC Storage Array that you are connecting to. PowerPath supports a wide variety of other storage arrays such as IBM ESS, Hitachi, HP StorageWorks, and HPXP storage arrays. Other arrays may be supported depending on the version of PowerPath you are looking to use. Check with an EMC reseller for more information as to if your array is supported by PowerPath. The array that you wish to connect to must be a supported array for EMC's PowerPath to manage the Logical Unit Numbers (LUNs) and allow you to configure the encryption. You can see this in Figure 2.13 where the PowerPath installer shows the various modules that can be installed so that the other storage array vendors' products can be installed.

The upside to using this sort of technique is that everything gets written encrypted without any changes to any of your code, either in your stored procedures or in your application layer. The downside is that because this is a software package this means that the work to encrypt and decrypt the data has to be done by your SQL Server's CPU. So as the load on the SQL Server goes up, and the amount of IO being done by the SQL Server goes up, the amount of CPU power needed by the MPIO driver will also increase. The other downside to using your MPIO driver for encryption is that you now have to manage the certificate used by the MPIO driver for encryption. However, this certificate management is done through an Enterprise Key Management system such as RSA Key Manager (RKM).

PowerPath Encryption with RSA Requirements and Setup

The encrypting and decrypting of data with PowerPath isn't as simple as installing the component and having it work. Using the PowerPath RSA Encryption requires installing and configuring some additional network components, including the RKM server software that is provided by RSA. Before you can begin configuring the system, you first need to request and install certificates from a certificate authority such as an internal Public Key Infrastructure (PKI). Both the server that will be encrypting the data using PowerPath and the server that will serve as the RKM server will need a certificate installed.

The certificates have some specific requirements that need to be met:

1. The certificate must be a password-protected PKCS#12 file, which contains the credentials that the PowerPath host uses. These credentials are the public key certificate and the associated private key that are used to secure the SSL communications.
2. The hosts are authenticated against the RKM server using a PEM (Privacy Enhanced Mail) encoded trusted root certificate.

After you have configured the RKM server and installed the needed certificates on the servers, the network administrator will need to configure a secure zone of the network for the servers that will be using PowerPath for encryption and the RKM server. A secure zone is a physical and logical area within a data center where all access to the devices within the zone is restricted. This restriction is implemented via a combination of user authentication and firewalls.

Note
Secure Zones Are Ultra-Secure

The Secure Zone within a company's network is going to be the most secured, isolated portion of the company network. This Secure Zone should be totally isolated using hardware firewalls preventing any unauthorized user from accessing the systems within it. General users would typically have no need to access the systems such as an Enterprise Key Management system, which would be housed within the secure zone. As users don't need access to this system, the firewall should be configured to blog any request into the Secure Zone other than the specific systems that need access to these systems.

The access that machines would need between themselves and the RSA Key Manager server is very straightforward to set up. By default the RSA Key Manager is accessed via HTTPS on TCP port 443, although this TCP port number can be changed by the systems administrator during the setup of the RSA Key Manager system. The RSA Key Manger is accessed via a website, which is protected by standard SSL encryption.

Once the secure zone is configured, you can install the RKM server on a server within the secure zone of the network. Walking through the process of installing RKM is beyond the scope of this book, and it is assumed that the RKM server is already setup and in working order.

In order to configure PowerPath to do data Encryption and Decryption, you have to install a newer version of PowerPath. To use the Encryption, you will want to have the newest version of

PowerPath. If you don't have access to the newest version, you will need to have PowerPath 5.2 or later. If when PowerPath was installed the default options were used, then the Encryption with RSA option was not installed and it will need to be installed to be used.

To install the Encryption with RSA feature, launch the PowerPath installer on the server and click next on the information screen. The second screen will ask you if you wish to modify, repair, or uninstall PowerPath; select the modify option and click the next button. The next page shows the features to install. Enable the "Encryption with RSA" as shown in Figure 2.15 and click next. The next screen informs you that the installation is ready to continue; click the Install button on the screen to complete the installation. Once the installation has completed, you will be prompted to reboot the server.

If you have not net installed PowerPath, the installation will be very similar to the upgrade process, with two additional steps. During the installation you will be prompted for your PowerPath key as well as for the folder to which you wish to install PowerPath.

After you have installed the RSA encryption module, you can launch the RKM Client Configuration tool by clicking on the Start button, then the EMC Folder, and then the Configuration folder. This will launch a wizard that will assist you define the Key Manager Client configuration, initialize your encryption LockBox, and initialize the Key Manager Client for PowerPath Encryption on the server.

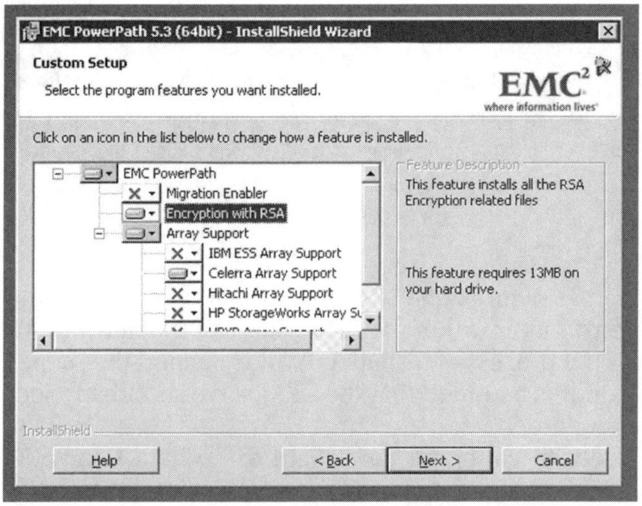

Figure 2.13 Updating an already installed PowerPath installation.

Before you can begin using PowerPath to encrypt your storage traffic, you need to tell the RKM how you wish to encrypt the data. You will want to start by creating a Key Class by logging into the RKM administration website and selecting the Key Class tab. If there is already a previously defined Key Class that you wish to use, then the process of creating a new class can be skipped; however, if you wish to use a class that is different from those that have already been created, you will need to create one. The Key Class stores the rules by which the keys that are generated for that key class must follow. This includes the algorithm, key size, and cipher mode, as well as the lifetime of the key.

Keys are controlled by Key Classes within the RKM. Optionally, these key classes can have the key specifications defined by a Crypto Policy (which is used by the Key Policy and is set when

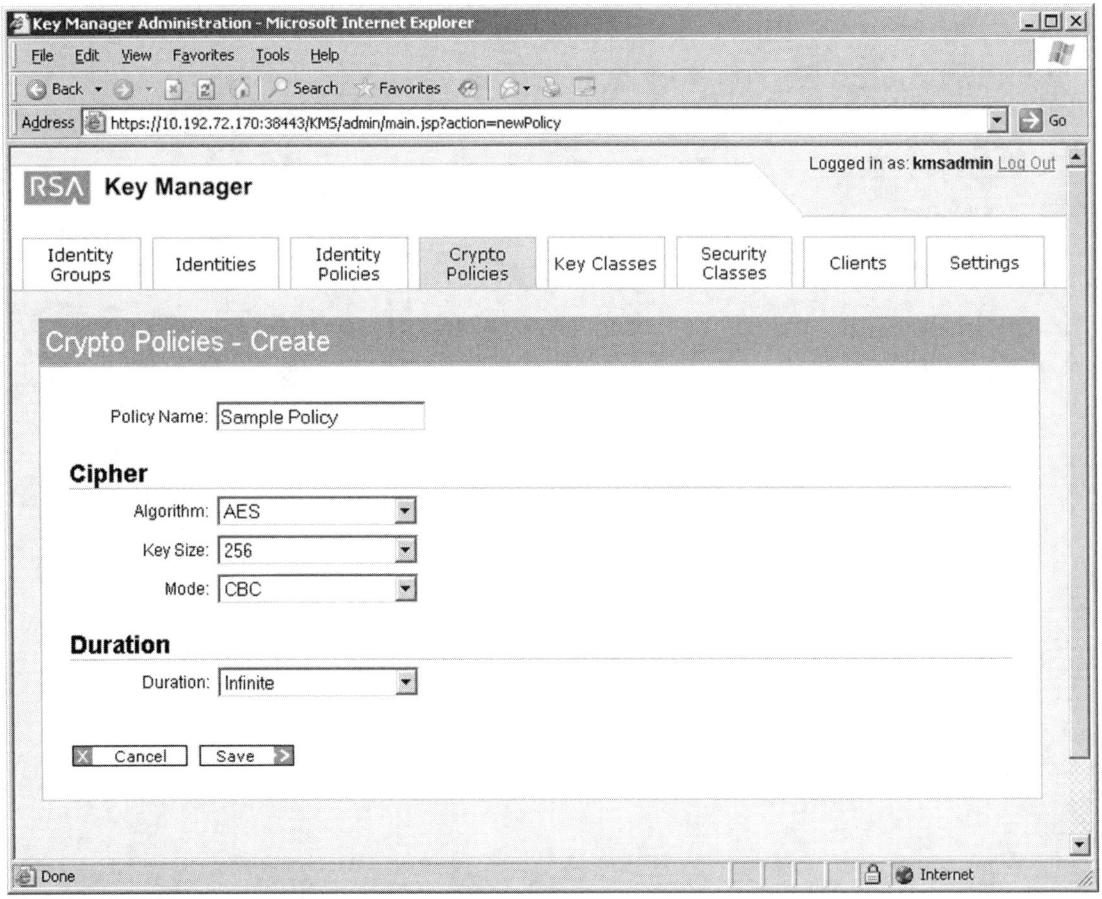

Figure 2.14 Creating a Crypto Policy in RKM's interface.

creating a new key policy later in this chapter). A crypto policy allows you to specify a fixed algorithm, key size, and cipher mode, as well as duration so that various classes have predefined values without having to set those values each time. To create a crypto policy, select the Create button on the Crypto Policy tab. Enter in the name of the Policy and set the values listed as shown in Figure 2.14.

To create a new key class, click on the Create button on the Key Classes tab that opens the first page of the five-page wizard as shown in Figure 2.15. On this first page you assign a name to the class, and assign the identity group that can use the Key Class. If the keys will expire, then you can check the box in the key duration option and optionally have the duration be controlled by a key class. This optional checkbox "Get Duration from a Crypto Policy" is shown in Figure 2.15 for reference only.

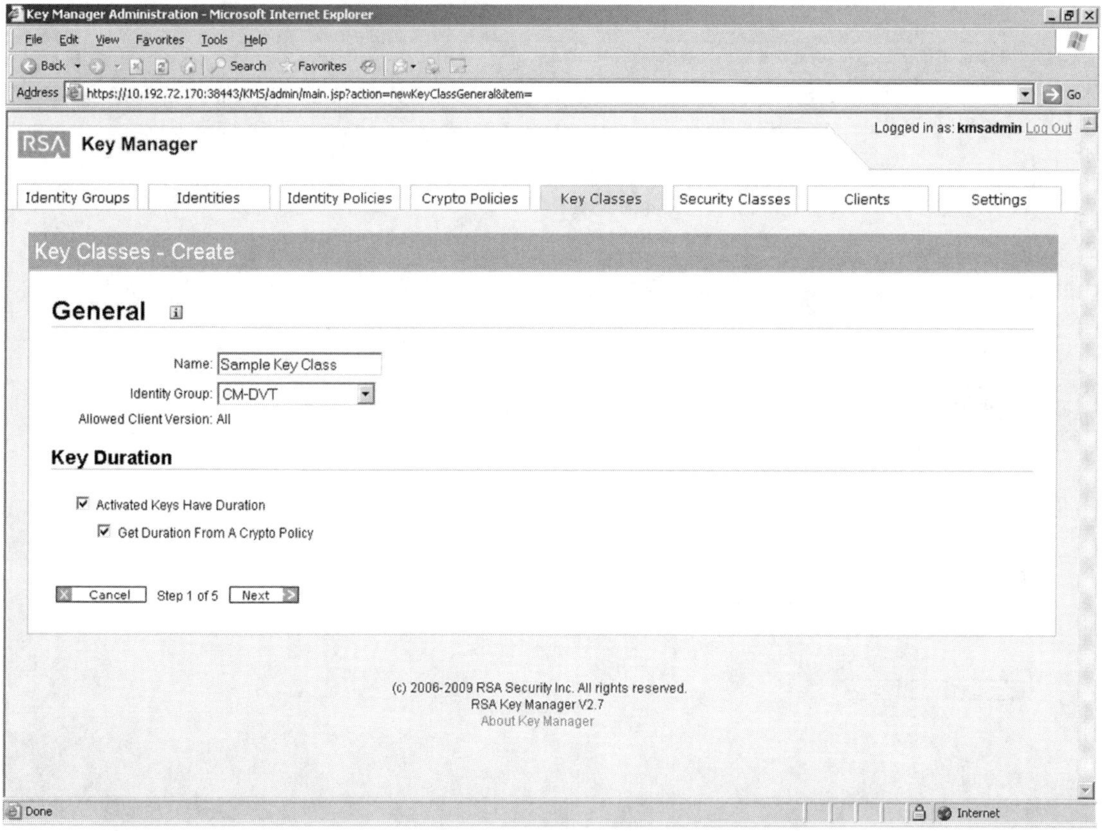

Figure 2.15 The first page of the Key Classes wizard setting the name and the identity group that can use the class.

On the second page of the new Key Class wizard you will set the algorithm, key size, and mode of the cipher, as well as the duration of the key, and if the current key can be reused if needed or if a new key should always be created as shown in Figure 2.16. If on the first screen you did select that the duration should be gotten from the Crypto Policy, then the screen will look as shown in Figure 2.16. If you did not select this option, then this page will look as shown in Figure 2.17.

The next page of the wizard allows you to assign attributes to the key class, which is an optional step. The next page of the wizard allows you to assign specifications to attributes, which is also an optional step. The last page of the wizard allows you to review all the various settings for the key class you are about to create.

After setting the key information into the system, you will need to configure the Key Management Server (KMS) to allow the client computer (in this case the SQL Server) to talk to it. This is done on the Clients tab of the RKM. After selecting the Clients tab, click

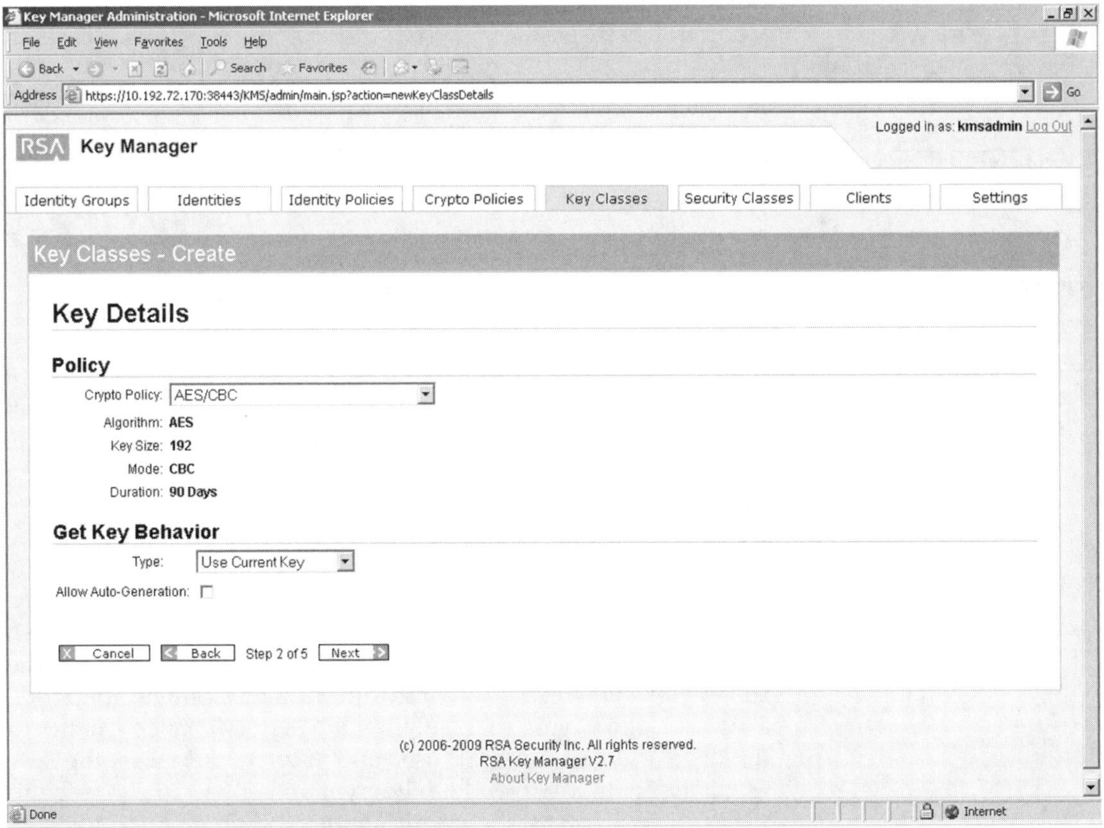

Figure 2.16 Setting the Crypto Policy to control the key details.

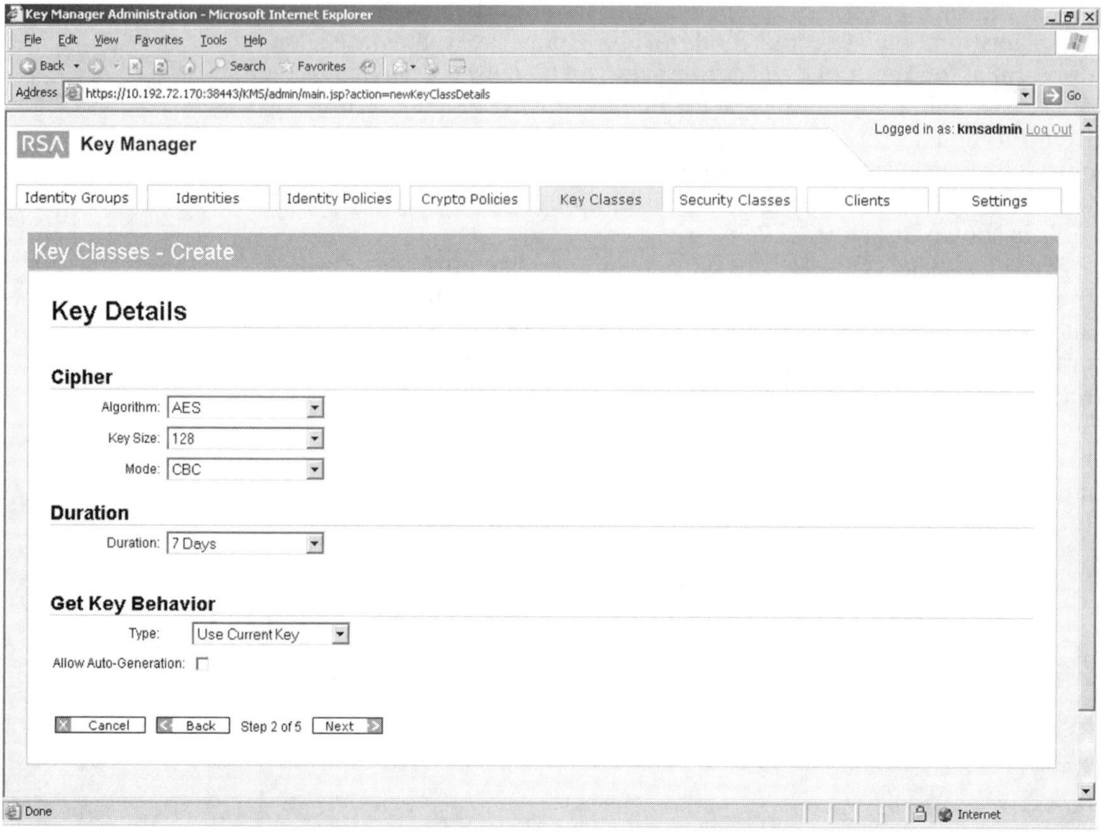

Figure 2.17 Setting the key details manually without the use of a Crypto Policy.

the Create button and on the Create Clients page enter the IP Address, Hostname, and Application Name of the server. You will also want to select the identity of the user that the server will use to log into the RKM, as well as the version of the client software that will be used to talk to the RKM as shown in Figure 2.18. The client version that you select will depend on the version of the MPIO driver that you are using, so please check with your software vendor before selecting.

Once you have set up the needed resources within the RKM, you can configure the server's MPIO driver for encryption. On the server you will be using, open the RKM Client Configuration tool. This will allow you to configure the Key Manager Client, to initialize the LockBox for use, and then to initialize the Key Manager Client for PowerPath Encryption between the server and the storage array as shown in Figure 2.19. Once this has been done, Power Path will begin encrypting all the traffic between the

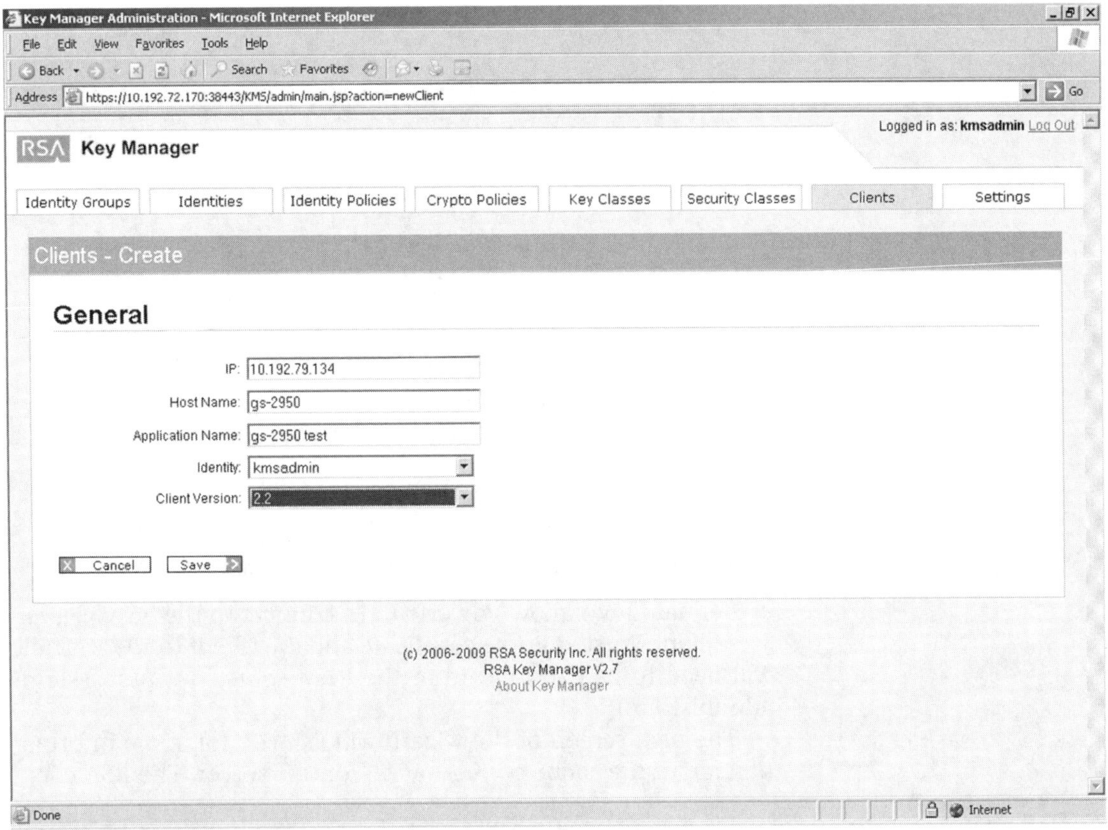

Figure 2.18 Showing the create client screen of the RKM.

server and the storage array so that when the data is written to the disk all the data will be written in an encrypted form.

To configure PowerPath open the RKM Client Configuration Wizard by clicking on Start > Programs > EMC > Configuration > RKM Client Configuration. This will bring up the wizard to configure PowerPath to talk to the RKM server. As part of the configuration you will need to supply the certificate and

Note
The Names Have Been Changed to Protect the Innocent

The screenshots shown in Figures 2.19 through 2.22 can be changed to match your environment. The same goes with all the various network paths. The names and paths shown in these screenshots are simply the paths and names that are used in the lab where the screenshots were taken.

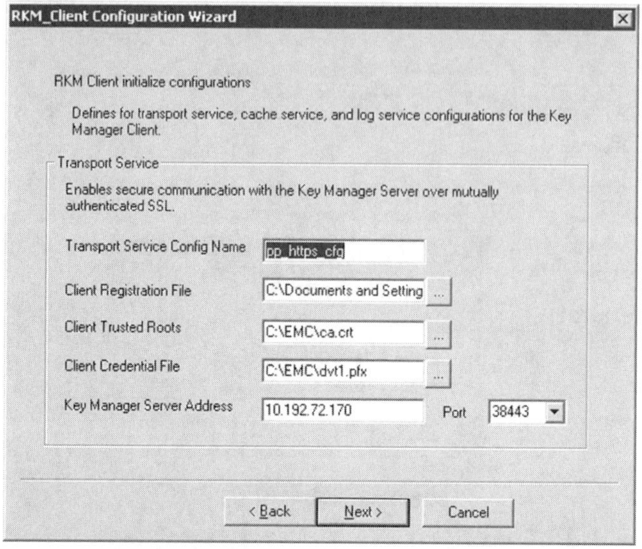

Figure 2.19 The first screen of the RSA configuration with EMC's PowerPath.

credential file to allow PowerPath to connect to the RKM Server. The Client Trusted Roots certificate and the Client Credential File will need to be exported from the RKM server by your systems administrator.

The next screen of the wizard will ask you for some information about the cache configuration for this server. The RSA client

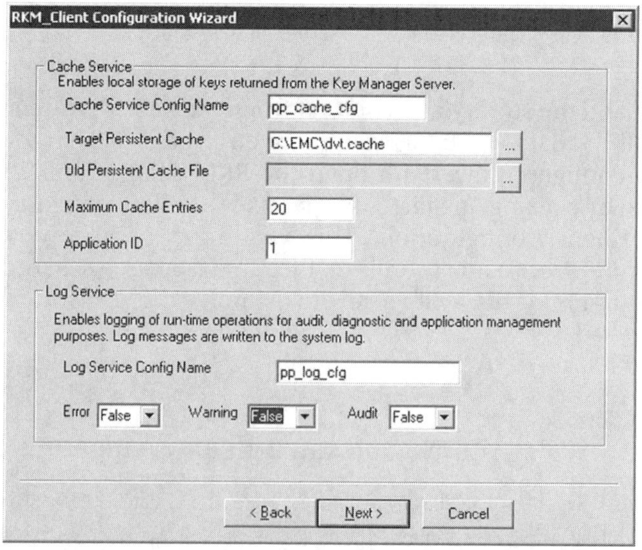

Figure 2.20 The cache and log configuration screen of the RKM setup for EMC's PowerPath.

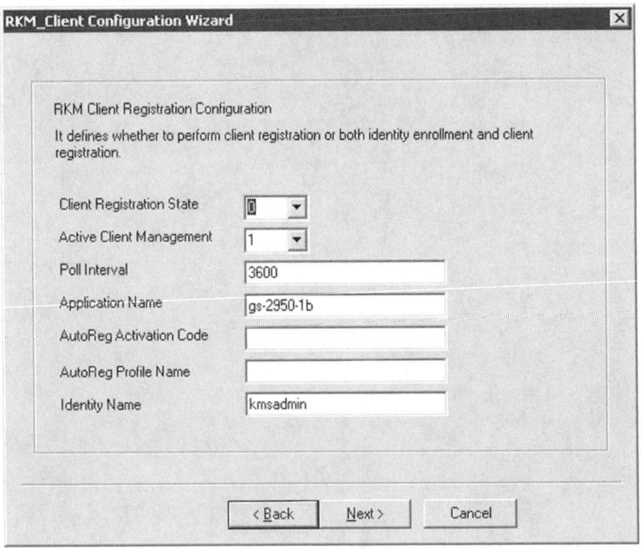

Figure 2.21 Screenshot showing the registration state, polling interval, and other registration settings.

uses this cache to store keys locally after they have been down-loaded from the RKM server. If you wish to enable logging of errors, warnings, and audit information to the system log, it is also configured on this page as shown in Figure 2.20.

The third screen of this wizard is the Client Registration Configuration screen. On this screen the registration state, polling intervals, and other registration settings are set as shown in Figure 2.21.

The fourth screen identifies the services based on the names you previously entered. This section is there in case you configure the service manually via the configuration files, and simply need to select the predefined services from the list. This screen also asks for the RKM Client Key Class. This value should be assigned by your systems administrator and will match a key class created within the RKM. As you can see in Figure 2.22, because we defined all the settings for the services, those options are grayed out and cannot be changed. This is because we are configuring the software through the wizard instead of selecting predefined settings from the prebuilt configuration files. The Key Class name shown in Figure 2.22 must match the Key Class that already exists within the RKM.

The next screen initializes the lockbox and sets the passphrase for the lockbox. The lockbox is where the keys are stored locally on the server. The next screen requests the password that will be used

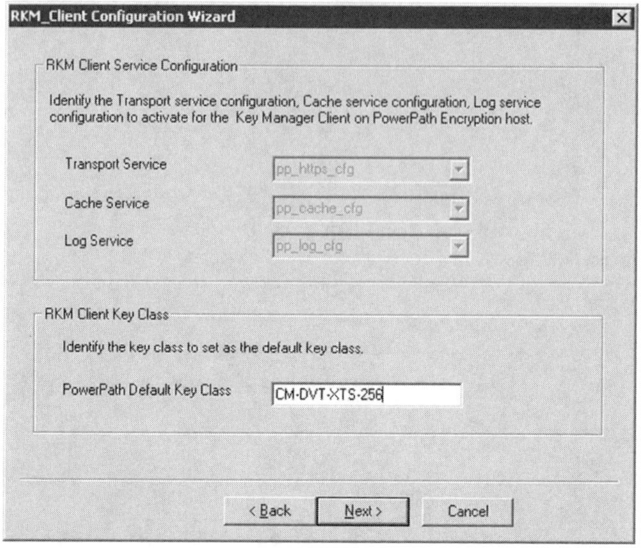

Figure 2.22 Assigning the Default Key Class that will be used to encrypt the LUNs.

for client credentials to the KMS. Once you have completed these last two password screens, the configuration is complete and you can click finish to close the wizard. At this point the PowerPath MPIO driver is ready to begin encrypting all data that is written to the volumes it manages and decrypting any encrypted blocks that it reads from the volume.

Before PowerPath will encrypt data, you need to tell Power-Path which volumes you want it to encrypt. This is done using the powervt command line utility. The syntax for this is very straight forward. Your pass is the xcrypt command telling powervt that you want to manage encryption. You then use the −on switch to tell powervt that you want to enable encryption on a LUN (Logical Unit Number). The −dev parameter tells powervt you want to specify a device, and then specify the device name as shown in the Example 2.5.

```
powervt xcrypt −on −dev harddisk2
```

Example 2.5: Sample code showing how to enable encryption on device harddisk2.

If you wish to view the status of a volume you also use the powervt command, this time switching the −on flag for the −info flag. This will return one of three return values. They are "encryp-ted," "encrypted with HBA assist," or "not encrypted." Not encrypted means that you have not encrypted the volume using PowerPath. A volume showing encrypted or encrypted with HBA

FAQ

But Denny, My System is Very Complex and Some LUNs Need to be Encrypted with Different Levels of Encryption?

There is no easy way to do this, but it can be done. When working your way through the wizard within PowerPath enter the Key Class to encrypt the first set of LUNs with, then use the powervt command to enable the encryption on those LUNs. After the encryption has been enabled on those LUNs, find the rkm_keyclass.conf file (located in the "C:\Program Files\EMC\RSA\Rkm_Client\config" directory by default) and open the file in notepad. Replace the value of the PowerPathDefaultKeyClass parameter with the name of the new Key Class that you want to use to encrypt the next set of LUNs. Repeat this process as needed until all your LUNs are encrypted with the correct Key Class.

If you use different Key Classes, you will need to document which Key Class is used for each LUN. As of the writing of this book in the summer of 2010, there is no way to query the system to find out which Key Class is being used to encrypt each LUN. PowerPath is able to do this because it writes some meta data to the front of the LUN where it stores which Key Class is used to encrypt that LUN; this is what allows you to encrypt different LUNs with different strengths of encryption.

assist means that the volume is being encrypted by PowerPath. Volumes that are encrypted with HBA assist are offloading the work of the encryption to the HBA, which is discussed later in this chapter.

Encrypting Data via HBAs

One of the newest ways to set up your encryption is to do the encryption via your HBA itself. This provides an interesting option for your encryption and decryption of data because all write and read requests are processed by the HBA so all the data stored on your disks is stored in an encrypted state (much like when you encrypt data via your MPIO driver). However, the workload of the actual data encryption and decryption is offloaded from the CPU of the SQL Server to the processors on the actual HBAs using a technique called HBA Assist.

Like everything else there is a potential downside to this. If you end up pushing so much IO through the HBA, you might overload the processor on the HBA, which would then slow down your IO requests that are queued by the HBA. However, if that were to become the case, you could simply add more HBAs to the server, giving you more processors to process the encryption and decryption of the data.

Another potential downside that you may see if encrypting data within the HBAs is that you are locked into a specific vendor's HBAs because, as of the summer of 2010, only one vendor can encrypt and decrypt data within the HBA, and that vendor is Emulex. Emulex currently supports only encryption and decryption of data when using the Emulex OneSecure adapters. This lock-in to a specific vendor may be offputting to some companies, but if you have already standardized on Emulex HBAs then this may not be a turnoff for you. If you need to replace the HBAs to HBAs that don't support encryption, the workload will then be pushed from the HBA back to the CPU of the server.

The Emulex OneSecure adapter encryption works with the PowerPath RSA Encryption configuration, so PowerPath will need to be configured to support encryption. The PowerPath encryption engine then hands off the Encryption work to the processor on the HBA instead of the CPU of the server being used to handle the encryption and decryption.

Setting up the encryption of the Emulex HBAs is incredibly easy. Once the encryption is configured through PowerPath, the HBAs will automatically begin encrypting the data. There is no configuration that must be managed or set up on the HBAs to begin the process. As you switch to the OneSecure HBAs, the output from the powervt command line utility will change from "encrypted" to "encrypted using HBA assist," which tells you that the HBAs are handling the encryption workload.

Summary

Data encryption can be done at many, many different points in the application depending on the goal that you are trying to meet. Some of these configurations are more complex to configure, such as encryption using the PowerPath MPIO driver, than others, such as the Transparent Data Encryption. There is no single answer to the question "How should I encrypt my database?" because each database is different. This is why it is so important that there are so many options as to how you can encrypt your database. Each option will load on some part of the database-driven application; it just depends on which part of your database-driven application you want to put the additional CPU load on. You can select from the client computer, the middle tier, the database server's CPU, or the HBAs in the SQL Server as long as where you want to place the processor workload corresponds to the layer where you want to encrypt the data for the SQL Server database.

When using SQL Azure as your database instance, the encryption options are extremely limited as SQL Azure does not support most of the options described in this chapter. With SQL,

Azure encryption can be handled within the application tier without issue. However, as of the summer of 2010, SQL Azure does not support any encryption within the SQL Azure database. SQL Azure does, however, support hashing using the same algorithms as the onsite SQL Server instances.

References

Levy Steven. *Crypto: How the Code Rebels Beat the Government Saving Privacy in the Digital Age*, 1st ed. Boston: Penguin (Non-Classics). 2002. Print.

"Net-Library Encryption." *MSDN | Microsoft Development, Subscriptions, Resources, and More.* N.p., n.d. Web. August 22, 2010.

"z/OS V1R9 Information Center—Beta." IBM Support & downloads—United States. N.p., n.d. Web. October 21, 2010.

3

SQL PASSWORD SECURITY

INFORMATION IN THIS CHAPTER

- SQL Server Password Security
- Strong Passwords
- Encrypting Client Connection Strings
- Application Roles
- Using Windows Domain Policies to Enforce Password Length

SQL Server Password Security

One of the key ways to protect your SQL Server is to use strong, secure passwords for your SQL Server login accounts. One of the biggest security holes in the SQL Server 2000 and older versions of Microsoft SQL Server was that the server installed with a blank system administrator (SA) password by default and would allow you to use a blank password, thereby permitting anyone to connect without much work at all.

Even with newer versions of Microsoft SQL Server, the SA account is still a potential weakness, as is any SQL Server Authentication based login. This is because SQL Accounts can be easily broken into by brute force password attacks. When using SQL Azure there is no SA account available to you the Microsoft customer work with. The SA account is reserved for the exclusive use of Microsoft.

When using SQL Azure as your database instance, only SQL Authentication is available. SQL Azure doesn't support Windows Authentication for use by Microsoft's customers as the SQL Azure database server doesn't support being added to a company domain. The Azure database servers do support Windows Authentication buy only for use by the Azure administration team within Microsoft.

SQL Authentication Logins are more susceptible to these login attacks than a Windows Authentication login because of the way that these logins are processed. With an SQL Authentication login, each connection to the SQL database passes the actual username and password from the client computer to the SQL Server Engine. Because of this, an attacker can simply sit there passing usernames and passwords to the server until a connection is successfully made.

With a Windows Authentication Login the process is much, much different from the SQL Authentication process. When the client requests a login using Windows Authentication, several components within the Windows Active Directory network are needed to complete the request. This includes the Kerberos Key Distribution Center (KDC) for when Kerberos is used for authentication, and the Windows Active Directory Domain Controller for when NTLM (NT LAN Manager) authentication is used. The Kerberos KDC runs on each domain controller within an Active Directory domain that has the Active Directory Domain Services (AD DS) role installed.

The process that occurs when a Windows Authentication connection is established is fairly straightforward once you know the components that are involved. When the client requests a connection, the SQL Server Native Client contacts the KDC and requests a Kerberos ticket for the Service Principal Name (SPN) of the Database Engine. If the request to the KDC fails, the SQL Server Native Client will then try the request for a ticket again using NTLM Authentication. This ticket will contain the Security Identifier (SID) of the Windows domain account, as well as the SIDs of the Windows groups that the domain account is a member of.

Once the SQL Server Native Client has received the ticket from the KDC, the ticket is passed to the SQL Server service. The SQL Server then verifies the ticket back against the Kerberos or NTLM server service on the domain controller to verify that the SID exists and is active, and was generated by the requesting computer. Once the Windows ID is confirmed against the domain, the SIDs for the local server groups that the user is a member of are added to the Kerberos ticket and the process within the SQL Server is started. If any of these checks fail, then the connection is rejected. The first thing that the SQL Server will verify is if there is a Windows Authenticated login that matches the user. If there is no specific Windows login, the SQL Server then checks to see if there is a Windows Domain Group or Windows Local Group to which the user belongs. The next check is to see if the login or domain group that has the login as a member is enabled and has been granted the right to connect. The next check is to ensure that the login or domain group has the right to connect to the specific endpoint. At this point the Windows Login has successfully connected to the SQL Server Instance. The next step in the process is to assign the Login ID of the Windows Login as well as any authorized domain groups. These login IDs are put together within an internal array within the SQL Server engine to be used by the last step of the authentication process as well as various processes as the user interacts with the objects within the SQL Server databases. The last step of the connection process takes the database name that was included within the connection string (or the login default database if no connection string database is specified) and checks if any of the login IDs contained with the internal array that was just created exist within the database as a user. If one of the login IDs exists within the database, then the login to the SQL Server is complete. If none of the login IDs exist within the database and the database has the guest user enabled, then the user will be connected with the permission of the guest user. If none of the login IDs exist within the database and the guest login is not enabled, then the connection is rejected with a default database specific error message.

Extended Protection

Expended Protection is a feature of the Windows operating system that was introduced with the release of Windows 2008 R2 and Windows 7. This new feature provides an additional level of preauthentication protection for client-to-server communications when both the client and server software support it. As of the writing of this book, the only version of the Microsoft SQL Server product that supports this new feature is Microsoft SQL Server 2008 R2. Patches are available from the website http://www.microsoft.com/technet/security/advisory/973811.mspx for the older Operating Systems. This new feature enhances the protection that already exists when authenticating domain credentials using Integrated Windows Authentication (IWA).

When Extended Protection is enabled, the authentication requests are both to the Service Principal Name (SPN) of the server which the client application is connecting to, as well as to the outer Transport Layer Security (TLS) channel within which the IWA takes place. Extended Protection is not a global configuration; each application that wishes to use Extended Protection must be updated to enable the use of Extended Protection.

If you are using Windows 7 and Windows Server 2008 R2 or later for both the client and server and if the SQL Server 2008 R2

Native Client or later are being used to connect to an SQL Server 2008 R2 SQL Server or later instance, and Extended Protection is enabled, then Extended Protection must also be negotiated before the Windows process can be completed. Extended Protection uses two techniques—service binding and channel binding—in order to help prevent against an authentication relay attack.

Note
Authentication Relay Attack Details

An authentication relay attack can take two different forms. The first, called a luring attack, refers to the situation where the client is tricked into connecting to an infected server passing its Windows authentication information to the attacked. The second is called a spoofing attack (or a man-in-the-middle attack) and refers to the situation where the client intends to connect to a valid service, but the connection is redirected to the attacker service via Domain Name Service (DNS) redirection or IP routing, and the spoofing server then captures the login information and passes the connection to the machine which the client is attempting to connect to.

These Authentication Relay attacks allow the user to connect to the expected resource. However, the man in the attacking computer (the one to which the user's connection has been redirected) will then capture the username and password (or other authentication information) before passing the login information to the requesting computer. The attacking computer will then either store or forward the authentication information to the person who has set up the attack, allowing them to access the internal data with the authentication information that has been captured.

Service Binding is used to protect against luring attacks by requiring that as part of the connection process, the client sends a signed Service Principal Name (SPN) of the SQL Server service to which the client is attempting to connect. As part of the response, the server then validates that the SPN that was submitted by the client matches the one that the server actually connected to. If the SPNs do not match, then the connection attempt is refused.

The service binding protection works against the luring attack as the luring attack works by having another service or application (such as Outlook, Windows Explorer, a .NET application, etc) connect to a separate valid compromised connection (such as a file server or Microsoft Exchange server). The attacking code then takes the captured signed SPN and attempts to pass it to the SQL server to authenticate. Because the SPNs do not match and the signed SPN is for another service, the connection to the SQL Server from the compromised server is rejected. Service binding requires a negligible one-time cost as the SPN signing happens only once when the connection is being made.

The channel binding protection works by creating a secure channel between the client and the SQL Server Instance. This is done by encrypting the connection using Transport Layer Security (TLS) encryption for all of the traffic within the session. The protection comes by the SQL Server Service verifying the authenticity of the client by comparing the client's channel binding token (CBT) with the CBT of the SQL Service. This channel binding protects the client from falling prey to both the luring and the spoofing attacks. However, the cost of this protection is much higher because of the TLS encryption, which must be maintained over the lifetime of the connection.

To enable Extended Protection, you first need to decide whether you wish to use service binding protection or channel binding protection. In order to use channel binding, you must force encryption for all SQL Server connections (more information about enabling SQL Server encryption can be found in Chapter 2). With SQL Server encryption disabled, only service binding protection is possible.

Note
What Extended Protection Type Should I Select?

The type of protection selected is completely up to the administrator depending on the needs of the specific environment. However, because of the CPU load differences that each option uses, the service binding protection is expected to become the more popular of the two. This becomes even more probable when it is noted that service binding protection requires the use of SSL encryption on the SQL Server connection.

Extended Protection is enabled from within the SQL Server 2008 R2 Configuration Manager for all editions of the Microsoft SQL Server 2008 R2 database engine. Within the SQL Server Configuration Manager select "SQL Server Services" from the left-hand pane and double click on the SQL Server Service you wish to enable Extended Protection for on the right, selecting the Advanced tab from the window that pops up. The Extended Protection option has three values from which you can select. The setting of "**Off**" will disable Extended Protection and will allow any connection whether or not the client supports Extended Protection. The setting of "**Allowed**" forces Extended Protection from Operating Systems which supported Extended Protection, while allowing Operating Systems, which do not support Extended Protection to connect without error. The setting of "**Required**" will tell the SQL Server to accept from client computers only those connections that have an Operating System that supports Extended Protection.

If your SQL Server has multiple Service Principal Names (SPNs) requested within the Windows domain, you will need to configure the Accepted NTLM SPNs setting. This setting supports up to 2048 characters and accepts a semicolon-separated list of the SPNs that the SQL Server will need to accept. As an example, if the SQL Server needed to accept the SPNs MSSQLSvc/ server1.yourcompany.local and MSSQLSvc/ server2. yourcompany.local, then you would specify a value of "MSSQLSvc/server1.yourcompany.local;MSSQLSvc/server2.yourcompany.local" in the Accepted NTLM SPNs setting as shown in Figure 3.1. After changing any of the Extended Protection properties, you will need to restart the SQL Server Instance for the settings change to take effect.

As SQL Azure servers are not installed on Microsoft's domain and not the company's server, Extended Protection is not available when using SQL Azure as of the writing of this book.

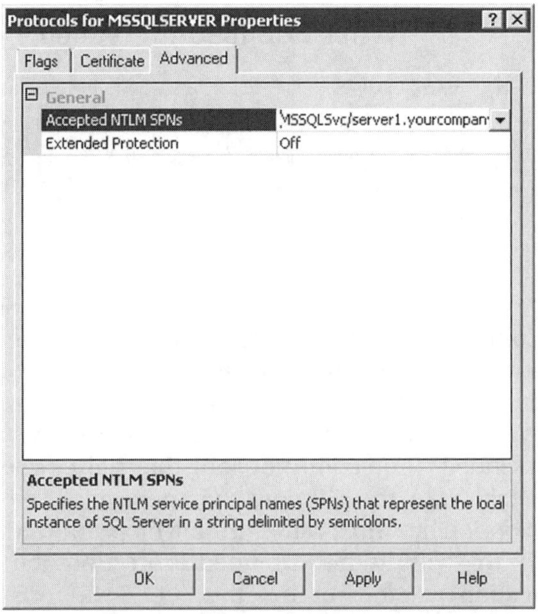

Figure 3.1 Configuring the Accepted NTLM SPNs setting in Microsoft SQL Server 2008 R2 or higher.

SPNs

Service Principal Names (SPNs) are unique service names within a Windows domain that uniquely identify an instance of a service regardless of the system that the service is running on, or how many services are running on a single machine. While a single SPN can only reference a single instance of a service, a single instance of a service can have multiple SPNs registered to it. The most common reason for multiple SPNs for a service would be that a service needs to be accessed under multiple server names.

Before an SPN can be used by Kerberos authentication, it must be registered within the Active Directory. The SPN when created is registered to a specific account within the domain. The account to which the SPN is registered must be the one under which the Windows service will be running. Because an SPN can only be registered to a single service, this means that an SPN can only be registered to a single Windows account. If the account will be running Windows service changes, then the SPN must be removed from the original account and assigned to the new account. When the client software attempts to connect using Kerberos authentication, the client locates the instance of the service and creates the SPN for that service. The client software then connects to the remote service and presents the created SPN for the service to authenticate. If the authentication fails, the client disconnects returning an error message to the end user.

The client computer is able to create an SPN for the remote service very easily as the format for an SPN is very simple. The format for an SPN is <service class>/ <host>: <port>/ <service name>. The <service class> and <host> values are required while the <port> and <service name> values are optional. In the case of Microsoft SQL Server the <service class> value will be MSSQLSvc, while the <host> value will be the name that the client computers will use to connect to the SQL Server. As an example, for an SQL Server instance listening on the default TCP port 1433 on a server named DB1.contoso.local and a Windows account named CONTOSO\sqlserver would look like "MSSQLSvc/DB1.contoso.local:1433/CONTOSO\sqlserver".SPNs are created automatically when the SQL Service starts up, but only for the default name under which the service will be running. Typically this would be the name of the SQL Server. Other SPNs can be manually registered as needed by a member of the "Domain Administrators" group by using the setspn command line application with the -A switch followed by the SPN that should be created. If the DB1.contoso.local server needed to also support the name mydatabase.contoso.local, then the command as shown in Example 3.1 would be used.

```
setspn -A MSSQLSvc/mydatabase.contoso.local:1433/CONTOSO
    \sqlserver
```

Example 3.1: Creating an SPN for mydatabase.contoso.local.

Once the SPN has been created and the SPN has replicated to all the domain controllers, the clients will be able to successfully authenticate against the new SPN. This replication can take anywhere from a few seconds to several hours, depending on how the domain replication is configured and the speed of the network links between sites.

SPNs do not need to be used with SQL Azure instances as you must use SQL Authentication with SQL Azure, and SPNs are used when using Windows Authentication with Kerberos.

Strong Passwords

Today there is no excuse for having an insecure password for your SQL Server. Most websites to which you connect, such as your bank and credit card websites, all require that you use a strong password of some sort. It is shocking the number of companies that don't take these same techniques to heart for their internal security.

A strong password is typically defined as a password that contains at least three of the following four categories and is at least eight characters in length, although some companies may require longer passwords.

1. Lower-case letters
2. Upper-case letters
3. Numbers
4. Special characters

Now when it comes to passwords for accounts like the SA account, which are rarely if ever actually used by people, there's no reason to stop there. The longer the password and the more special characters that you use in your password, the less chance that someone will be able to break into your SQL Server using this account. This same use of strong passwords should be used for any SQL Login that you create so as to better secure these SQL Logins against brute force attacks.

One thing that you can do to really secure your SA account is to use some high ASCII (American Standard Code for Information Interchange) characters within the password. This will basically make the account unbreakable to most of the people who use automated scripts to attack the SA password as all of them pretty much use the standard characters from the Latin alphabet. Inserting a character like a smiley face, which can be created by pressing <ALT>257 on your keyboard, will be outside the range of characters that are used by the password cracking program. By using this character, suddenly the word "Password" becomes a much more secure password as shown in Figure 3.2.

With a little creativity you could in fact turn the word "Password" into a truly strong and secure password. As shown in Figure 3.3, we've taken it to the extreme, replacing the letter S with the Hebrew Lamad, the letter O with a smiley face, and the letter D with a Dong Sign.

You can get more ideas on ways to replace characters with high ASCII characters from the character map that can be found within Windows. You can find the character map by clicking Start > Programs > Accessories > System Tools > Character Map. After the application loads, simply scroll down on the list of available characters until you find ones that you wish to use.

Now there is a catch with using these high ASCII characters for your SA password: If you ever need to log into the SQL Server using the SA account, you'll either need to use the character map to get the characters, or you'll need to know the <ALT> codes to access these characters.

The SA account needs to be the most secured account on your SQL Server for a few reasons, the most important of which is that the SA account has rights to everything and you can't revoke its rights to do anything that it wants. The second reason is that the SA account has a known username since you aren't able to change the username from SA to something else. Because of this, someone who is trying to break into your SQL Server doesn't need to guess the username; he or she only needs to guess the password that reduces the amount of work needed to break into the SQL Server by half.

The most secure way to secure your sa account is to not enable SQL Authentication, which requires that all connections to the SQL Server come from a trusted computer that is authenticated against your Windows domain. Disabling SQL Authentication is

Passw☺rd

Figure 3.2 The word password with a smiley face in place of the letter "a."

Paℓℓw☺rḏ

Figure 3.3 The word "Password" with the letters S, O, and D replaced with high ASCII characters.

a very easy change for you to make on your SQL Server. However, before you disable the SQL Authentication on an SQL Instance that is already in production, you'll need to ensure that there are no applications logging into the SQL Server using SQL Authentication. Once this is done you can disable the SQL Authentication. Whenever possible, new SQL Server installations should be configured to use Windows Authentication only. SQL Authentication can be disabled by connecting the object explorer in SQL Server Management Studio to the instance in question, then right clicking on the Server and selecting properties. Select the Security tab on the right. In the Server Authentication section, select the Windows Authentication radio button as shown in Figure 3.4 and click OK. If you are using Enterprise Manager to configure SQL Server 7 or SQL Server 2000, the properties screen will look similar.

Now there is T/SQL code available to change this setting. However, the change is not a simple change via the sp_configure settings like most server wide settings. You have to update the registry using the xp_instance_regwrite system stored procedure from within the master database. The T/SQL code needed to change this setting is shown in Figure 3.5. As with all changes made to the registry (either directly or via this T/SQL script), incorrect values or changes will cause the SQL Server to behave incorrectly or to not start at all.

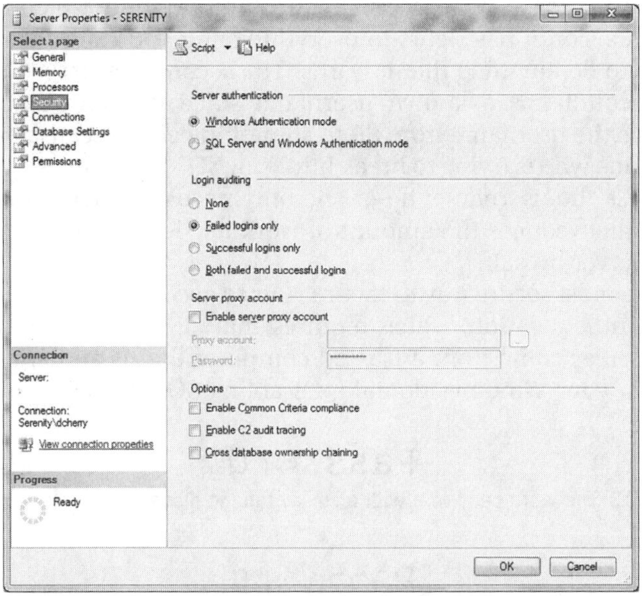

Figure 3.4 The security properties page of the server properties with Windows Only Authentication enabled.

```
SQLQuery1.sql - (l...nity\dcherry (54))*
   USE [master]
   GO
⊟EXEC xp_instance_regwrite N'HKEY_LOCAL_MACHINE',
      N'Software\Microsoft\MSSQLServer\MSSQLServer',
      N'LoginMode',
      REG_DWORD,
      1
   GO
```

Figure 3.5 The T/SQL Script to enable Windows Only Authentication.

If you find that you need to allow both SQL Server Authentication and Windows Authentication, then using T/SQL use the same code as shown in Figure 3.5, replacing the last parameters value of 1 with a value of 2.

When making changes to the Server Authentication mode, either with the UI (User Interface) or via T/SQL, you will need to restart the SQL Instance. This is because the setting is a registry setting that is only read on the start of the instance and is not refreshed by the instance while the instance is running.

When doing the initial install of the SQL Server 2005 or newer instance, if you select Windows Authentication only the SQL Server will automatically disable the sa account for you. It does this because you aren't prompted for a password for the SA account during the installation wizard when installing using Windows only authentication. Thus, if you were to later change from Windows Authentication to SQL Server Authentication, you would have the SA account enabled with no password allowing the SQL Server to be easily broken into.

Encrypting Client Connection Strings

While using Windows authentication is the best way to connect to the database server, this isn't always possible because the client machine that is connecting to the database server may not be connected do the Windows Domain.

Note
Encryption Isn't Microsoft SQL Server Specific

This technique can be used for connection strings to all your database platforms. You could also be using a database server such as NoSQL, MySQL, which may or may not support Windows Authentication. This technique will work for all database platforms equally well as no matter what the database platform is, the connection string is always a week spot.

This is most often the case when the web server is located in a DMZ network and the database server is located within the internal network as shown in Figure 1.3 in Chapter 1. In a case like this, the application development team should take extra care to secure the web server's connection string. Without this extra protection, someone could break into the web server and find the database server's connection information sitting in the web.config file and simply log into the database using the username and password, which are stored in plain text in the configuration file.

One great technique to do this is to have the web application on startup read the web.config file looking for an unencrypted connection string. Then read that string into memory, delete that node from the web.config file's XML, and then add a new node labeled as being the encrypted string, encrypt the string, and place the encrypted string within the XML document, saving it when done. On subsequent loads of the XML file, the unencrypted connection string would not be found, and the application would then load the encrypted version, decrypting it in memory, thereby making it much, much harder for someone who has broken into the SQL Server to find any useful connecting string information.

If you don't want to give the web application access to write to the web.config file (as this would technically be a security hole unto itself), the application team could create a small standalone app that takes the normal connection string and outputs an encrypted value, which the SA could then put within the web.config file during deployment of the application by the SA team.

SQL Reporting Services

SQL Reporting Services does an excellent job of protecting the connection information to the repository databases, as well as the connection strings that the reports use to connect to the source databases. All database connection strings that are used by SQL Reporting Services are encrypted and stored within the web.-config as the encrypted string. Within the SQL Server Reporting Services database, typically named ReportServer, all the connection information that the reports use to connect to the source databases is also stored as an encrypted value. Both of these encrypted values together form a very secure platform that makes it very difficult for an attacker to exploit the SQL Server Reporting Services platform to get any useful information from the database holding the Reporting Server catalog database, or the source data; getting access to the source data via the data stored within the SQL Server Reporting Service repository would require decrypting two layers of information.

Application Roles

When using Windows Authentication, there is an unfortunate side effect that needs to be considered: The user can now log into the database using any Open Database Connectivity (ODBC)-based application such as Microsoft Access, Microsoft Excel, and SQL Server Management Studio, and they have the same rights that they would have if they were logged in via the application. If the user logs into the database by supplying the SQL Login username and password, this name risk is there. However, if the application contains the username and password hard coded within the application, then the user won't have this ability as they will not have the username and password. This is probably something that you don't want to happen. Before you go and switch all your applications to using SQL Authentication and hard coding the password within the application, there's another solution that gives you the best of both worlds. This solution is to use an application role.

The application role is not a very well-understood, and therefore not very frequently used, security feature of Microsoft SQL Server, which allows a user to authenticate against the Microsoft SQL Server Instance, but not have any specific rights within the database. The rights to perform actions are granted to the application role, which would then need to be activated by the application before the user would be able to perform any actions.

Application roles are created by using the sp_addapprole system stored procedure in SQL Server 2000 and below or by using the CREATE APPLICATION ROLE statement in SQL Server 2005 and above. The application role has its own password that is used to ensure that only authorized applications are able to activate the application. The application role is activated by using the sp_setapprole system stored procedure, and then the application role is deactivated by using the sp_unsetapprole system stored procedure, or by simply closing the connection to the database engine.

```
EXEC sp_addapprole @rolename='MyAppRole', @password=
   'MyPa$$word'
CREATE APPLICATION ROLE MyAppRole WITH PASSWORD='MyPa$$word'
```

Example 3.2 Sample code using the sp_addapprole system stored procedure and CREATE APPLICATION ROLE statement to create an application role.

Tip
sp_addapprole Has Been Deprecated

If you are using SQL Server 2005 and above, you should use the CREATE APPLICATION ROLE statement as the sp_addapprole has been deprecated and will be removed in a future version of Microsoft SQL Server.

The sp_setapprole system stored procedure has four parameters that are of interest. The first and second parameters are the @rolename and @password parameters to which you supply the name and password that were specified when you created the application role. The third parameter is the @fCreateCookie parameter, which is a bit parameter and tells the SQL Server if it should create a cookie when the application role is activated (I'll explain the cookies in a moment). The fourth parameter is the @cookie parameter, which is a varbinary(8000) and stores the cookie that was created if the @fCreateCookie parameter was set to 1.

The @cookie parameter stores a cookie much in the same way that your web browser stores cookies when you browse the web, so that it can correctly identify the session that was used to activate the application role. Thus, when the application role is disabled, the SQL Server knows which session state to return the user's session to. If you don't plan to unset the application role and will simply close the connection to the SQL Server, then you don't need to set a cookie and can simply set the @fCreate-Cookie password to 0 telling the SQL Server to not create the cookie.

In the sample code shown in Example 3.3, we create a new database, and then we create an application role within that database. We then create a table within the database, as well as a user within the database. We next give the application role access to select data from the table. We then use the EXECUTE AS statement to change your execution context from that of our user to that of the user, which we just created and has no rights. Next we query the table, which returns an error message to us. After that we switch to using the application role and try and query the table again, this time receiving the output as a recordset. We then unset the application role using the cookie that was created by the sp_setapprole system stored procedure. We then use the REVERT statement so that we are no longer executing code as our MyUser database use, after which we drop the sample database.

```
USE master
GO
IF EXISTS (SELECT * FROM sys.databases WHERE name =
   'AppRoleTest')
   DROP DATABASE AppRoleTest
GO
CREATE DATABASE AppRoleTest
GO
USE AppRoleTest
GO
CREATE APPLICATION ROLE MyAppRole WITH PASSWORD='MyPa$$word'
GO
CREATE TABLE MyTable
 (Col1 INT)
GO
CREATE USER MyUser WITHOUT LOGIN
GO
GRANT SELECT ON MyTable TO MyAppRole
GO
DECLARE @cookie varbinary(8000)
EXECUTE AS USER = 'MyUser'
SELECT * FROM MyTable
EXEC sp_setapprole @rolename=MyAppRole, @password='My
   Pa$$word', @cookie=@cookie OUTPUT, @fCreateCookie=1
SELECT * FROM MyTable
EXEC sp_unsetapprole @cookie=@cookie
REVERT
GO
USE master
GO
DROP DATABASE AppRoleTest
GO
```

Example 3.3 Sample code showing the use of an Application Role.

When we run this script as shown in text output mode from within SQL Server Management Studio, we see the output shown in Figure 3.6. The first SELECT statement that we issued was rejected because the user didn't have rights to the table dbo.-MyTable in the AppRoleTest database. However, the second

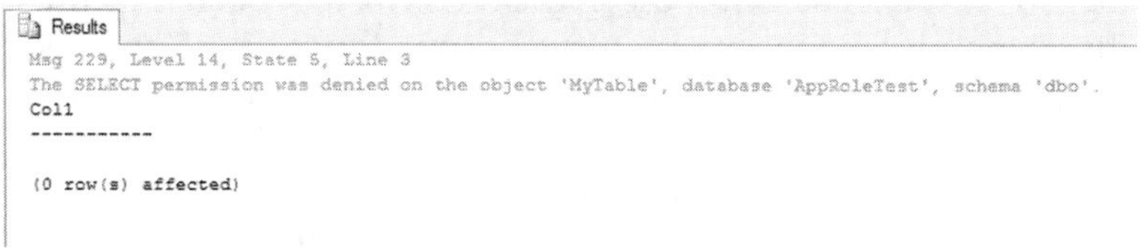

Figure 3.6 Output of the sample code as shown in Figure 3.5.

SELECT statement that we issued after we set the Application Role was accepted by the database, and the contents of the table were returned.

You can now see how use of the application role can enable the use of the very secure Windows authentication without requiring that the user's Windows account actually have rights to access any objects within the database directly, but the application can run once the application role has been activated.

Note
Application Roles and Linked Servers

Application roles and linked servers can start giving you problems if you expect the Windows account to be passed across the linked server, as you are now executing within the context of the application role and not the Windows account. Any mapping being done through a linked server would need to be done globally or through the application role name.

In addition, system functions such as the login name functions will also return incorrect information for the same reason—that is, the work is being done within the context of the application role, not within the user's context.

Another technique that can be used along the same lines of the application role is to create a user with no attached login as done in Figure 3.5 and use the EXECUTE AS statement to run commands as that user. While this will allow you to run all your statements without the user needing to have rights to the database objects, the problem with this technique is that any logging that is done via the username functions returns the dummy user that you created and not the login of the actual user. This is shown along with sample code in Figure 3.7 As you can see in the sample code, we create a dummy user, then output my username using the SUSER_SNAME() system function, then switch to running under the context of the MyUser database user, and then output the value of the SUSER_SNAME () function again with the output being the SID of the MyUser database user account. You can't even query the dynamic management views to get the correct username of the user logged in, because once the EXECUTE AS has been executed, the dynamic management views show the SID of the user instead of the name of the login that was originally connected to the database.

When using an application role, you don't have the database username return problem when using the system functions or the dynamic management views.

```
 1  USE tempdb
 2  GO
 3  CREATE USER MyUser WITHOUT LOGIN
 4  GO
 5  print 'normal login output'
 6  GO
 7  SELECT SUSER_SNAME()
 8  GO
 9  print 'Using EXECUTE AS'
10  GO
11  EXECUTE AS USER='MyUser'
12  SELECT SUSER_SNAME()
13  REVERT
14  GO
15  DROP USER MyUser
```

Results

```
normal login output
------------------------------------------------------------
Serenity\dcherry

Using EXECUTE AS
------------------------------------------------------------
S-1-9-3-2851743519-1315201071-3451601828-1822525857
```

Figure 3.7 Script and output showing how the EXECUTE AS statement is used.

Using Windows Domain Policies to Enforce Password Length

Starting with Microsoft SQL Server 2005, Microsoft introduced a new level of password security within the product, as this was the first version of Microsoft SQL Server that could use the domain policies to ensure that the passwords for the SQL Authentication accounts were long enough and strong enough to meet the corporate standards as set forth by the SAs. By default, all SQL Authentication accounts created within the SQL Server instance must meet the domain password security policies. You can, if necessary, remove these restrictions by editing the SQL Authentication account.

Within the Microsoft SQL Server, two settings can be applied to each SQL Authentication Login, which are shown in Figure 3.8.

1. The "Enforce password policy" setting tells the SQL Server engine to ensure that the password meets the needed complexity requirements of the domain, and that the password hasn't been used within a specific number of days, which is defined within the domain policy, and is explained later in this chapter.

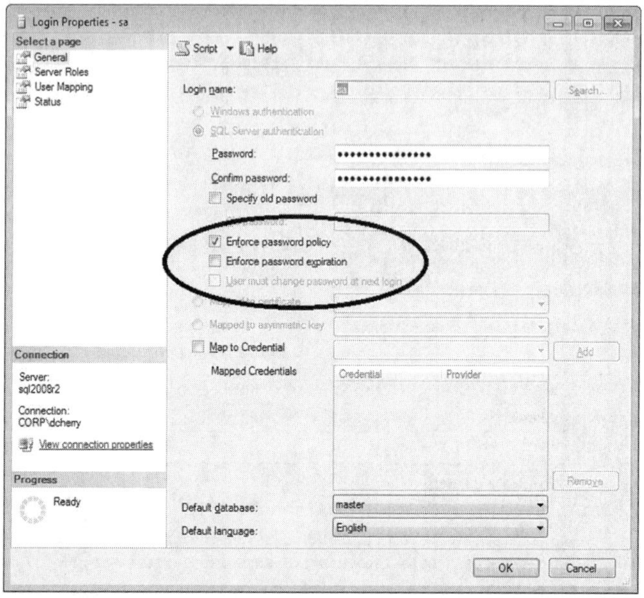

Figure 3.8 The SQL Authentication Login screen showing the two available domain policy settings with the "User must change password at next login" option disabled.

2. The "Enforce password expiration" setting tells the SQL Server that the password for the SQL Authentication Login should have expired based on the domain settings (also discussed in more detail later in this chapter).

The "User must change password at next login" option, shown disabled in Figure 3.8, will only become available when the logins password is manually reset and the "Enforce password policy" setting is enabled for the login.

Allowing the SQL Server to ensure that your passwords meet your domain policies has some distinct advantages, especially when it comes to auditing. Without this ability you would need to physically check each SQL server password to ensure that it meets the corporate standards when the Auditor asks you if all your SQL Authentication passwords meet the corporate standards. In a worst case situation, this would require that you either keep a list of all the usernames and passwords somewhere (which would probably cause you to fail the audit) or you would need to contact each person that uses the SQL Authentication login and ask them how long the password is, and if it meets the company policies, and so on. Now with this feature built into the product, a quick and simple SQL query is all that it takes to verify the information.

```
SELECT name, is_policy_checked
    FROM sys.sql_logins
```

Example 3.4 Querying the sys.sql_logins catalog view will show you any logins that may not meet the domain password policies.

While the T/SQL shown in Example 3.4 works great for a single SQL Server, if there are dozens or hundreds of SQL Servers that need to be verified, a T/SQL script may not be the best way to check all those servers. In this case a Windows PowerShell script may be more effective. Within the Windows PowerShell script shown in Example 3.5, the SMO (Server Management Object) is used to get a list of all the available instances on the network. After this list has been returned from the network, SMO is used to return the SQL Logins along with the value of the PasswordPolicyEnforced setting.

```
[System.Reflection.Assembly]::LoadWithPartialName('Micro-
    soft.SqlServer.Smo') | out-null
foreach ($InstanceList in [Microsoft.SqlServer.Management.
    Smo.SmoApplication]::EnumAvailableSqlServers())
{
$InstanceList;
$instanceName = $InstanceList.Name;
$instanceName;
$SMOserver = New-Object ('Microsoft.SqlServer.Management.
    Smo.Server') $instanceName
$db = $SMOserver.Logins | where-object {$_.loginType -eq
    "sqllogin"} | select name, PasswordPolicyEnforced
$db;
}
```

Example 3.5: Using SMO to return the PasswordPolicyEnforced setting for all SQL Logins for all SQL Server Instances available on the network.

By setting the is_policy_checked flag to true (shown as the number 1 when you run the sample query in Example 3.4), this tells you that any password that is assigned to the SQL Authentication Login must meet the password requirements of the domain. Expanding on the query shown in Example 3.4, an SQL Server Reporting Services report could be configured that runs against each SQL Server in the environment, giving a simple report that can be run as needed for auditing purposes.

When you have the is_policy_checked flag set to true, there are several domainwide settings that will be evaulated each time the password is changed. These policies can be found by editing the Group Policy Object (GPO) on the domain that holds these settings, or by editing the local security policies for the server in question if that server is not a member of a Windows domain. While you can set these settings on a server that is a member of the domain, doing so won't have any effect as the domain policies but will overwrite any local settings you have set.

If all the SQL Server Instances that need to be polled are registered within SQL Server Management Studio, this select statement can be run against all the instances at once returning a single record with all the needed information. This can be done by opening the registered servers panel within SQL Server management studio by clicking on the View dropdown menu and then the "Registered Servers" menu item. Right click on the folder that contains the SQL Server Instances you want to execute the query against and select "New Query" from the context menu that opens. This opens a new query window which, when executed, will execute the query against all the servers that are within the registered servers folder with all the data from all the servers being returned as a single recordset. SQL Server Management Studio will automatically add in a new column at the beginning of the recordset, which contains the name of the instance; this will allow you to use the same query shown in Example 3.4 against all the SQL Servers at once and giving back a single recordset that can be reviewed or handed off as needed.

Windows Authentication Group Policies

There are a total of six policies that you can set within Windows that affect the domain or local password policy. However, Microsoft SQL Server only cares about five of them. The policy with which the SQL Server is not concerned is the "Store passwords using reversible encryption" policy. This policy tells Windows if it should store the user's password using a two-way encryption process, instead of a one-way hash. Enabling this policy presents a security vulnerability on your domain as an attacker could download the list of all users and passwords, then break the encryption on the passwords and have full access to every user's username and password. Due to the security issues with this setting, the setting is disabled by default and should remain so unless there is a specific reason to enable it. The typical reasons to enable it include using Challenge Handshake Authentication Protocol (CHAP) through Remote Access or Internet Authentication Services (IAS). It is also required if one or more Internet Information Service (IIS) servers within the Windows Domain are using Digest Authentication.

The five password policies that the SQL Server does recognize and follow are the following:

1. Enforce password history;
2. Maximum password age;
3. Minimum password age;
4. Minimum password length;
5. Password must meet complexity requirements.

Each of these settings has a specific effect on what the passwords can be set to and should be fully understood before changing the password of an SQL Authentication Login.

The "Enforce password history" setting on the domain (or local computer) is not a boolean, although the name sounds as though it would be. It is in fact the number of old passwords for the account that the SQL Server should track so that passwords cannot be reused. The setting has a valid range of 0 (or no passwords) to 24 passwords. The more passwords that are kept, the greater the chance that the user will forget their password, but the lesser the chance that someone will break into the system via an old password. The default on the domain is 24 passwords.

The "Maximum password age" setting tells the SQL Server how many days a password is valid. After this number of days has passed since the last password change, the user will be prompted to change the password. If the password is not changed, the user will not be able to log into the database instance. This setting accepts a value from 0 (never expires) to 999 days, with a default value of 42 days.

The "Minimum password age" setting tells the SQL Server how many days from the time a password has been changed until it can be changed again. This setting prevents the user from rapid-fire changing their passwords to eat up the number of passwords specified by the "Enforce password history" setting. Without this setting, or with this setting set to 0, when the user's password expires, the user can simply change the password 24 times and then change it to the same password that it was before effectively breaking the password requirement feature. This setting accepts a value from 0 (allows immediate password changes) to 998 days, with a default value of 1; however, this setting has a practical upper limit of one day lower than the setting for the "Maximum password age." If you were to set this setting to the same value or higher than the "Maximum password age" setting, then the users wouldn't ever be able to login until after their passwords had expired.

The "Minimum password length" setting tells the SQL Server how many characters need to be in the password for the password to be acceptable. This setting can be any value from 0 (allowing a blank password) to 14 characters, with a default value of

7 characters. It is typically recommended to increase this value from the default of 7 to a higher number such as 9 characters. While this will make the password harder for the user to remember, it will also make it exponentially harder for an attacker to guess. The "Password must meet complexity requirements" setting tells the SQL Server that all passwords must be considered "strong" passwords. There are several requirements to having a strong password beyond what one would normally consider. By default this setting is enabled.

1. The password cannot contain the username within it.
2. The password must be at least six characters in length.
3. The password must contain characters from at least three of these four categories:
   a. Lower-case letters (a through z);
   b. Upper-case letters (A through Z);
   c. Numbers (0 through 9);
   d. Symbols ($, #, @, %, ^ for example).

When you enable the "Enforce password policy" setting for an SQL Authentication Login, this enforces the "Enforce password history," "Minimum password length," and "Password must meet complexity requirments" settings against that login. When you enable the "Enforce password expiration" setting for an SQL Authenticaiton Login, this enforces the "Maximum password age" and the "Minimum password age" settings against that login. In order to enable the "Enforce password expiration" setting against an SQL Authenticaiton login, you must also enable the "Enforce password policy" setting. However, you do not need to enable the "Enforce password expiration" setting if you enable the "Enforce password policy" setting.

When working on an SQL Azure database, the login must meet the password complexity settings that Microsoft has defined. As of the summer of 2010, this means that the password must be 8 characters in length, and meet the complexity requirements shown above. There is no way to configure a login to an SQL Azure instance to not meet these requirements, for the SQL Azure instances do not support using the check_policy parameter to disable the policy checking.

Windows Domain Requirements to Use Domain Policies to Manage SQL Authentication Logins

In order for these settings to be available, specific requirements from the Windows domain must be met. Notably, the domain must be a Windows 2003 domain or higher, and the domain functional level must be Windows 2003 Native or higher.

If the domain is a Windows 2000 domain, or a Windows NT 4.0 domain (or older), then these settings will not be available for you to change and will effectivly always be set to false.

There are two ways to configure these settings for an SQL Server login. You can use the SQL Server Management Studio to edit the login, or you can use T/SQL to change the settings. To edit a login within the SQL Server Management Studio, follow these five steps:

1. Connect to the server within the object explorer;
2. Navigate to Security;
3. From Security navigate to Logins;
4. From Logins navigate to the login that you want to configure;
5. Right click on the login, and select properties from the context menu which opens.

The window that opens, as shown in Figure 3.9, will allow you to configure which of the two properties you wish to enable.

If you prefer to use T/SQL to edit these settings, then you will need to use the ALTER LOGIN command as shown in Example 3.6.

```
ALTER LOGIN YourLogin
WITH CHECK_POLICY = on,
CHECK_EXPIRATION = off
```

Example 3.6 T/SQL Code setting the policy and expiration settings for an SQL Authentication Login.

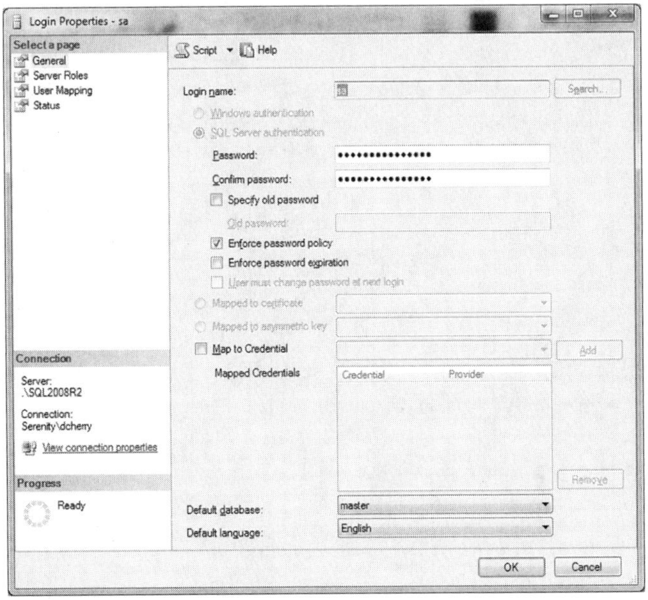

Figure 3.9 The login properties dialog box.

Summary

One of the biggest problems in today's IT world is that once you have created your nice secure passwords, how do you track them? Those usernames and passwords are probably going to be documented somewhere, typically within an Excel sheet that is kept on a network share so that all the database administrators within the group have quick and easy access to them. However, by doing this you now have placed all the passwords that you have taken the time to ensure that are strong and secure within your web.config and app.config files are easily readable and usable by anyone who has access to the network share. Typically, not just the database administrators would have access to the network share. In addition to the database administrators, the SAs, backup software, and monitoring system would all have access to the network share. And this is in addition to whoever has found the lost backup tape for your file server. In other words, be sure to store that password list in a nice, safe place and not in the public arena available to everyone to read and network share.

References

Choosing an Authentication Mode. (n.d.). *Microsoft TechNet: Resources for IT Professionals.*

Connecting to the Database Engine Using Extended Protection. (n.d.). *MSDN | Microsoft Development, Subscriptions, Resources, and More.*

4

SECURING THE INSTANCE

INFORMATION IN THIS CHAPTER

- What to Install, and When?
- SQL Authentication and Windows Authentication
- Password Change Policies
- Auditing Failed Logins
- Renaming the SA Account
- Disabling the SA Account
- Securing Endpoints
- Stored Procedures as a Security Measure
- Minimum Permissions Possible
- Linked Servers
- Using Policies to Secure Your Instance
- SQL Azure Specific Settings
- Instances That Leave the Office

What to Install, and When?

When building a new Microsoft SQL Server, proper security planning starts even before you launch the SQL Server installer. Each component of the Microsoft SQL Server product suite adds another piece that needs to be managed and patched regularly. Each additional component that is installed also provides a potential for additional security holes that could provide an attacker with an entry point into the SQL Server instance.

In Microsoft SQL Server 2000 and older, it was standard practice among most database administrators (DBAs) as well as Microsoft to install more components than were needed, such as the database engine, full-text search, DTS, and replication on the server hosting the database. This is because these subcomponents were not separate components but were all part of the

Note
We Protect Against Potential Attacks

Fortunately, in the Microsoft SQL Server world, we are pretty lucky when it comes to security problems. In the last several versions of the database engine, Microsoft has done a very good job when it comes to securing the instance, and not having any security flaws that need to be patched. However, as ultraparanoid DBAs we don't guard against actual threats; we want to guard against any potential threat that we can conceive of. When this approach is taken, even if a security vulnerability is found, the SQL Server instances won't be susceptible to attack because the component that has the security problem isn't installed or available on the server.

database engine. This technique, however, leads to install components that you don't need; this can lead you to having security problems on the SQL Server's server that you may not realize are there because the component isn't ever used.

In Microsoft SQL Server 2005 and later, this is becoming less and less the case, as each major function within the SQL Server product is now a separate component that can be installed or uninstalled as needed, so that only the minimum components that are needed are installed on the SQL Server. If you do end up with components installed that you don't need, for the most part you can simply stop the service that corresponds to this component, as without the service running, any potential security holes in that component are not available to the attacker. Only installing the services that are needed requires some additional planning and understanding of what will be used on the SQL Server so that the correct components are installed. This additional research and understanding is the price for reducing the potential attack surface.

This can be seen by default when a single instance of the Microsoft SQL Server 2008 engine (or newer) is installed as the default instance. When you install any instance of the Microsoft SQL Server engine, the SQL Browser is installed. When you only have a single instance installed, and that instance is the default instance, the SQL Browser is installed by default in a disabled state. This is because the SQL Browser is not used when connecting to the default instance.

There are two reasons that the SQL Browser is disabled by default when only a default instance is installed and that it should be disabled on older versions unless it is needed. The first reason is to reduce the number of components running on the server to reduce the attack surface. The second is to limit attacks like the SQL Slammer Worm that went around in 2003.

FAQ
What Does the SQL Browser Do?

The SQL 2000 driver and the SQL Native Client use the SQL Browser to identify the TCP port number that a named instance is listening on when a connection to a named instance is requested. This is because, by default, named instances are configured to use a dynamic port number.

When connecting to the default instance of Microsoft SQL Server, unless a specific TCP port is specified in the connection string, the SQL 2000 driver and the SQL Native Client will assume that the SQL Server is running on TCP port 1433. Because this assumption is made, the SQL 2000 driver and the SQL Native Client will not make a request to the SQL Browser to get the TCP port number. This assumption is made to save a round trip between the client and the server to save time when connecting to the default instance.

The SQL Browser works by listening on UDP port 1434 for connections from the SQL 2000 driver and the SQL Native Client. When the SQL 2000 driver or the SQL Native Client connects to the UDP port, they inform the SQL Browser of the name of the instance they are attempting to connect to. The SQL Browser will then respond with a TCP port number, which the SQL driver will then use to attempt to connect to the correct instance. As each Microsoft SQL Server instance on the server is started, it informs the SQL Browser of its name, and the TCP port number on which it is listening for requests.

Note
SQL Slammer Was a Major Embarrassment

The SQL Slammer Worm was unleashed on the world in January 2003 to the dismay of DBAs everywhere. The SQL Slammer attacked a vulnerability in the SQL Browser service, which was installed and running on every computer running Microsoft SQL Server 2000, including MSDE instances, which were installed by default by a variety of products including Visual Studio and Office Business Contact Manager.

The basic attack consisted of a 376-byte UDP packet being sent to the SQL Browser. Depending on the response from the SQL Browser, a remote privilege execution bug was used to grant the attacking code to upload the SQL Slammer Worm onto the server and launch it. Once infected, the server would begin scanning the local network and the Internet for other machines with which to infect, making the virus self-replicating. Because of the self-replicating nature of the virus, simply removing the virus from the SQL Server wasn't enough, for the server would become infected often within just a few minutes.

Fortunately, the SQL Slammer Worm didn't have any additional payload other than to infect other machines with itself. It is assumed that the SQL Slammer worm was a test run to see how well the replication code would work. However, the replicate code worked a little too well, as within minutes of being infected, the Internet connection for the infected machine would run up to 100% utilization (or as close to 100% utilization as the worm could get) as the worm looked for more servers to infect. If the self-replication code was a little better behaved, it could have been months

Note—*Cont'd*

before anyone noticed the worm, this time with a dangerous payload running on SQL Servers and desktops in almost every company. The worm was able to make its way into most companies, not by going through corporate firewalls, but by infecting company laptops that had the MSDE edition installed on them (often without the user's or the DBAs' knowledge). The employee would then bring the infected laptop onto the company network where it would begin looking for internal and external SQL Servers to infect.

Microsoft's saving grace with regard to the SQL Slammer worm was that the patch for the problem had been released in October 2002. However DBAs were slow to install the patch on their servers, leaving them open to SQL Slammer attack, which came three months later.

While the SQL Slammer worm didn't do any damage with regard to data loss or data theft, several companies were unable to operate for days or weeks while they patched and cleaned hundreds or thousands of computers, all of which had been infected with the SQL Slammer worm. This included at least one of the major banks in the United States, which was unable to process debit card transactions for several days while the SQL Slammer cleanup proceeded.

You can read more about SQL Slammer by looking at the cert advisory published for the worm at http://www.cert.org/advisories/CA-2003-04.html or by looking at the Microsoft Security Bulletin MS02-061, which can be found at http://www.microsoft.com/technet/security/bulletin/MS02-061.mspx.

SQL Slammer was a wakeup call to SQL Server DBAs who, until this time, were known to install Service Packs only when there was a specific reason for installation. After the SQL Slammer was released on the world, DBAs became much more willing to install Service Packs and hotfixes more regularly on the database servers. Because of the extent of the problems, damage, and lost revenue that SQL Slammer caused, business users became more willing to accept the small amount of downtime that SQL Server patching required in order to protect themselves.

When installing a new Microsoft SQL Server, only install those components that are actually necessary for the application or applications that will be using the instance to function. If SQL Reporting Service and SQL Integration Service aren't needed, then do not install those components. The same applies to the SQL Server Management tools. If you don't have a need to run the SQL Server Management Tools on the server's console, there is no need to install them. This is especially true on SQL Server 2005 and newer as installing the management tools also installs the Visual Studio shell, which gives yet another product that needs to be patched to ensure that it is safe to have installed.

SQL Authentication and Windows Authentication

Microsoft SQL Server has for many years now, going back to 6.0 if not further, given two different authentication methods when connecting to the SQL Server Engine. These authentication methods are SQL Authentication and Windows Authentication.

SQL Server Authentication takes place when the username and password for the account are both stored within the database engine. These accounts don't have any relation to any local or domain user account and can be used by any number of people to connect to the database engine.

Windows Authentication is based on an account being created and managed either on the operating system that is running under the SQL Server or on the Windows Active Directory domain that the server running the SQL Server is a member of, or has access to through domain trusts.

Windows Authentication is more secure than SQL authentication because with Windows Authentication the username and password are not sent between the client application and the SQL

FAQ
Domain Trusts?

Domain Trusts are used to allow multiple Windows domains access to each other. Several different kinds of trusts can be created between domains, the more advanced of which are beyond the scope of this book. The key points to remember about domain trusts is that any domains within the same domain tree (contoso.local and newyork.contoso.local, for example) have an automatic two-way transitive trust, which means that users in either domain can access resources in the other domain. The transitive part means that if the newyork.contoso.local domain had a child domain such as queens.newyork.contoso.local then because that domain has a two-way transitive trust to its parent, the trust is implied all the way up and down the tree. Thus, users in queens.newyork.contoso.com and contoso.com can access resources in the other domain as the authentication will be passed to the other domain via the newyork.consoso.local domain, as shown in the Active Directory diagram in Figure 4.1.

The same applies to domains that are within the same Active Directory forest, but are not members of the same Active Directory Tree. If you have a forest with two trees in it, consoso.local and adventureworks.local, the root domains of those trees would have a two-way transitive trust between them, automatically allowing any user in either domain, or any subdomain, to access resources within any domain or subdomain of the other tree as shown in the Active Directory diagram in Figure 4.2.

Systems administrators can also create external trusts between domains or forests to other domains or forests, allowing partner companies Windows Authentication to be used against internal resources. These trusts can be one way or two way, and can be either transitive or intransitive (the trust is not shared with other domains in the forest).

Now from a technical standpoint there are no two-way trusts. When a two-way trust is created (either a transitive or nontransitive trust), two one-way trusts are created between the two domains. There is no way to convert a two-way trust into a one-way trust. In order to do this, the two-way trust would need to be deleted and a new one way trust created.

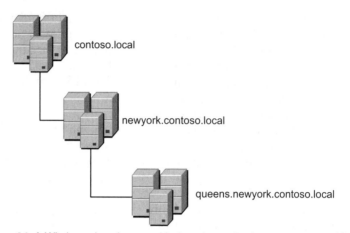

Figure 4.1 A Windows domain tree with three layers having two-way transitive trusts between them.

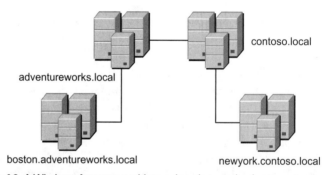

Figure 4.2 A Windows forest tree with two domain trees having two-way transitive trusts between them.

Server. Instead, a ticket is generated on the domain controller and passed to the client, who then passes it to the SQL Server instance for authentication. This ticket is then verified against the domain controller to ensure that it is valid and that it was passed to the SQL Server from the correct computer.

When you install SQL Server, several accounts are created by default. As for SQL Accounts, only one account has always been created, which is the system administrator (SA) account. Newer versions of SQL Server starting with SQL Server 2005 will create two additional accounts, which are "##MS_PolicyEvent ProcessingLogin##" and "##MS_PolicyTsqlExecutionLogin##". These logins, among others that may be created, depending on what features are installed on the instance, are for internal use by the database engine and should be left disabled. They should not

Note
More Information About the Windows Authentication Process

The Windows Authentication process is rather lengthy when you include the various local and domain groups that are possible, as well as handling for both Kerberos and NTLM authentication. The process is fully documented in Chapter 3 of this book for your reference if you would like to read up further on the internal processes that happen between clicking connect and actually getting connected.

be deleted, as the parts of the database engine that require them will not work correctly without them. These special logins that start with ## are certificate logins, so they are bound to a specific certificate each and that certificate is required in order to log in to the instance using that login.

Several Windows logins are created on a database instance by default. SQL Server 2005 and older will create a login for BUILTIN\Administrators, which allows anyone who is a member of the Administrators group on the Windows OS to log into the SQL Server. By default, this group is a member of the sysadmin fixed-server role, meaning that anyone in the local Administrators group is a member of the sysadmin fixed-server role. SQL Server 2008 and newer do not create this Windows login, as this login is considered to be a security violation inasmuch as it grants people other than the DBA system administrator (SA) rights to the database instance, and also allows people other than the DBA to grant other people SA rights on the database server by placing them within the local Administrators group. For database instances that have the BUILTIN\Administrators login, it is recommended that you, after granting SA rights to the DBAs, remove the BUILTIN\Administrators from the sysadmin fixed-server role. Some services such as the full-text service expect the BUILTIN\Administrators login to exist. If rights are removed from the BUILTIN\Administrators login, or the BUILTIN\Administrators login is removed, the "NT AUTHORITY\SYSTEM" login must be added so that these services will continue to function correctly.

The versions of Microsoft SQL Server starting with the SQL 2008 version will also create some other Windows logins by default. While these logins shouldn't be removed, they should be understood. These logins are:
- NT AUTHORITY\SYSTEM
- NT SERVICE\MSSQLSERVER
- NT SERVICE\SQLSERVERAGENT

The "NT AUTHORITY\SYSTEM" service is used to allow applications running under the local system account access to the database instance. This is used for services such as the full-text indexing service that runs under the local system account. The "NT AUTHORITY\SYSTEM" login is a member of the sysadmin fixed-server role, which can present a security risk because any application running under the local system account will have SA rights to the database instance. Unfortunately, the full-text service cannot be run under an account other than the local system account, as running under an account other than the local system account is an unsupported configuration.

The "NT SERVICE\MSSQLSERVER" and "NT SERVICE\SQL SERVERAGENT" Windows logins are service-specific logins that are used to run the SQL Service and the SQL Server Agent when the services are configured to run under the local system account. When the services are configured to run under a domain or local account, these logins will not exist; instead Windows logins will exist for the accounts that are running the services.

When installing SQL Server 2008 or higher, the installer will ask you to specify the Windows accounts, either accounts or groups, that should be members of the sysadmin fixed server role. The installer will add these Windows accounts as logins as the installation process is completed so that those Windows logins are members of the sysadmin fixed server role.

With SQL Accounts there is more to worry about than just having to protect from brute force attacks. Depending on what access someone can get to the database server there are other ways into the system. Some examples include shutting down the instance and editing the master.mdf file directly with a hex editor and changing the password to an encrypted value for a known password. Another technique that can be used is to attach a debugger to the SQL Engine process and capture the password as it comes into the engine and is processed.

Editing the Master.mdf File

Editing the master.mdf file to change the password is the least sneaky of the techniques, as it requires an outage to the database instance to complete, but it is the easiest. To break into the SQL Server using this technique simply backup the master database file, and restore it to another machine as a user database (called master_old or something similar). Query from another SQL Server Instance the hash for the password of an account that has a known password. The password can be queried from the syslogins catalog view in the master database. On the database that has been restored, update the password for the SA account in the master_old database to update the value to the password for the SA account (or other account that needs to be changed). Once the password has been changed, detach the master_old database. Stop the instance you wish to get into and replace the master.mdf with the master_old.mdf file. When the instance starts up, attempt to log in to the SQL Server instance using the password you just changed.

Using a Debugger to Intercept Passwords

As the SQL Server Engine is just a computer process (albeit a very complex one), you can attach a debugger to the instance and get access to some of the data that the instance is passing around within the engine. This can be done by attaching a debugger to the instance and waiting for someone to log into the instance using an SQL Login. When this happens, the SQL Server will have the password in plain text in a variable that can be viewed through the debugger and used to now log into the SQL Server.

You can use a memory debugger such as Olly Debugger to capture the memory pages owned by the SQL Server process. Within these memory pages you can simply search for the login name that you want to find the password for.

FAQ
More Information

The process of gathering passwords with a debugger is a rather complex process that doesn't explain well on paper. Fortunately, Sean and Jen McCown have published a video on the MidnightDBA.com website in which Sean walks you through the process of capturing a user's password as it comes through on the wire from a client. The video can be viewed or downloaded from http://bit.ly/RecoverSQLPasswords. The really interesting part of the video is about 6 minutes, which is where Sean finds the password in the memory dump.

Purchased Products

All the truly lazy hacker needs is a copy of the master.mdf either by taking it from the database server itself or the backup server and a copy of a program like Advanced SQL

Password Recovery by Elcomsoft, which allows you to view or reset the passwords in SQL Server 2000, 2005, or 2008. Once the hackers have the SA password, it is simple to now log into your servers and export and/or destroy the data that the server protects.

Password Change Policies

After installing the SQL Server engine on the server, you will probably begin creating SQL Server accounts. Using SQL Server 2005 or newer, creating accounts that use SQL Server Authentication will give you a few checkboxes, shown in Figure 4.3, which you need to understand so that you know how these options work. If you are in a Windows NT 4 domain, then these options will not be available to you and they will be grayed out as Windows NT 4 domain's password policies are not used by Microsoft SQL Server.

The first checkbox, "Enforce password policy," tells the SQL Server that the password must fit within the password requirements of the Windows domain, or the local security policy defined on the server (if the server is not in a Windows domain). The password policies that are being enforced by the first checkbox are the "Enforce password history," "Minimum password length," and "Password must meet complexity requirements" policy settings.

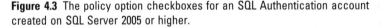

Figure 4.3 The policy option checkboxes for an SQL Authentication account created on SQL Server 2005 or higher.

Note
Group Policy Definitions

All six of the group policy settings—the five that SQL Server uses and the one that SQL Server doesn't look at—which control password policies within a Windows domain are explained in Chapter 3 in greater detail. Because they are covered there, they are only discussed at a high level in this chapter.

The second checkbox, "Enforce password expiration," tells the SQL Server that this account must change its password based on the "Minimum password age" and "Maximum password age" settings that come from the domain or the local security policy.

The third checkbox shown in Figure 4.3 is the "User must change password at next login" option. In Figure 4.3 the option is disabled because the "Enforce password expiration" option is not selected. If the "Enforce password expiration" option were checked, then the "User must change password at next login" option would be available. By checking this option and clicking OK the next time the user attempts to log into the database engine, the user will need to change their password.

FAQ
How the Password Change Process Works

If the user connects to the SQL Server with an account that has an expired password, then they will need to be prompted to change their password. If the user is using SQL Server Management studio, they will be prompted to change they password automatically as shown in Figure 4.4. The same will happen when using the SQLCMD command line tool.

However, when using your own application to log into the database, such as a Windows Forms application, the application will need to know how to prompt the user for a new password, as well as what to do with the new password in order to change the password for the SQL Account.

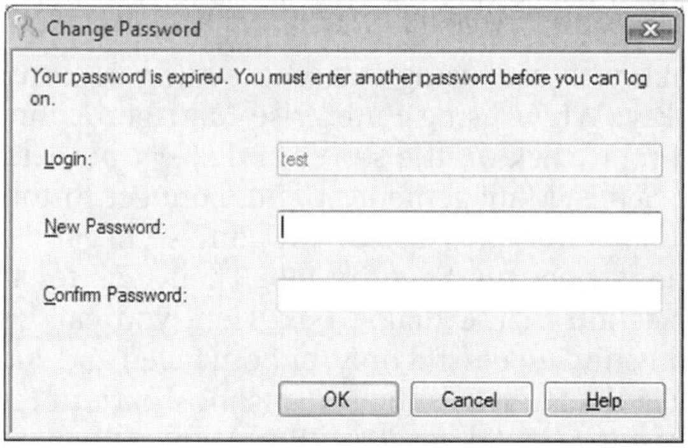

Figure 4.4 The Change Password dialog shown in SQL Server Management Studio.

The advantage of having and using these policies is that all the SQL Authentication accounts that are configured to follow the policies meet the password policies that have been defined on the domain.

Auditing Failed Logins

Microsoft SQL Server has, since at least version 6.5, included the ability to audit failed login connections to the ERRORLOG file. This auditing allows the DBA to know when someone is attempting to log into the database using an account for which they have no password. While this feature has been around for many versions, it was enhanced with the release of Microsoft SQL Server 2005 to include the IP Address of the computer that attempted the login. Before this change, the only information provided was the username that was being used to attempt to log into the database. This information is important to log so that you know when someone is attempting to break into the database.

You can also log successful login attempts to the database, which is information that can also be useful to track. If you don't track successful login attempts, you don't know why attempts to break into the SQL Server have stopped. If you do track this information and you see the login attempts stop, followed by successful logins, you know that the password was found and you need to change your password. If you see the login attempts stop, and no successful logins are found, then you know that the person gave up the attempt. The downside to logging the successful attempts is that all successful attempts are logged; thus on a very busy SQL Server instance that has hundreds or thousands of connections per second, the ERRORLOG file will get very full, very quickly.

Changing this setting is easiest done via the Enterprise Manager or SQL Server Management Studio (depending on the version that you are using), as the setting is controlled via a registry key. When using Enterprise Manager, connect to the server and right click on the server and select properties. When using SQL Server Management Studio, connect to the server in the object explorer and select properties. Regardless of the version, then select the Security tab. Then look for the "Login auditing" section in the dialog box. Here you can select from None, failed only, successful only, or both failed and successful as shown in Figure 4.3. While the screenshot shown in Figure 4.5 is from Microsoft SQL Server 2008 R2s Management Studio, the dialog from SQL Server 7 and 2000s Enterprise Manager looks very similar to the one shown.

If you want to change this setting via T/SQL, you will need to use the xp_instance_regwrite system stored procedure to do this passing in an integer that defines what the setting should be set to, as shown in Example 4.1. A setting of 1 indicates that successful login only should be logged. A setting of 2 indicates

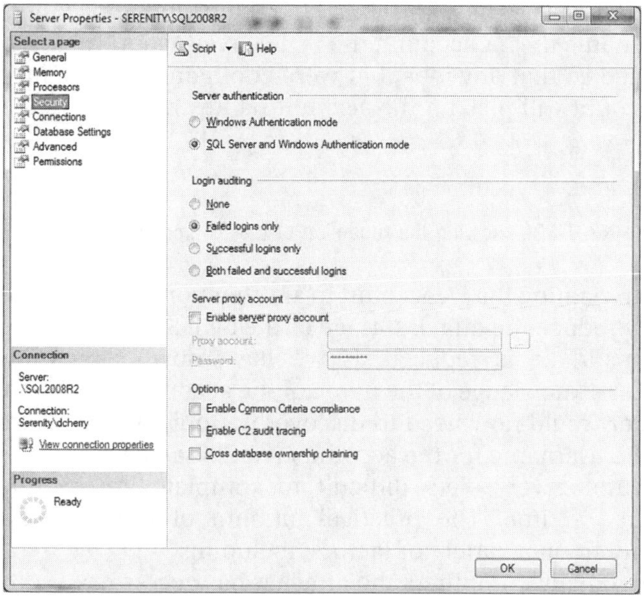

Figure 4.5 The security tab of the server properties dialog from a the 2008 R2 version of the SQL Server Management Studio.

that failed logins only should be logged. A setting of 3 indicates that both successful and failed logins should be logged. A setting of 0 indicates that neither failed nor successful logins should be logged.

No matter if you change this setting via T/SQL or the management tool, a restart of the SQL Instance is required before the setting change will take effect.

```
EXEC xp_instance_regwrite N'HKEY_LOCAL_MACHINE',
N'Software\Microsoft\MSSQLServer\MSSQLServer',
   N'AuditLevel', REG_DWORD, 2
GO
```

Example 4.1 Sample T/SQL code on how to change the logging level.

Renaming the SA Account

Starting with SQL Server 2005, you have the ability to rename the SA account to another username to make the account more difficult for an attacker to use. This is an important security step to take, especially if the SQL Server is available on the public Internet. To rename the SA account use the ALTER LOGIN command as shown in Example 4.2. Microsoft SQL Server 2000 and older will not have the ability to rename the SA account. After you rename the SA account, the SQL Server Agent will need to be restarted so that any jobs that were configured to run under the SA account will pick up the account name change.

```
ALTER LOGIN sa
WITH NAME = SomeOtherName
```

Example 4.2: T/SQL showing the renaming of the SA account.

By renaming the SA account to another nonstandard name, we greatly reduce the attack surface of the SQL Server Instance. The attack surface is reduced as we have now taken away the attacker's knowledge of the name of the account to login with. An attacker would now need to discover not only the password, but also the username for the account as well making a remote brute force attack very, very difficult to complete in any practical amount of time. The practical amount of time, however, is dependent on a variety of factors, including:

- How many computers the attacker has access to;
- How long the username is;
- How many characters the attacker starts with when attacking the SQL Server;
- If the user is able to get someone to tell them the username.

A typical attacker will start with the username SA and will try a large number of passwords before starting to try different usernames. The longer the username is the longer it will take an attacker to gain access to the database instance, with most attackers giving up long before finding the actual username and password. The biggest reason that this attack will take so long is that the SQL Server returns the same error message if the wrong username and password is used or if just the wrong username is used. In either case error 18456 will be returned with a level of 14 and a state of 1, with the wording of the error message simply stating "Login failed for user '{username}'" where {username} is the username that has attempted to log into the database instance.

Disabling the SA Account

An important security procedure that many people do not follow is disabling the SA account. By having this account enabled, you have done half of the work for an attacker as the username for the SA account is well known by attackers. This means that the attacker just needs to figure out the password. While there is hopefully a very strong password on the SA account, with the account enabled the attacker can sit there and

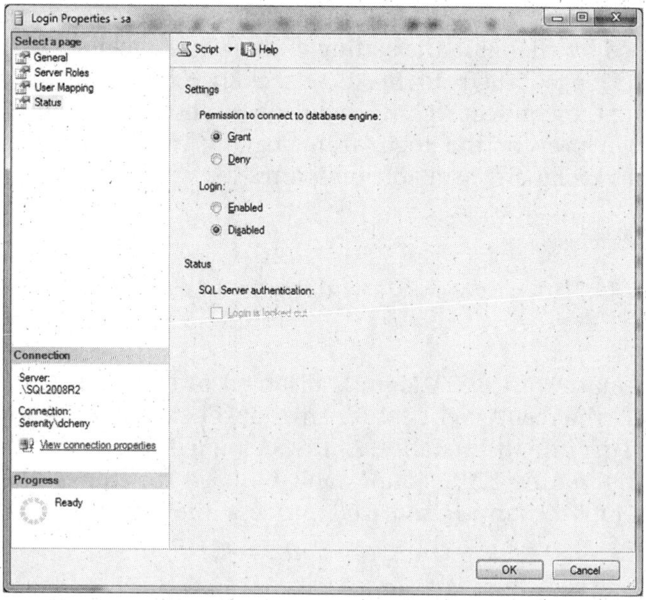

Figure 4.6 How to disable the SA account using the SQL Server Management Studio.

hammer away on the SA account until getting the password correctly. Where you disable the SA account doesn't matter if the attacker gets the password correct; regardless, the account won't allow the attacker into the SQL Server instance.

If the SQL Instance is configured for Windows Only Authentication, then there is no need to disable the SA account as the SA account is an SQL login and when Windows Only Authentication is used the SA account can't be used.

Disabling the SA account is a fairly easy process to complete. Connect to the server in question using the object explorer and expand the security node. Double click the SA account from the list and select the status tab. Select the disabled radio button and click OK as shown in Figure 4.6.

If you prefer to use T/SQL to disable the SA login you can do so with the ALTER LOGIN statement as shown in Example 4.3.

```
ALTER LOGIN [sa] DISABLE
```

Example 4.3: T/SQL showing how to disable the SA login.

If you wish to leave the SA account enabled, but prevent it from connecting to the instance you can deny the account access to the instance. This can also be done either in the SQL Server Management Studio or via T/SQL. You can see in Figure 4.6 that the SA login is granted login rights, but this permission can be removed by changing the setting to deny and clicking OK. If you prefer to use T/SQL to make this change, you can do so by denying the connect right to the login as shown in Example 4.4. This will prevent the login from logging into the SQL Server instance using any available endpoint.

```
DENY CONNECT SQL TO [sa]
```

Example 4.4: T/SQL code showing how to deny the SA account rights to connect to the SQL Server.

No matter if the SA login is disabled or denied, the right to connect the result is the same. An attacker can't use the login to try and get into the instance. As the SA login is disabled or denied login rights, the SA account can't be used for things like SQL Agent jobs or any authorized process that does use the SA account.

Securing Endpoints

By default, Microsoft SQL Server 2005 and higher have several endpoints on each instance. These default endpoints are what users will normally be connecting to. If users are connecting using TCP, then they will connect to the "TSQL Default TCP" endpoint. If users are connecting using Named Pipes, then they will connect to the "TSQL Named Pipes" endpoint. If users are connecting using VIA, then they will connect to the "TSQL Default VIA" endpoint.

To provide an additional layer of security, you can create an endpoint that is an application-specific endpoint and configure it so that the endpoint will only allow the application account to use the endpoint. This way if an attacker is able to get into the web server and attempts to initiate his or her own connections to the SQL Server, the connection information coming from the applications connection string will reference an endpoint that the attacker can't connect to with any account other than the application account. Attempted logins using other accounts to that endpoint would then fail to allow the user to connect.

By default, when you create a new endpoint on your SQL Server, the fixed-server role public has its rights to connect to the T/SQL Default TCP endpoint removed as an additional security measure. You can correct this by running the code shown in Example 4.5.

```
GRANT CONNECT ON ENDPOINT::[TSQL Default TCP] to [public]
```

Example 4.5: T/SQL code showing how to restore the default connection rights to the default TCP endpoint.

After you have created a new TCP endpoint for the application account to use for a connection, you will need to revoke the public rights to connect to that endpoint, grant the application account rights to connect to that endpoint, and deny the application account rights to connect to the default endpoint as shown in Example 4.6.

```
/*Create the new endpoint*/
CREATE ENDPOINT SampleEndpoint AS TCP (LISTENER_PORT=12345,
    LISTENER_IP=ALL)
FOR TSQL()
/*Remove default rights for all users to connect to the new
    endpoint.*/
REVOKE CONNECT ON ENDPOINT::[SampleEndpoint] to [public]
/*Prevent application account from connecting to default
    endpoint*/
DENY CONNECT ON ENDPOINT::[TSQL Default TCP] to
    [ApplicationAccount]
/*Allow application account to connect to Sample Endpoint.*/
GRANT CONNECT ON ENDPOINT::[SampleEndpoint] to
    [ApplicationAccount]
```

Example 4.6: T/SQL code showing how to secure an application account so that it can only connect to the specified endpoint.

Regardless of what permissions that are granted to a T/SQL endpoint, all members of the sysadmin fixed-server role can connect to the endpoint, as can the owner of the endpoint.

Stored Procedures as a Security Measure

Stored procedures make an excellent security measure for a couple of reasons:
1. Users don't need access to base tables to execute a stored procedure that uses the tables.
2. When calling stored procedures, the amount of access to the database is defined by the database developer.

Access to Base Tables Isn't Required

When a stored procedure is run, the user account that runs the stored procedure only needs access to execute the stored procedure. No access to the underlying tables or views that are used by the stored procedure is needed for the stored procedure to execute. This is because of a concept within the database called a database permission chain. Database permission chaining is enabled by default and cannot be disabled.

Permissions chaining is what allows the user to access the tables via the stored procedure without the user having the ability to access the tables from outside the stored procedure. This is done because the SQL Server assumes that because the owner of the stored procedure has created the procedure to access these tables, and the stored procedure creator has access to the tables and views that are used by the procedure, so it is assumed that the user running the stored procedure should have access to those tables.

Note
Dynamic SQL versus Hardcoded SQL

Dynamic SQL within the stored procedure makes things work a little differently when it comes to permissions. When you run dynamic SQL, the dynamic SQL command is run out of scope from the call to the stored procedure. Because the dynamic SQL is run out of scope, this breaks the permissions chain as permission chains cannot survive a change of scope. What this means is that the application account will need to have access to perform whatever operation the dynamic SQL specifies. If the dynamic SQL is a simple select, then the application account will need to have the select right granted to the table or view being accessed. The same goes for insert, update, or delete statements. Typically, the only commands that would be run through dynamic SQL are going to be select statements, as dynamic SQL is used to allow for dynamic sorting where the application layer can tell the database what column to sort the data with. However, in some cases, database developers have found reasons to use dynamic SQL for insert, update, and delete statements.

If the stored procedure needs to access tables or views within another database on the instance, the security chain can still be maintained. This is done by enabling cross database chaining, which was introduced in SQL Server 2000 Service Pack 3. When cross database chaining is enabled, it will allow the object security chain to pass from one database to another, removing the requirement of granting permissions to the tables and views that are being accessed in the second database.

Enabling Cross Database Chaining

By default, cross database chaining is disabled and needs to be enabled on the instance, as well as the databases that will be participating in the cross database chain. At the instance level this change is made by using the sp_configure system stored procedure, while the database level changes are made with the ALTER DATABASE command as shown in Example 4.7.

```
EXEC sp_configure 'cross db ownership chaining', 1
RECONFIGURE
GO
ALTER DATABASE YourFirstDatabase
    SET DB_CHAINING ON
GO
ALTER DATABASE YourSecondDatabase
    SET DB_CHAINING ON
GO
```

Example 4.7: Enabling cross database chaining at the instance as well as the database level.

After enabling cross database chaining at the instance and database level, one last change to the database needs to be made. The login that will be using the stored procedure in the first database needs to be a member of the public fixed database role within the database that contains the tables. Without the login being mapped to a user within the second database, the user won't be able to log into the database to use cross database chaining. No other security permissions are needed in the second database.

Minimum Permissions Possible

A technique that has been alluded to in places throughout this book is the technique on giving users and applications only the minimal permission needed to get done whatever job needs to be done. By granting only the minimum permission to the user account, the user isn't able to accidentally (or intentionally) change data that they shouldn't be able to, or to see data that they aren't authorized to see.

The most complex part of granting minimum permissions is typically the discovery process where you work with the application developers or business users (when the business users have direct database access) to determine the correct permissions that the users need. This is because business users and developers often don't want to take the time to figure out what they *need* access to and will instead request what they *want* access to, which is everything. And everything usually translates to being a member of the dbo (database owner) fixed database role or the sysadmin fixed-server role, both of which more than likely are more rights than are actually needed.

There is no easy technological solution to finding the permissions that users or applications need. You can use Microsoft SQL Profiler to help with this process. You can use SQL Server profiler to gather the commands that the user executes against the database. This captured information can then be used to document the objects that are being accessed. This documentation can then be used to determine what permissions the user or application needs, at which point the higher level permissions and rights that the user does not need are to be revoked. For this technique to work successfully, the SQL Profiler trace should be run for several weeks or months to ensure that all month-end, quarter-end, and year-end processes are captured to ensure that nothing is missed.

The other easy technique would be to start granting select permissions to the known table objects and then have a user begin using the application granting rights as needed to fix the various errors that come up. While this will eventually fix the permissions problem, it is a time-consuming and frustrating process, but it will work.

Note
And How Many Members of the Sysadmin Fixed Server Role Do You Have?

The sysadmin fixed-server role grants a massive amount of control to the database instance. A member of the sysadmin fixed-server role has rights to everything within the database instance, and these rights cannot be revoked using any method. Due to the massive amount of power that can be wielded by the members of the sysadmin fixed-server role, the number of SQL or Windows logins that are members of this role should be kept to a minimum. By keeping this to a minimum, it becomes much easier to see changes made to the membership of the sysadmin fixed server role.

In a perfect world, the answer to the question "which is the name of this sidebar?" is two. No more, no less. These two members should be the SA account (after having been renamed) and a Windows Domain (or local) group that allows the DBAs to have administrative rights to the instance. The Windows group that is a member of the sysadmin fixed-server role should not be the BUILTIN\Administrators group, nor should it be the local administrators group referenced by the computer name or domain name. By using this group, other employees who have no business being within the database, such as the SAs, storage administrators, and network administrators, would have access to the database instance.

Linked Servers

Linked servers are a place where security problems can really pop up. Linked servers, which were introduced in SQL Server 7, allow a T/SQL statement or stored procedure to access database objects in the remote server. This remote server can be an SQL Server database, an Oracle database, an Excel sheet, and so on. The limits are basically driven by what ODBC (Open Database Connectivity) drivers are installed on the server.

When you configure a linked server, mappings are defined to grant security so that logins to the server to which the user is connected has a way to authenticate against the remote database instance. When you create a new login mapping, you specify the local login, as well as the remote login and password for the remote instance. Logins can be mapped from a Windows login or an SQL Login to a login of the same name by checking the Impersonate checkbox, or the login can be mapped to a different SQL login. When mapping to a different login, the remote login must be an SQL login and not a Windows login. The only way mapping to a Windows login can be done is when mapping is being done to the same Windows login, the user is logged into the system on the local server.

When a linked server is configured, a global mapping can be defined that covers all users that don't have specific mappings defined. Four options can be selected for this global mapping:
1. Not be made;
2. Be made without using a security context;
3. Be made using the login's current security context;
4. Be made using this security context.

When selecting the "Not be made" option, access to the remote server will be denied. When selecting the "Be made without using a security context," which will attempt to log into the remote database instance without a username. When selecting the "Be made without using a security context" the SQL Server will attempt to log into the remote database instance without specifying a username or password. The fourth option allows a specific SQL login to be used for all users that don't have specific login mappings defined.

Where linked servers can start to cause trouble is when some companies use linked servers to perform administrative tasks against all the SQL Servers within the environment from a central database server. Often when this is done the "Be made using this security context" option is selected, with a highly privileged account used as the remote login, often using a login that is a member of the sysadmin fixed-server role, if not the SA account itself. This causes any user who connects to the database instance to then be able to connect via that linked server and execute tasks on that remote SQL Server with the high-level permissions of the mapped account.

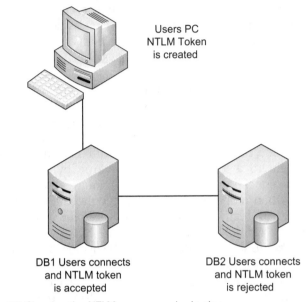

Figure 4.7 Showing the NTLM process and rejection.

NTLM Double Hop Problems

When configuring linked servers to pass Windows Authentication between instances, you can get into what is called the NTLM Double Hop problem. Where this problem comes into play is a limitation of the NTLM authentication process (some call it a bug, but it is really a design limitation) where NTLM does not allow a login token to be passed from the one server to another. The NTLM process will pass the login token from the user's computer to the database instance, which is the first hop. However, the database instance cannot pass that login token to the next database instance, which is the second hop. The second instance will reject the token because the token was created by a different computer other than the one that passed it the token. This is documented in Figure 4.7.

Using Policies to Secure Your Instance

Starting with SQL Server 2008 you can now use Policy Based Management to ensure that users don't have permissions that they shouldn't have. While Policy-Based Management was introduced with Microsoft SQL Server 2008, Microsoft has made is possible to use Policy Based Management against Microsoft

SQL Server 2005 and Microsoft SQL Server 2000 instances, as well just in a limited function.

FAQ
Some Policy-Based Management Features Do Not Work in Microsoft SQL Server 2000 and 2005

Because Policy-Based Management is a new feature of Microsoft SQL Server 2008, not all the features of Policy-Based Management work on older versions of Microsoft SQL Server.

Policy Creation on an SQL Server 2008 or 2008 R2 instance can be done using the online technique shown within this section of the chapter. The second technique is called disconnected authoring. With disconnected authoring, the policies are saved to the file system of the SQL Server as an XML file. This disconnected authoring requires use of the Microsoft SQL Server 2008 (or higher) Management Studio, but does not require that the SQL Server 2008 database engine be installed, allowing you to deploy the policies to an SQL Server 2000 or SQL Server 2005 instance.

In SQL Server 2008 and higher, you can store the policies within the database instance or you can store the configuration within an XML file on the SQL Servers hard drive. SQL Server 2000 and 2005 can only store the configuration within an XML file.

SQL Server 2008 and up support the ability to automate policy evaluation. The automated policy evaluation requires features that are only available in SQL Server 2008 and higher, including SQL CLR, SMO, SQL Agent, and DDL Eventing. Additionally automated policy evaluation requires that the policy configuration be stored within the database instead of an XML document, which is a function which is only supported within SQL Server 2008 and higher.

Policy-Based Management is a new feature that allows the DBA to create conditions and policies that can monitor hundreds of different metrics within the database instance either blocking changes or logging changes for later action by a DBA. Policy-Based Management can be configured through SQL Server Management Studio or through T/SQL. The configure Policy-Based Management follows these three steps:

1. Connect to the server in object explorer.
2. Navigate to the Management Folder.
3. Navigate to the Policy Management Folder.

In order to configure Policy-Based Management, you first need to configure conditions. Conditions are logical checks that are made when the policy is evaluated. You can define multiple conditions within each instance of Microsoft SQL Server, and each policy can have one condition associated with it.

The third piece of Policy-Based Management are the Facets. Facets are used when creating a condition so that the condition knows what part of the database instance the condition will

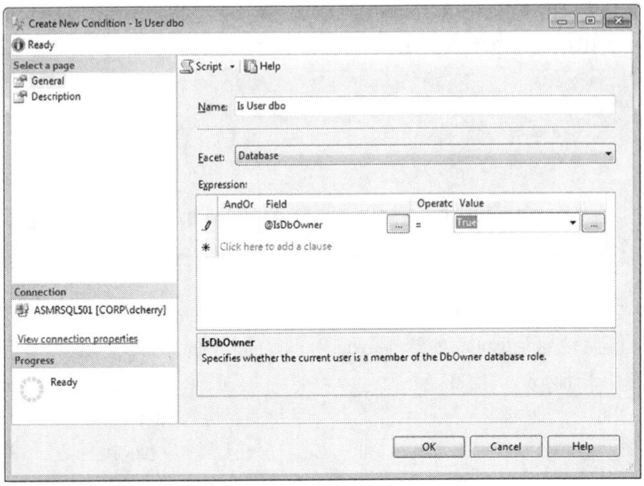

Figure 4.8 The "Create New Condition" dialog box configured to log that a user is a member of the dbo fixed database role.

apply to. There are a couple dozen facets defined within the Policy-Based Management system. The list of available facets can be found in the Facets folder under the "Policy Management" folder.

If you wanted to define a condition that checked to see if the logged in user was a member of the dbo fixed database role in the object explorer, select "Conditions" from the tree under the "Policy Management" folder. Right click on conditions and select "New Condition" from the context menu. This will open the "Create New Condition" dialog. In this example select "Database" from the Facet drop down menu. In the Field column select "@IsDbOwner" and set the Value column to "True" as shown in Figure 4.8. Name the policy as required in the Name field.

In addition to creating conditions through the SQL Server Management Studio UI, they can also be created using T/SQL by using the sp_syspolicy_add_condition stored procedure in the msdb database. This procedure takes a series of parameters, all of which are pretty straightforward with the exception of the @expression parameter, which takes an XML document showing how the condition should be evaluated as shown in Example 4.8.

```
Declare @condition_id int
EXEC msdb.dbo.sp_syspolicy_add_condition @name=
   N'Is User dbo',
@description=N", @facet=N'Database', @expression=
   N'<Operator>
```

```
<TypeClass>Bool</TypeClass>
<OpType<EQ</OpType>
<count>2</Count>
<Attribute>
  <TypeClass>Bool</TypeClass>
  <Name>IsDbOwner</Name>
</Attribute>
<Function>
  <TypeClass>Bool</TypeClass>
  <FunctionType>True</FunctionType>
  <ReturnType>Bool</ReturnType>
  <count>0</Count>
</Function>
</Operator>', @is_name_condition=0, @obj_name=N'',
@condition_id=@condition_id OUTPUT
```

Example 4.8: Creating the same condition shown in Figure 4.8.

After creating a condition, a policy needs to be created which uses the condition. Like the condition, this can be done either within the SQL Server Management Studio UI or by running a T/SQL script. Within the Management Studio UI, after navigating to the Policy Management folder, right click on Policies and select "New Policy" from the context menu. In the "Create New Policy" window name the policy and select the check condition that you wish to use as shown in Figure 4.9.

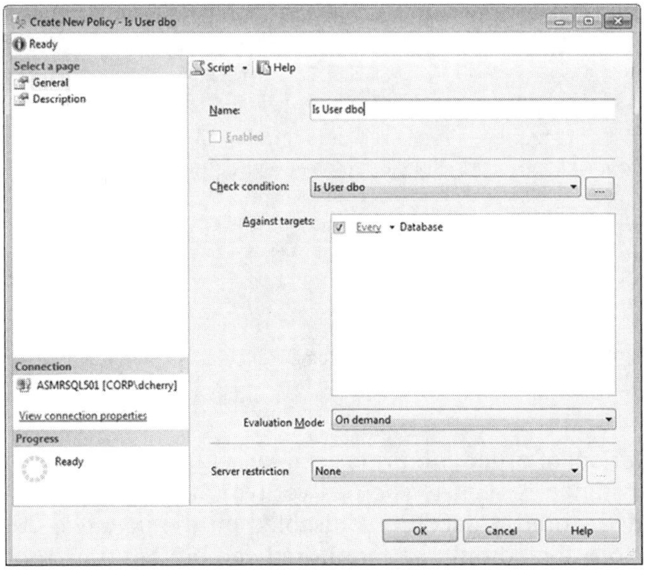

Figure 4.9 Creating a new policy using the "Is User dbo" condition.

Policies can also be created using T/SQL instead of the SQL Server Management Studio using a series of stored procedures in the msdb database:

1. sp_syspolicy_add_object_set creates an object set which is an internal undocumented object;
2. sp_syspolicy_add_target_set creates a target set which says what type of condition target will be called, binding the object set to the target set;
3. sp_syspolicy_add_target_set_level assigns a target set level to the previously created target set;
4. sp_syspolicy_add_policy creates the policy specifying the object set name.

```
Declare @object_set_id int
EXEC msdb.dbo.sp_syspolicy_add_object_set
   @object_set_name=N'policy_ObjectSet', @facet=N'Database',
   @object_set_id=@object_set_id OUTPUT
Declare @target_set_id int
EXEC msdb.dbo.sp_syspolicy_add_target_set
   @object_set_name=N'policy_ObjectSet', @type_skeleton=
   N'Server/Database',
   @type=N'DATABASE', @enabled=True, @target_set_id=
   @target_set_id OUTPUT
EXEC msdb.dbo.sp_syspolicy_add_target_set_level
   @target_set_id=@target_set_id, @type_skeleton=N'Server/
   Database',
   @level_name=N'Database', @condition_name=N'', @target_set_
   level_id=0
GO
Declare @policy_id int
EXEC msdb.dbo.sp_syspolicy_add_policy @name=N'Is User dbo',
   @condition_name=N'Is User dbo', @execution_mode=0,
   @policy_id=@policy_id
   OUTPUT, @root_condition_name=N'',
   @object_set=N'policy_ObjectSet'
Select @policy_id
GO
```

Example 4.9: T/SQL code creating the same Policy as shown in Figure 4.9.

A variety of other conditions can be set to help ensure that an SQL Instance is secure, such as verifying that the xp_cmdshell extended stored procedure is disabled on the instance. A list of conditions that should be monitored can be found in Table 4.1, along with the value to monitor for.

Table 4.1 Various Conditions that Should Be Monitored to Ensure a More Secure SQL Server Installation.

Facet	Field	Operator	Value
Server Security	@CmdExecRights ForSystemAdminsOnly	=	False
Server Security	@ProxyAccountEnabled	=	True
Server Security	@PublicServerRoleIs GrantedPermissions	=	True
Server Security	@XPCmdShellEnabled	=	True
Database Security	@IsOwnerSysadmin	=	True
Login	@PasswordExpiration Enabled \ @LoginType	= \ =	False \ SqlLogin
Server	@AuditLevel	!=	All

Note
Conditions Can Have Multiple Checks Within Them

Table 4.1 shows the PasswordExpirationEnabled and LoginType values within the same line. This condition is configured in this way so that this condition only logs an issue when the password expiration is disabled and the user is an SQL Login. Setting this condition requires that two values be set within a single condition. The Password ExpirationEnabled should be set to False, and the LoginType should be set to SqlLogin.

SQL Azure Specific Settings

Note
SQL Azure Is a Moving Target

Do keep in mind that in any book about SQL Azure, including this one, the information about SQL Azure can get out of date very quickly as the SQL Azure product is a constantly moving target. This is because the SQL Azure team releases new versions of the database engine every few months, so what you see here may not be relevant after the summer of 2010.

Figure 4.10 Showing how to enable the SQL Azure Firewall to other Microsoft Services servers.

Microsoft has done an excellent job of securing SQL Azure databases, but that doesn't mean that they can't be screwed up by someone who doesn't know how to set up the SQL Azure instance correctly.

When you sign up for an SQL Azure account, you control the firewall to the database server. By default, no one has access to the instance, including other servers within the Microsoft Services platform. This is easy enough to change by checking the "Allow Microsoft Services access to this server" checkbox, as shown in Figure 4.10. You can access the Firewall settings by logging into SQL Azure and clicking on the Firewall Settings tab for the server you selected.

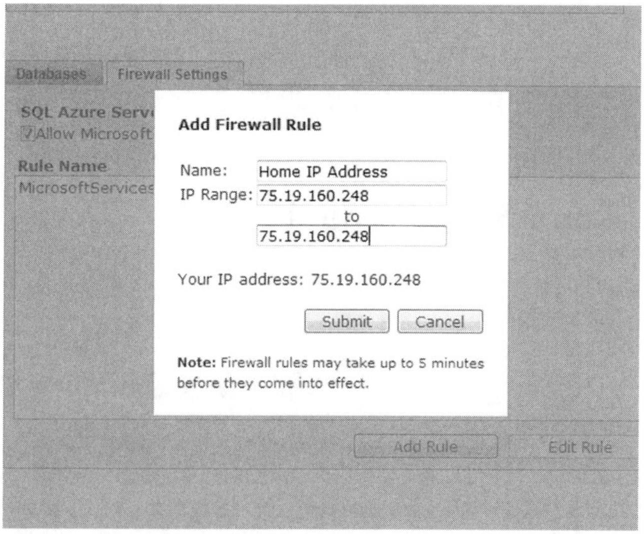

Figure 4.11 Showing how to allow a single IP Address access to the SQL Azure database.

To add rules to the firewall list, click the Add Rule button, which will open a window that allows you to set an IP range that will have direct access to the database. When adding database rules, add as small sets of IP Addresses as possible in order to prevent unauthorized people from accessing the database. When the screen opens, it will display the public IP Address that you are using to access the management portal. The best firewall rules are the rules that only allow a single IP Address, as shown in Figure 4.11.

Configuring a firewall rule that allows all IP Addresses (0.0.0.0 to 255.255.255.255) would be a bad idea because any attacker would be able to attempt a brute force attack against the database engine.

Instances That Leave the Office

The most difficult instances within any company to properly secure are instances that leave the office on a regular basis. These instances are usually located on developers or DBAs laptops and are taken home daily. These laptops present an interesting challenge in that they need to be able to leave the office and be usable by the employee, but the data needs to be useless in the event that the computer is stolen.

Using Transparent Data Encryption, which is discussed in detail in "Encrypting Data at Rest" in Chapter 2, can help mitigate this risk, for it will prevent the computer thief from taking the database and attaching it to another instance of the SQL Server. As the laptop will more than likely be a member of the domain, the accounts on the machine will have a strong password, making it very hard to break into the Windows OS. This leaves the thief the option of removing the hard drive from the laptop and installing it within another computer as a secondary hard drive. This would allow the thief access to the physical files, but without the certificates from the master database, the attacker wouldn't be able to attach the database.

An additional step that could be taken would be to secure the entire hard drive using the Windows bit locker technology. Bit locker encrypts the entire folder on the hard drive so that only the OS that is installed on the computer can access the data within the folder. This prevents the laptop thief in this scenario from being able to access the files within the folder.

To enable the bit locker on a folder to navigate to the folder within the Windows Explorer, right click on the folder and select the Advanced button on the General tab. On the Advanced

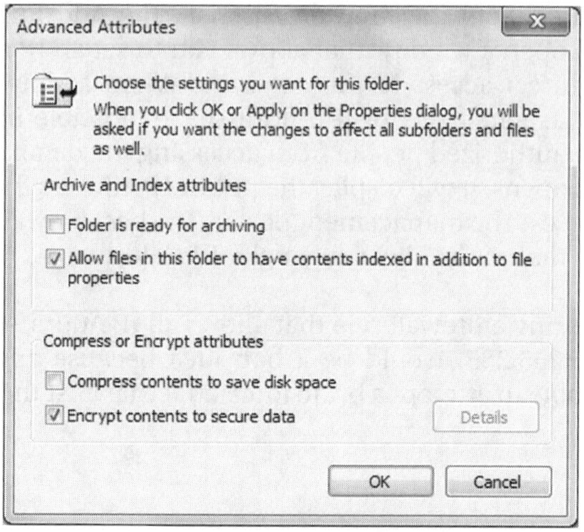

Figure 4.12 Screenshot showing the "Encrypt contents to secure data" option.

Attributes screen which opens, as shown in Figure 4.12, check the "Encrypt contents to secure data" and click OK and apply the changes to all subfolders if prompted (and desired).

Summary

Properly securing a single instance of Microsoft SQL Server isn't always the easiest task. However, with good company wide policies in place, as well as using newer features like Policy-Based Management, securing all the instances within the enterprise becomes easier over time and eventually becomes second nature. When it comes to dynamic SQL and cross database object security time, a methodical approach, combined with closely working with application and database developers (as well as business users and data analysts who have direct database access) will be the best approach to keeping the database objects properly secured.

ADDITIONAL SECURITY FOR AN INTERNET FACING SQL SERVER AND APPLICATION

INFORMATION IN THIS CHAPTER

- SQL CLR
- Extended Stored Procedures
- Protecting Your Connection Strings
- Database Firewalls
- Clear Virtual Memory Pagefile
- User Access Control (UAC)
- Other Domain Policies to Adjust
- Reporting Services

SQL CLR

When the SQL CLR was introduced in Microsoft SQL Server 2005, it was probably one of the most misunderstood and misused features of SQL Server. Part of this was due to the dual marketing message that Microsoft was putting out. When you spoke with those from the .NET and database developer side of Microsoft, they said that SQL supported the CLR and that you could use it to solve all your database problems. When you spoke with those from the Database Administration side of Microsoft, they said that SQL CLR was very limited and should almost never be used. This made proper implementation of the SQL CLR quite difficult, especially in environments where security was important.

The SQL CLR allows you to take an existing .NET CLR and load the compiled module into the SQL Server database as an assembly. Stored procedures and functions can then be created that call into the .NET assembly, allowing for the power and function of the .NET language to be used with the SQL Server

Back when SQL CLR was introduced to Microsoft SQL Server 2005, Microsoft had two very distinct stories they would present. The first story was being told to the database administrators and systems administrators, and the second to application and database developers. Neither story told the entire story, and these different stories created a lot of arguments between developers who wanted to use the SQL CLR and database administrators who were scared to death of it.

The story that the database administrators were being told was that the SQL CLR was very dangerous and that it had the ability to crash the SQL Server instance if things weren't done correctly. Database administrators were told of limitations, but at the time most database administrators didn't know much about programming, especially in .NET. Because of this lack of .NET knowledge, these limitations didn't mean much to most database administrators.

The story that the developers were being told was that SQL CLR was very safe to use and that it would be able to do anything that you needed it to do: Need to load data from a file, use the SQL CLR. Need to export data on the fly from a T/SQL stored procedure, use an SQL CLR procedure instead. Need to connect to a web service from a stored procedure, use an SQL CLR procedure to reach out to the web method. During the developer sessions, there was no mention of the limitations of the SQL CLR.

Due to these massively different messages, some interesting "discussions" were held at companies all over the world between developers who wanted to implement SQL CLR procedures, but they didn't understand the consequences of running SQL CLR assemblies in modes other than in the SAFE mode. Database administrators didn't like the idea of running SQL CLR procedures that they didn't have any visibility into, and even if they did, many of the database administrators wouldn't know how to read the code even if they could see it.

database by calling them with T/SQL. When you create an assembly within the SQL Server database, you can choose from three security levels; these tell the SQL Server engine how much access the .NET assembly should have to the host system, which are SAFE, EXTERNAL_ACCESS, and UNSAFE.

Assemblies that are considered to be safe are only allowed to access resources within the SQL Server Instance. These assemblies may not access the file system, system registry, variables, or network resources. These safe assemblies would typically be used to pass values into the procedure to do some sort of string manipulation or advanced math returning a value back to the database.

Assemblies that are created with the EXTERNAL_ACCESS permission have the same scalability and reliability features of the SAFE permission set, while giving the assembly rights to access the objects outside of the SQL Server instance. Unless impersonation is being used within the .NET assembly, the assembly will be launched under the same account that the SQL Server service is running. This means that the .NET assembly will have access to any object that the SQL Server service account has access to. If the SQL Server runs as a local administrator, and there is a .NET procedure within the assembly that accepts a file name to read, then the .NET assembly would have access to read any file on the server. If the SQL Server runs as a domain administrator with that same procedure, then the .NET assembly would have access to read any file (and probably write to any file) on the entire Windows domain.

Assemblies that are created with the UNSAFE permission can perform actions that could comprise the robustness of the SQL Server Instance. Procedures that are run in the UNSAFE mode could potentially compromise the security features within the operating system or the SQL Server Instance. This is the case as assemblies that are run in the UNSAFE mode can reference any native or third party .NET assembly that allows them to have effectively unfettered access to the Windows operating system. Like assemblies that are created with the EXTERNAL_ACCESS permission, assemblies that are created with the UNSAFE permission run under the account that the SQL Server service is running unless impersonation is used to access objects under a different account.

Note

Debugging Can Kill You

Never ever, under any circumstance, attach a debugger to a .NET assembly that is running on a production SQL Server. The .NET assembly runs within the process space of the SQL Server process, which means that if you sent a breakpoint in the debugger to pause the execution of the .NET assembly, the entire SQL Server process would be paused, causing the SQL Server to stop all processing and stopping all new connection requests to the database engine. This debugging can be very handy when debugging SQL CLR procedures against a development instance, or against a developer's personal sandbox instance, but against a production instance it would be catastrophic.

There are many horror stories of people attaching a debugger, setting a breakpoint in an obscure branch of code, then going to lunch waiting for the breakpoint to be hit and having the database come grinding to a halt for 30 minutes until the code can be restarted.

It is recommended that assemblies be created using only the SAFE or EXTERNAL_ACCESS permissions, preferably the SAFE permission, so that the assembly cannot cause problems or access .NET assemblies that are not considered safe. Only certain assemblies are thought to be safe for use in SQL CLR assemblies. As of the writing of this book, the list of assemblies to be SAFE are:

- Microsoft.VisualBasic.dll
- Mscorlib.dll
- System.Data.dll

- System.dll
- System.Xml.dll
- Microsoft.VisualC.dll
- CustomMarshalers.dll
- System.Security.dll
- System.Web.Services.dll
- System.Data.SqlXml.dll
- System.Transactions.dll
- System.Data.OracleClient.dll
- System.Configuration.dll

Note
Microsoft Has Special Support Policies for SQL CLR

Microsoft has special support policies for databases which have SQL CLR assemblies on them. If a .NET assembly references assemblies that are not included on the list above and Microsoft's Support department feels that the SQL CLR assembly is related to the performance problem, then they may require that the assembly be removed from the SQL Server before troubleshooting can continue.

In addition, Microsoft's support department may request that unsupported SQL CLR assemblies be temporally removed from the SQL Server instance while troubleshooting is performed. More information about the Microsoft support policy can be found at http://support.microsoft.com/kb/922672/en-us.

Assemblies can be created using either the SQL Server Management Studio User Interface (UI) or T/SQL via the CREATE ASSEMBLY statement. To create an assembly within SQL Server Management Studio, use these five steps:

1. Connect to the server in the Object Explorer.
2. Navigate to the database to put the assembly in.
3. Open the programmability folder.
4. Open the Assemblies folder.
5. Right click on the Assemblies and select "New Assemblies" from the context menu.

The screen that opens is the "New Assembly" window. Set the "Assembly owner," "Permission set," and "Path to assembly" similar to what is shown in Figure 5.1. The "Assembly name" and "Additional properties" values will be filled in automatically.

When you are creating an assembly using T/SQL, you use the CREATE ASSEMBLY statement. When using the CREATE ASSEMBLY statement, either the path to the assembly can be specified as shown in Example 5.1 or the bits that make up the binary can be included as shown in Example 5.2.

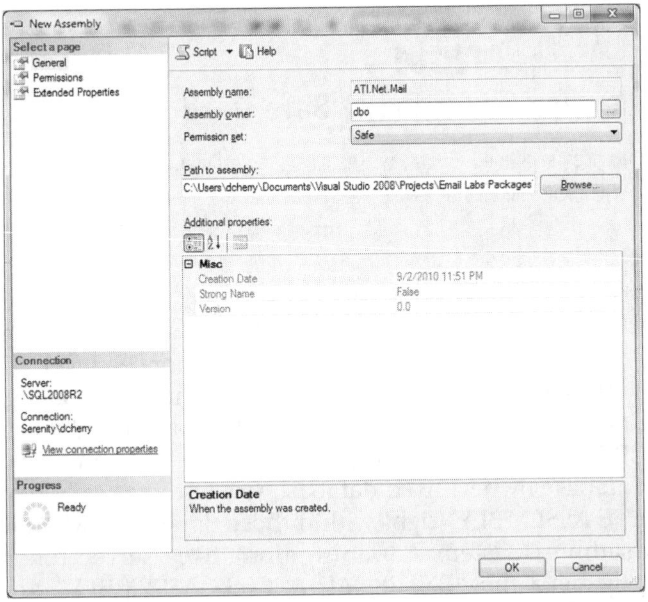

Figure 5.1 Showing the creation of a SAFE .NET Assembly using SQL Server Management Studio.

```
CREATE ASSEMBLY [ATI.Net.Mail]
AUTHORIZATION [dbo]
FROM 'C:\Users\dcherry\Documents\Visual Studio 2008\Projects
    \Email Labs Packages\mrdenny.Net.Mail.dll'
WITH PERMISSION_SET = SAFE
```

Example 5.1: T/SQL code showing the creation of an assembly using the path to the .NET assembly.

```
CREATE ASSEMBLY [mrdenny.Net.Mail]
AUTHORIZATION [dbo]
FROM
0x4D5A9000030000004000000FFFF0000B80000000000000000400000
  000000000000000000000
...
0000000000000000000000000000
WITH PERMISSION_SET = SAFE
```

Example 5.2: T/SQL code showing the creation of an assembly using the binary value of the assembly.

When creating assemblies, specific rights need to be had. In order to create an assembly, the user creating that assembly must have the "CREATE ASSEMBLY" right within the database. In order to create an assembly with the EXTERNAL_ACCESS permission, the login must have the "EXTERNAL ACCESS

Note
Sample Code Was Shortened to Save Dead Trees

This code, shown in Example 5.2, has been shortened for brevity. The binary representation of this .NET assembly is over 11 pages long. It was shortened for the sole purpose of saving dead trees that did not need to be chopped down.

ASSEMBLY" right at the instance level. In order to create an UNSAFE assembly, the login for the user must have the "UNSAFE ASSEMBLY" right at the instance level. These instance-level rights will allow the login that has the right to create an assembly at that level in any database that the user has the "CREATE ASSEMBLY" right assigned to it. Members of the dbo (database owner) fixed database role automatically have the "CREATE ASSEMBLY" right within those databases. Members of the sysadmin (System Administration) fixed-server role automatically have the "EXTERNAL ACCESS ASSEMBLY" and the "UNSAFE ASSEMBLY" right within that instance. These high-level rights are not needed to run the procedures and functions within the assembly; they are only needed to create the assembly within the database.

Note
Combining an Unsafe Procedure with an SQL Injection Attack Gives Some Interesting Possibilities

If an application account was configured with these higher level permissions and the application was susceptible to an SQL Injection attack, serious damage could be done very quickly and easily. An attacker could write a .NET dll, create an assembly within the database, and mark it as unsafe. Then an attacker could call the assembly and have the assembly download and install any software that the attacker wanted. The assembly could also log back into the database and elevate the permissions of the login that the application account uses, giving the attacker easier and greater access to the database instance.

Extended Stored Procedures

Even though Extended Stored Procedures are scheduled for removal from Microsoft SQL Server in a future version (after Microsoft SQL Server 2008 R2), they can still be a useful tool. When you create an extended stored procedure, the dll must physically exist on the database server, which makes it a little more complex for attackers to create an extended stored procedure on the fly as they can with an SQL Server Assembly.

In order to create an extended stored procedure, the login that the user uses to log into the database must be a member of the sysadmin fixed server role. Extended stored procedures are always created within the master database, but can be referenced from any database. Typically, an extended stored procedure would be created with a name starting with xp_ or sp_ so that the database engine would automatically look in the master database for the object if there was no object with that name in the user database.

Note

Getting a New dll Onto the Server Isn't All That Hard

Once attackers have figured out that they can use SQL Injection attacks to gain access to the system, it isn't hard to determine what sort of access they have to the database server. If the attacker is able to gain access to xp_cmdshell, even if it is without admin rights, the attacker can still do a decent amount of damage to the system.

As an example, an attacker could create text file that has FTP (File Transfer Protocol) commands and then run ftp.exe using xp_cmdshell passing ftp.exe the name of the text file, which has the commands to run. The text file with the commands could be set up to log into the attacker's FTP server and download various files. If attackers have sysadmin rights to the SQL Server instance, then they can simply attack an extended stored procedure to the instance. If they don't have sysadmin rights to the instance, the attacker could install software on the machine and configure it to start up automatically either via a service (probably hidden by a rootkit), or in the run registry key for either one or all users. At this point this software could be configured to do anything the attacker wants to and will probably be hidden from the view of the database administrator and system administrators.

Like .NET assemblies, extended stored procedures can be written to access anything on the local system or the Internet, limited only by the coding knowledge of the developer who writes the dll that is attached as an extended stored procedure. Extended stored procedures run within the SQL Server, meaning that the code is executed within the SQL Server memory space. As the extended stored procedures run within the SQL Server process, bugs within the extended stored procedure can surface within the SQL Server as it crashes or core dumps, even causing the SQL Server engine processes to stop completely.

Extended stored procedures can be added to an SQL Server instance by using the sp_addextendedproc system stored procedure within the master database. The system stored procedure accepts two parameters, @functname and @dllname, as shown in

Example 5.3. @functname is the name of the function to call within the DLL and is a nvarchar(517) parameter. @dllname is the full path to the DLL and is varchar(255). There can be multiple functions within a single DLL, each one with a different name and exposed as a separate extended stored procedure.

```
EXEC sp_addextendedproc @functname='MyFunction',
    @dllname='c:\Program Files\Microsoft SQL Server\MSSQL\binn
    \myfile.dll'
```

Example 5.3: Adding an extended stored procedure to an SQL Server Instance.

Protecting Your Connection Strings

Applications use connection strings to identify the server instance and database to connect to and to determine how to connect to the instance. Typically, the connection string will be stored in a configuration file somewhere within the application or web server. This connection string is typically stored in plain text to make it easy to edit and easy to change as the application is moved from development, to QA, to staging, and to production.

When the connection strings are stored in plain text, they provide a wealth of information to an attacker, typically everything that an attacker would need to break into a database. In order to protect the database, you have to protect the connection string, so that if an attacker is able to get access to the files on the web server or application server, the attacker isn't able to use the connection string to attack the database. The best way to secure the database connection string is to encrypt the value within the configuration file. The application would then load the encrypted value from the config file, decrypt the value, and then use the decrypted value as the connection string to connect to the database.

Securing the connection string could be done through a separate application that the systems administrator could use during the deployment process to encrypt the string, or the application could be configured to automatically encrypt the string the first time the application launches. This automatic encryption of the connection string is a better method for the systems administrator because it doesn't require the systems administrator to use a separate application to encrypt the connection string.

In either case, troubleshooting the application is made a little bit harder as the connection string isn't easily visible without decrypting the connection string to ensure that the connection string is correct, which would require a separate application.

Even with the connection string stored in the configuration file in an encrypted format, there is still a risk of an attacker getting the connection string. However, it is much more difficult for the attacker. For the attacker to get the connection string, the attacker would need to dump the memory for the application, be it a Windows Service, Win32 application, or web-based application, and read through the memory dump looking for the connection string. The application would have to store the connection string in a variable in memory, which means that it would be contained within a full memory dump.

Database Firewalls

There is a special set of firewall products out there that are called Database Firewalls. These database firewalls monitor and track all connections that are made to the database engine. Many of them, such as "SecureSphere Database Firewall," can take proactive action if the firewall detects SQL injection attacks, buffer overflow attacks, and denial of service attacks. Depending on the Database Firewall, they can either monitor the network connection remotely, usually by using a feature on the network switch called port mirroring where all network traffic going to one physical Ethernet port is sent to a second mirrored port for analysis. The second method involves installing an agent on the database server and using that agent to inspect all the database calls. The mirrored port method doesn't put any load on the database server at all, but this method typically doesn't allow for the monitoring of encrypted database connections.

These Database Firewall applications can go a long way toward preventing attacks as they monitor every command that is sent to the database server, no matter whether that statement is a DML (Data Modification Language) statement that is selecting, deleting, or updating data; or whether it is a DDL (Data Definition Language) statement that is dropping tables full of data. You can create policies that define which statements can be run, which would trigger an alert to be sent, or which statements should be blocked.

Clear Virtual Memory Pagefile

When you have a server that can be accessed from the Internet, the possibility exists that an attacker could access a memory dump to gain access to data they normally wouldn't be able to access. This includes the virtual memory page file, as well as system dumps that Windows has taken.

To protect the virtual memory page file, a policy setting can be enabled which upon shutdown of Windows will cause the page file to be rewritten with 0s. This setting is called "Shutdown: Clear virtual memory page file." It can be set via a group policy or via the "Local Security Policy" MMC (Microsoft Management Console) within the Administrative Tools menu off of the Start Menu. To set it on a single server, open the "Local Security Policy" and then navigate to the Local Policies folder and the Security Options folder. Then double click on the policy "Shutdown: Clear virtual memory pagefile" and set the setting to enabled as shown in Figure 5.2.

In order to set this setting on all computers on a domain (or a subset of computers on a domain), the setting should be enabled within a group policy that is applied to the computers, which should have the setting enabled. To do this, open the Group Policy Editor and edit the correct policy that affects the correct computers, then navigate to:

1. Computer Configuration
2. Policies
3. Windows Settings
4. Security Settings

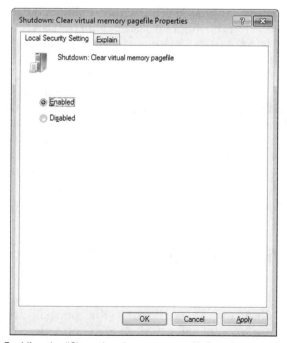

Figure 5.2 Enabling the "Clear virtual memory pagefile" setting on a single server.

5. Local Policies

6. Security Options

After navigating to the Security Options folder, locate and edit the "Shutdown: Clear virtual memory page file" policy, setting the value to enabled as shown in Figure 5.2. Closing the Group Policy Editor will save the settings back to the domain controller, allowing the setting change to replicate to all domain controllers within the domain, then eventually to all the computers affected by the group policy.

There is a downside to enabling the "Shutdown: Clear virtual memory page file" setting: Notably, computers will begin taking a much longer time to shut down or reboot. This longer time occurs because before Windows will complete the shutdown process, the page file will be overwritten with zeros so that no data from within the page file can be accessed. The more RAM a server has, the longer this process will take, with servers with a gig or two taking just a few minutes and servers with hundreds of gigs of RAM taking hours to complete the process. In addition to the amount of RAM in the server changing the amount of time it takes, the speed of the hard drives that hold the operating system will also impact the performance of the process.

In order to prevent an attacker from getting access to a memory dump, Windows' ability to dump the memory to disk should be disabled on a server unless it needs to be enabled for a specific reason. On a single server, this is done through the system control panel. After opening the system control panel, select the Advanced tab and click the Settings button within the "Startup and Recovery" section. In the new Window that opens, change the "Write debugging information" dropdown menu to "(none)" as shown in Figure 5.3.

There is no group policy setting that can be used to disable the setting over all computers in a domain. However, a group policy can still be used to make the needed registry change. The registry setting that needs to be changed is HKEY_LOCAL_MACHINE\SYSTEM\CurrentControlSet\Control\CrashControl\CrashDumpEnabled. The setting is a DWORD value, which should be set to 0. To set a registry value within a group policy, edit the group policy and navigate to:

1. Computer Configuration

2. Preferences

3. Windows Settings

4. Registry

Right click on Registry and select "New" from the context menu then select "Registry Item". Set the Hive to HKEY_LOCAL_MACHINE and the key path to "SYSTEM\CurrentControlSet

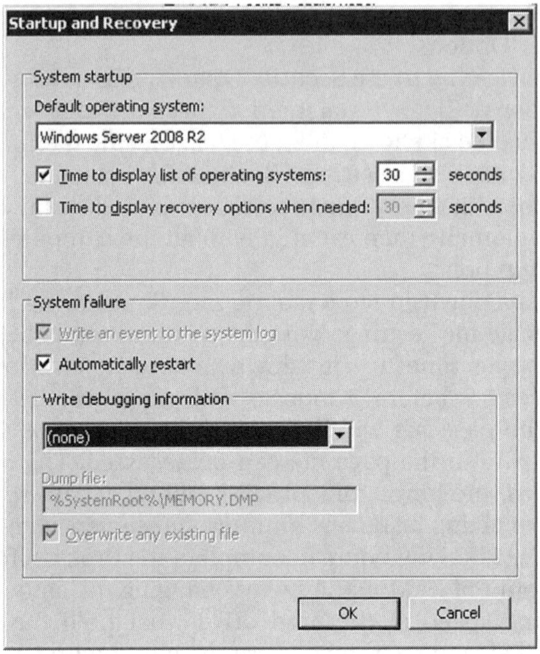

Figure 5.3 How to disable the writing of memory dumps in Windows.

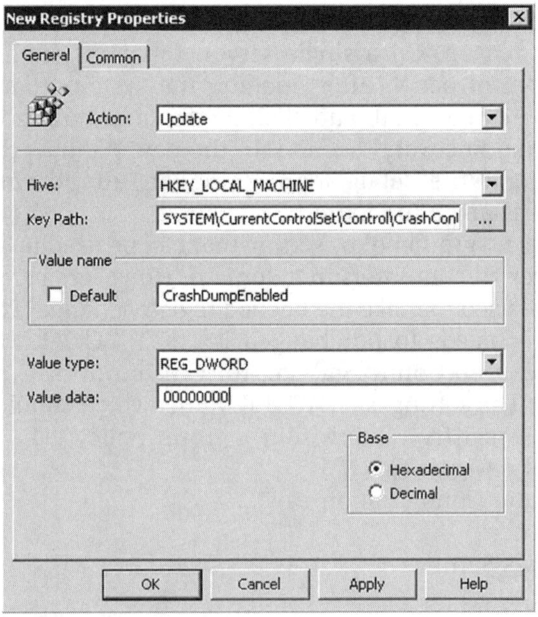

Figure 5.4 The registry setting change needed to disable memory dumps on a server through a group policy.

\Control\CrashControl" as shown in Figure 5.4. Set the "Value name" to ChashDumpEnabled, the "Value type" as REG_DWORD and set the "Value data" to 00000000 as shown in Figure 5.4.

No matter how this setting is disabled, either on the local server or globally through a group policy, the server(s) will need to be rebooted in order for the setting change to take effect. The reboot can either be done at the time the change is made manually or upon the next normal reboot which happens.

While changing these settings will increase the security of the server, it will greatly decrease the ability to troubleshoot system problems. The first troubleshooting technique when attempting to resolve Windows instability issues would normally be to analyze the system memory dump. In the event that these memory dumps are not available, these settings will need to be reversed so that memory dumps can be created and used for debugging. After this debugging has been completed, the settings would then need to be put back into place in order to resolve the problem.

User Access Control (UAC)

User Access Control (UAC) was first introduced to Windows in Windows 2008 and Windows Vista. UAC is often considered to be a pain and more trouble than it is worth. However, UAC serves an important function in that it requires a second approval to complete administrative actions on the computer, such as accessing the registry or various protected files and folders such as the Windows operating system and the Program Files folder. This extra approval is meant to prevent applications from being able to successfully access parts of the operating system that shouldn't be accessed.

While on the desktop this can be annoying at best and downright troublesome at worst, on a server this extra protection can prevent things from running that shouldn't be running and making administrative level changes to the system such as installing applications, adding services, or making registry changes.

To make changes on a single computer, open the control panel and then the User Accounts control panel icon. From there click on the "Change User Account Control settings" link. From here you can adjust the level of interaction UAC will have with the desktop. On a production server this setting should be set as high as possible, as shown in Figure 5.5.

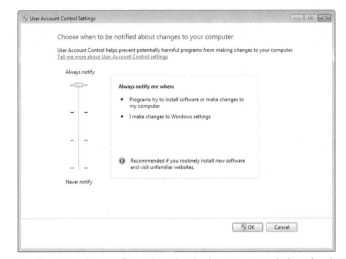

Figure 5.5 The User Access Control setting in the recommended setting for servers.

Beyond the simple slider setting shown in Figure 5.5, a variety of settings can be set via group policy. These can all be found under:

1. Computer Configuration
2. Policies
3. Windows Settings
4. Security Settings
5. Local Policies
6. Security Options

Within the Security Options folder there are 10 User Account Control settings that can be controlled for greater control of UAC than the normal control panel interface. Of these 10 settings, 3 of them will have a noticeable effect on servers. These settings are:

1. User Account Control: Detect application installations and prompt for elevation
2. User Account Control: Virtualize file and registry write failures to per-user locations
3. User Account Control: Behavior of the elevation prompt for standard users

It is very important to enable the "User Account Control: Detect application installations and prompt for elevation" setting. When this setting is enabled, the UAC subsystem of the operating system will detect the installation of applications and will trigger a UAC authentication prompt when an installer is run. With this setting disabled, this check is not in place and installers are able to run without prompting.

The "User Account Control: Virtualize file and registry write failures to per-user locations" is another good setting to disable on production servers. This setting, which is enabled by default, when disabled causes applications that attempt to write to the %ProgramFiles% (typically "C:\Program Files\"), %WinDir% (typically "C:\Windows\"), and %WinDir%\System32 (typically "C:\Windows\System32\") folders and to the HKEY_LOCAL_MACHINE\Software registry key to fail instead of redirecting those writes to protected user-specific locations such as C:\UserData\. When the setting is enabled, the writes are automatically disabled, and when the setting is disabled, the writes will fail. Many rouge applications would be written to hide themselves and their data in the %WinDir% and %WinDir%\System32 folders. By preventing these rouge applications from writing to these protected locations, many of these rouge applications will fail to run correctly, causing them to simply crash.

Note
Be Very Careful When Adjusting UAC Settings

Making changes to the UAC settings should not be done to production servers at random. These changes should first be fully tested on development and QA systems to ensure that all applications that are installed on the server can function as expected with these changes. There is nothing worse than changing settings to improve security and having the production systems crash days or weeks later after the next system reboot. As a result, large amounts of time are required to figure out what change, which happened days or weeks before (months possibly depending on how often you reboot), caused the problem.

A third setting that should be adjusted, assuming that the SQL Server service or the website is running under a non-administrator account, is the "User Account Control: Behavior of the elevation prompt for standard users." This setting controls how UAC will react when a standard user (a user who isn't a member of the local Administrators group) attempts to perform an action that is protected by UAC. By default, UAC will prompt the user to enter a username and password that have the rights to perform the action. It is recommended that this setting be changed from "Prompt for credentials on the secure desktop" to "Automatically deny elevation requests," which will tell the Windows OS to simply fail the request to perform the protected action.

Other Domain Policies to Adjust

Beyond User Account Control (UAC), other security policies should be adjusted in order to reduce the surface area that a potential attacker could use to attack the server. The more of these settings that are configured, the smaller the surface area of the server that can be attacked. These settings are as follows:

1. Accounts: Rename administrator account
2. Accounts: Guest Account Status
3. Accounts: Rename guest account
4. Devices: Prevent users from installing printer drivers

The "Accounts: Rename administrator account" policy allows you to globally change the username of the local Administrator account. This will help reduce the attack surface area by making an attacker guess the username of the local administrator account. Like the SA (system administrator) account in Microsoft SQL Server that has a known username, making it easier for an attacker to break into the database, leaving the Administrator account with the default name poses the same potential vulnerability. When selecting a new username to use for the local administrator account, the same syntax should be used that is used for the local administrator account. For example, if the company username syntax is first name dot last name, then a username of James.Kirk would be a good username to use. If the company username syntax is first initial followed by the last name, then a username of jkirk would be a good username to use.

The "Accounts: Guest Account Status" policy allows you to disable the guest account to ensure that no one is able to log into the server using the local guest account. While this is a very low privileged account that does not have rights to access much of the operating system, there is always the potential that an attacker could use this account along with a privilege elevation attack to increase their privileges. By forcing the account to always be disabled, no user can authenticate using the guest account even with the correct username and password.

The "Accounts: Rename guest account" policy allows you to globally change the username of the local guest account. It is recommended that you change the guest account so that the username is set to "Administrator." This way if someone attempts to log into the server using the local account with the name "Administrator" and that account is enabled, then the user will get a very low privileged account. If the account is disabled, then the potential attacker will receive a message about the account being disabled and the login will be denied.

The "Devices: Prevent users from installing printer drivers" privilege can be used to ensure that users do not have the right to install printer drivers on the server. One potential attack that could be used via a print driver would be to install an Internet print driver, which could then be used to print company documents to that print driver, sending the documents to a remote printer service. The service could then store the documents or print them on the attacker's printer. In either case, the attacker would have access to internal company documents, which they shouldn't have.

Reporting Services

Other than the database engine (which hopefully isn't ever configured directly connected to the Internet), SQL Reporting Services would be the only SQL Server Service that would be directly connected to the Internet. As SQL Reporting Services provides a wide variety of information, it should be properly configured to prevent unauthorized access to the reports.

SQL Server Reporting Services 2005 and below require Internet Information Services (IIS) in order to function. When installing these older versions of SQL Server Reporting Services on Windows 2008 or newer, there is a much more granular control about what IIS features are being installed on the server. As with the SQL Server Services, only install the features that you will be using. If the server hosting the SQL Server Reporting Services will not be using classic ASP (as an example), then do not install and/or configure classic ASP. The same goes for the other native features that the Reporting Services does not need to use. The features that SQL Server Reporting Services uses that should be installed are the following:

- .NET Extensibility
- ASP.NET
- ISAPI Extensions
- Default Document
- Directory Browsing
- HTTP Errors
- HTTP Redirection
- HTTP Logging
- Request Filtering
- Windows Authentication

Other features can be installed as needed, but only when needed.

When configuring SQL Reporting Services to be accessed from the public Internet, it is always recommended to use SQL Reporting Services over SSL (or HTTPS) instead of HTTP. When using HTTP and SQL Reporting Services prompts for authentication, the username and password that the end user submits will be transmitted in plain text between the web browser (or other application that is calling the SQL Reporting Services website) and the web server. When SQL Reporting Services is configured to use SSL and the user uses SSL by putting HTTPS in front of the SQL Reporting Services website name, instead of HTTP, then the username and password are encrypted before being sent from the web browser (or other client application) and the web server that is hosting the SQL Reporting Services application. This holds true for SQL Reporting Services 2008 and higher, even though these versions do not rely on IIS in order to run.

Anonymous Authentication

Whenever possible, Anonymous Authentication should be disabled on all SQL Server Reporting Services instances. When Anonymous Authentication is enabled, anyone who connects to the reporting services instance will have access to the reports that are configured to be viewed by the account to which the Anonymous Authentication account is mapped. When using SQL Reporting Services 2000 or 2005, Anonymous Authentication can be easily enabled within the IIS Manager. However, when using SQL Reporting Services 2008 and above, Anonymous Authentication is very difficult to configure as SQL Reporting Services 2008 and above no longer are hosted by the Windows IIS. This is because SQL Reporting Services 2008 and above use the Windows APIs and host the web service within the SQL Reporting Services service directly. When configuring SQL Reporting Services 2005 and below, always ensure that Anonymous Authentication is disabled, as shown in Figure 5.6. This is done by following these X steps on Windows 2003:

1. Right click on the "Reports" or "ReportServer" virtual folder within IIS Manager (the folder names may be different depending on your configuration).
2. Select properties from the context menu that opens.

When using Windows 2008 or newer, the steps are a little different, with the final result shown in Figure 5.7.

1. Navigate to the reports folder in the menu tree.
2. Double click Authentication from the menu on the left.
3. Select Anonymous Authentication from the new screen on the right.

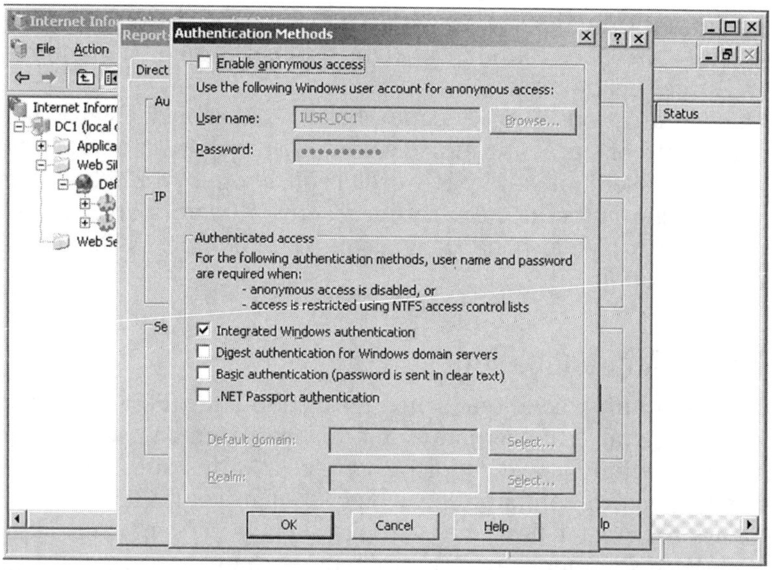

Figure 5.6 Internet Information Manager showing Anonymous Authentication being disabled for the Reporting Services web application when using Windows 2003 or lower.

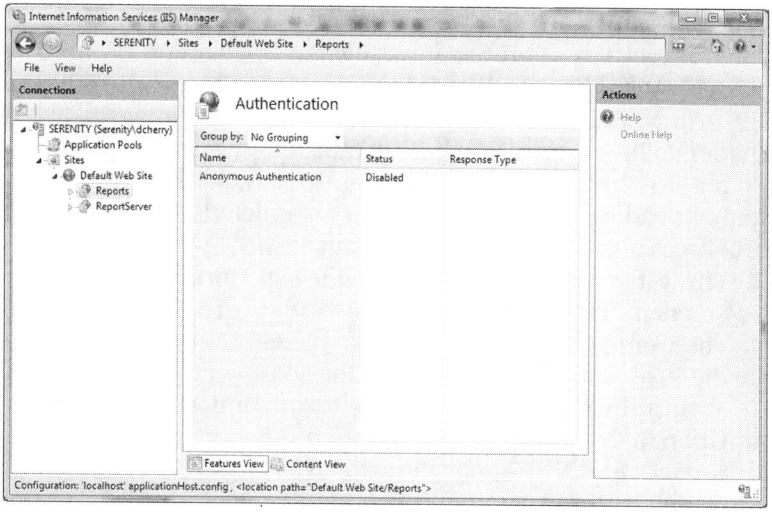

Figure 5.7 Internet Services Manager for Windows 2008 or higher showing Anonymous Authentication being disabled for the Reporting Services web application.

4. From the "Actions" menu on the far right, select disable (this can also be found by right clicking on "Anonymous Authentication").

Once Anonymous Authentication has been disabled, ensure that some sort of authentication is used that requires the user to specify a username and password. Typically this would be done via domain authentication through active directory authentication, but it can also be done using a technique called forms authentication.

Forms Authentication

The security technique called forms authentication allows for a database table of usernames and passwords to be used for the authentication against reporting services. Forms authentication is an advanced configuration which, though complex to set up, allows for greater flexibility when designing the reporting solution. Forms authentication permits users to use a username and password that are stored securely within a database table, or LDAP database, and so on, allowing for the reporting services authentication to be keyed off of another application's authentication provider.

When using Windows credentials to handle Reporting Services authentication, the process is very straightforward. The login process happens in the same way that is described within the "SQL Server Password Security" section of Chapter 3. After the normal Windows Authentication process is completed, the Reporting Services ASP.NET application passes the user's information to the reporting services database to see what folders and/or reports the user should be able to view. When using forms authentication, however, the process is much different.

1. The user browses to the Reporting Services website.
2. The website redirects the user to the login form where the user enters in the username and password.
3. The username and password are passed from the website to the user-supplied security extension, which then checks against the database table or other authentication source.
4. Upon a successful authentication attempt, the Reporting Services ASP.NET application creates an authentication ticket (which is stored within a web browser cookie) and verifies the role that the user has been assigned to within the Reporting Services environment.
5. The cookie created in the prior step is passed to the user's web browser, and the user's reporting services page is displayed.

6. When the user navigates throughout the SQL Reporting Services website, the cookie is uploaded for each request, and the reporting services application checks with the user-defined security extension to determine whether the user has the right to perform the requested action.
7. If the user has the needed right, then the report or the menu is displayed to the user.

> # Note
> ## Sample Source Code
>
> Putting sample source code for Forms Authentication into this book would take a very large number of pages full of C# code, which is not something the author is very good at writing. Fortunately, Microsoft has provided some excellent examples that can be referenced at "http://msdn.microsoft.com/en-us/library/aa902691(SQL.80).aspx." This page also includes several diagrams of the workflow that result when forms-based authentication is used to make understanding the workflow process easier when building your own forms-based authentication.

Security within Reporting Services

Once SQL Reporting Services is set up and is prompting users for authentication, the security job is not done. In most Reporting Services environments, not all users have the need to view all the reports within the SQL Server Reporting Services environment. When this is the case, the native security should be used to enforce security on the folders and reports.

Probably the easiest way to secure the reports and folders is to create domain (or local) groups for each group of people who need access to a group of reports (you can use existing domain groups if those exist aready). You can then edit the security properties of the folders, or the specific reports, and remove the rights for all users to view the objects; you can also add in the specific groups that need to have access to the objects. When removing rights from the groups, be sure to leave in (or put in) the group that contains the database administrators (or other users who have the rights to deploy reports), so that report deployment isn't blocked.

If forms-based authentication is being used, then the permission to view folders and reports must be controlled through the security provider, which is developed in house.

Summary

Every server needs to have some protections done to it. Servers that are customer (or Internet) facing need some extra protections in order to secure the server from attackers. This includes only hosting known code within an SQL Instance through the extended stored procedures and SQL CLR assemblies. The server can be further protected by limiting the amount of data that an attacker can gather by limiting the amount of memory data that can be written to the hard drive at any time through crash dumps and the Windows page file.

When working within SQL Azure, the only section of this chapter that applies is that on securing your connection string. As of 2010, SQL Azure does not support SQL CLR assemblies of any type, nor does it support extended stored procedures. The other information in this chapter is related to Windows-specific settings that must be set by logging into the Windows OS ,which cannot be done on SQL Azure instances. If the application requires SQL CLR or extended stored procedures, then SQL Azure is not a good solution for hosting that application.

6

SQL INJECTION ATTACKS

INFORMATION IN THIS CHAPTER

- What Is an SQL Injection Attack?
- Why Are SQL Injection Attacks So Successful?
- How to Protect Yourself from an SQL Injection Attack
- Cleaning Up the Database After an SQL Injection Attack

What Is an SQL Injection Attack?

An SQL Injection Attack is probably the easiest attack to prevent, while being one of the least protected against forms of attack. The core of the attack is that an SQL command is appended to the back end of a form field in the web or application front end (usually through a website), with the intent of breaking the original SQL Script and then running the SQL script that was injected into the form field. This SQL injection most often happens when you have dynamically generated SQL within your front-end application. These attacks are most common with legacy Active Server Pages (ASP) and Hypertext Preprocessor (PHP) applications, but they are still a problem with ASP.NET web-based applications. The core reason behind an SQL Injection attack comes down to poor coding practices both within the front-end application and within the database stored procedures. Many developers have learned better development practices since ASP.NET was released, but SQL Injection is still a big problem between the number of legacy applications out there and newer applications built by developers who didn't take SQL Injection seriously while building the application.

As an example, assume that the front-end web application creates a dynamic SQL Script that ends up executing an SQL Script similar to that shown in Example 6.1.

```
SELECT * FROM Orders WHERE OrderId=25
```

Example 6.1: A simple dynamic SQL statement as expected from the application.

This SQL Script is created when the customer goes to the sales order history portion of the company's website. The value passed in as the OrderId is taken from the query string in the URL, so the query shown above is created when the customer goes to the URL http://www.yourcompany.com/orders/orderhistory.aspx?Id=25. Within the .NET code, a simple string concatenation is done to put together the SQL Query. So any value that is put at the end of the query string is passed to the database at the end of the select statement. If the attacker were to change the query string to something like "/orderhistory.aspx?id=25; delete from Orders," then the query sent to the SQL Server will be a little more dangerous to run as shown in Example 6.2.

```
SELECT * FROM Orders WHERE ORderId=25; delete from Orders;
```

Example 6.2: A dynamic SQL String that has had a delete statement concatenated to the end of it.

The way the query in Example 6.2 works is that the SQL database is told via the semicolon ";" that the statement has ended and that there is another statement that should be run. The SQL Server then processes the next statement as instructed.

While the initial query is run as normal now, and without any error being generated but when you look at the Orders table, you won't see any records in the Orders table because the second query in that batch will have executed against the database as well. Even if the attacker omits the value that the query is expecting, they can pass in "; delete from Orders;" and while the first query attempting to return the data from the Orders table will fail, the batch will continue moving on to the next statement, which will delete all the records in the Orders table.

Many people will inspect the text of the parameters looking for various key words in order to prevent these SQL Injection attacks. However, this only provides the most rudimentary protection as there are many, many ways to force these attacks to work. Some of these techniques include passing in binary data, having the SQL Server convert the binary data back to a text string, and then executing the string. This can be proven by running the T/SQL statement shown in Example 6.3.

```
DECLARE @v varchar(255)
SELECT @v = cast(0x73705F68656C706462 as varchar(255))
EXEC (@v)
```

Example 6.3: Code showing how a binary value can be used to hide a T/SQL statement.

When data is being accepted from a user, either a customer or an employee, one good way to ensure that the value won't be used for an SQL Injection attack is to validate that the data being returned is of the expected data type. If a number is expected, the front-end application should ensure that there is in fact a number within the value. If a text string is expected, then ensure that the text string is of the correct length, and it does not contain any binary data within it. The front-end application should be able to validate all data being passed in from the user, either by informing the user of the problem and allowing the user to correct the issue, or by crashing gracefully in such a way that an error is returned and no commands are sent to the database or the file system. Just because users should be sending up valid data doesn't mean that they are going to. If users could be trusted, most of this book wouldn't be needed.

Note
The Database Isn't the Only Weak Spot

If a file name is going to be generated based on the user's input, a few special values should be watched for. These values are Windows file system key words that could be used to give attackers access to something they shouldn't have, or could simply cause havoc on the front-end server.

- AUX
- CLOCK$
- COM1-COM8
- CON
- CONFIG$
- LPT1-LPT8
- NUL
- PRN

By allowing an attacker to create a file path using these special names, attackers could send data to a serial port by using COM1 (or whatever com port number they specify) or to a printer port using LPT1 (or whatever printer port they specify). Bogus data could be sent to the system clock by using the CLOCK$ value, or they could instruct the file to be written to NUL, causing the file to simply disappear.

The same technique shown in Example 6.3 can be used to send update statements into the database, causing values to be places within the database that will cause undesirable side effects on the websites powered by the databases. This includes returning javascript to the client computers causing popups that show ads for other projects, using HTML iframes to cause malicious software to be downloaded, using HTML tags to redirect the browser session to another website, and so on.

SQL Injection attacks aren't successful against only in-house applications. A number of third-party applications available for purchase are susceptible to these SQL Injection attacks. When purchasing third-party applications, it is often assumed that the product is a secure application that isn't susceptible to the attack. Unfortunately, that isn't the case, and any time a third-party application is brought into a company, it should be reviewed, with a full code review if possible, to ensure that the application is safe to deploy. When a company deploys a third-party application that is susceptible to attack and that application is successfully attacked, it is the company that deployed the application that will have to deal with the backlash for having an insecure application and their customer data compromised, not the company that produced and sold the insecure application.

Many people think that SQL Injection attacks are a problem unique to Microsoft SQL Server, and those people would be wrong. SQL Injection attacks can occur against Oracle, MySQL, DB2, Access, and so on. Any database that allows multiple statements to be run in the same connection is susceptible to an SQL Injection attack. Now some of the other database platforms have the ability to turn off this function, some by default and some via an optional setting. There are a number of tickets open in the Microsoft bug-tracking website http://connect.microsoft. com that are requesting that this ability be removed from a future version of the Microsoft SQL Server product. While doing so would make the Microsoft SQL Server product more secure, it would break a large number of applications, many of which are probably the ones that are susceptible to SQL Injection attacks.

Another technique that is easier to use against Microsoft SQL Server 7 and 2000 is to use the sp_makewebtask system stored procedure in the master database. If the attacker can figure out the name of the webserver, which can usually be done pretty easily by looking at the sysprocesses table, or the path to the website, then the sp_makewebtask procedure can be used to export lists of objects to HTML files on the web server to make it easier for the attacker to see what objects are in the database. Then they can simply browse to the website and see every table in the database.

```
exec master.dbo.sp_makewebtask '\\web1\wwwroot\tables.html",
  "select * from information_schema.tables"
```
Code that an attacker could execute to export all table objects to an HTML file.

If xp_cmdshell is enabled on the server, then an attacker could use xp_cmdshell to do the same basic thing just by using Bulk Copy Protocol (BCP) instead of sp_makewebtask. The advantage to sp_makewebtask is that xp_cmdshell doesn't need to be enabled, while the downside to sp_makewebtask is that it doesn't exist on Microsoft SQL Server 2005 and up. The downside to xp_cmdshell is that, unless the application uses a login that is a member of the sysadmin fixed server role, the xp_cmdshell procedure will only have the rights that are granted by the proxy account. An attacker can use the xp_cmdshell procedure to send in the correct commands to give the account that is the proxy account more permissions, or even change the account to one that has the correct permissions. At this point BCP can be used to output whatever data is wanted. The attacker could start with database schema information, and then begin exporting your customer information, or they could use this information to change or delete the data from the database.

The catch to either of these techniques is that the NT File System (NTFS) permissions need to allow either the SQL Server account or the account that the xp_cmdshell proxy account uses to have network share and NTFS permissions to the web server. On smaller applications where the web server and the database server are running on the same machine, this is much, much easier as the SQL Server is probably running as the local system account that gives it rights to everything.

Note
There Are Lots of Protection Layers to Make Something Secure

Hopefully, by now you are starting to see how the various layers of the Microsoft SQL Server need to be secured to make for a truly secure SQL Server. In this case we look specifically at NTFS permissions combined with the xp_cmdshell proxy account, combined with the Windows account that the SQL Server is running under, combined with the application account that logs into SQL having the minimum level of rights, and combined with parameterizing the values from the web application all to create a more secure environment.

To fully protect from an SQL injection attack, the application account should only have the minimum rights needed to function; it should have no rights to xp_cmdshell, which should be disabled (or removed from the server). The SQL Server service should be running under a domain or local computer account that only has the rights needed to run as a service and access the SQL Server folders. That Windows account should have no rights to the actual files that are the website files, and it shouldn't be an administrator on the server that is running the SQL Server service

Note—*Cont'd*

or the web server. The resulting effective permissions that an SQL Server has are to access the database files and do nothing else. Any other functions that the SQL Server instance is expected to perform either via an SQL Agent job or a CLR procedure should be controlled through some sort of account impersonation.

At the application level the actual SQL Server error messages should be masked so that they aren't returned to the client. If you have done these things, then even if attackers were able to successfully complete an SQL Injection attack against the SQL Server they wouldn't be able to do much to the server as they wouldn't have any way to get information back from the SQL Server (as the error messages are masked) and they wouldn't be able to get to the shell and get software downloaded and installed from the outside. Once these things fail a few times, attackers will probably just move on to an easier target.

The amount of time that an attacker will spend trying to successfully use an SQL Injection attack against a web-based application will for the most part depend on the amount of value the target has. A smaller company such as a wholesale food distributor probably won't be attacked very often, and the attacker will probably leave after a short period of time. However, a bank or other financial company will provide a much more enticing target for the attacker, and the attack will probably last much longer, with many more techniques being tried, as well as many combinations of techniques until they successfully break into the database application.

Why Are SQL Injection Attacks So Successful?

SQL Injection attacks are so successful for a few reasons, the most common of which is that many newer developers simply don't know about the problem. With project timelines being so short, these junior developers don't have the time to research the security implications of using dynamic SQL. These applications then get left in production for months or years, with little to no maintenance. These developers can then move through their career without anyone giving them the guidance needed to prevent these problems.

Now developers aren't solely to blame for SQL Injection attack problems. The IT Management should have policies in place in order to ensure that newer developers that come in don't have the ability to write dynamic inline SQL against the database engine. These policies should include rules like the following:

1. All database interaction must be abstracted through stored procedures.
2. No stored procedure should have dynamic SQL unless there is no other option.

3. Applications should have no access to table or view objects unless required by dynamic SQL, which is allowed under rule #2.
4. All database calls should be parameterized instead of being inline dynamic SQL.
5. No user input should be trusted and thought of as safe; all user interactions are suspect.

Warning
SQL Injection Happens at All Levels

Unfortunately, not just small companies can have problems with SQL Injection attacks. In 2009, for example, ZD Net reported that some of the international websites selling Kaspersky antivirus, specifically Kaspersky Iran, Taiwan, and South Korea, were all susceptible to SQL Injection attacks. In the same article (http://bit.ly/AntiVirusSQLInject) ZD Net also reported that websites of F-Secure, Symantec, BitDeffender, and Kaspersky USA all had problems with SQL Injection attacks on their websites.

These are some of the major security companies of the day, and they are showing a total lack of security by letting their websites fall prey to the simple injection attack. Considering just how simple it is to protect a website from an SQL injection attack, the fact that some of the biggest security companies in the industry were able to have SQL Injection problems on their production customer facing websites is just ridiculous.

Because of how intertwined various websites are with each other, real-estate listing providers and the realtors which get their data from the listing providers, a lot of trust must exist between these companies and the people who use one companies site without knowing that they are using another companies data. This places the company that is showing the real-estate listings to their users in a position of trusting the advertising company to have a safe application. However, this trust can backfire as on a few occasions various partner companies have suffered from SQL Injection attacks, in some cases pushing out malicious software to the users of dozens, hundreds, or thousands of different websites that display the data.

With the introduction of Object Relational Mappings (ORM) such as Link to SQL and nHybernate, the SQL Injection problems are greatly lessened as properly done ORM code will automatically parameterize the SQL queries. However, if the ORM calls stored procedures, and those stored procedures have dynamic SQL within them, the application is still susceptible to SQL Injection attacks.

How to Protect Yourself from an SQL Injection Attack

Once the command gets to the database to be run by the database engine, it is too late to protect yourself from the SQL

Injection attack. The only way to truly protect your database application from an Injection attack is to do so within the application layer. Any other protection simply won't be anywhere nearly as effective. Some people think that doing a character replacement within the T/SQL code will effectively protect you, and it might to some extent. But depending on how the T/SQL is set up and how the dynamic SQL string is built, it probably won't, at least not for long.

NET Protection Against SQL Injection

The only surefire way to protect yourself is to parameterize every query that you send to the database. This includes your stored procedure calls, as well as your inline dynamic SQL calls. In addition, you never want to pass string values that the front-end application has allowed the user to enter directly into dynamic SQL within your stored procedure calls. If you have cause to use dynamic SQL within your stored procedures (and yes, there are perfectly legitimate reasons for using dynamic SQL), then the dynamic SQL needs to be parameterized just like the code that is calling the stored procedure or inline dynamic SQL Script. This is done by declaring parameters within the T/SQL statement, and adding those parameters to the SQLCommand object that has the SQL Command that you will be running, as shown in Example 6.4 and Example 6.5.

```
Private Sub MySub()
    Dim Connection As SqlConnection
    Dim Results As DataSet
    Dim SQLda As SqlDataAdapter
    Dim SQLcmd As SqlCommand
    SQLcmd = New SqlCommand
    SQLcmd.CommandText = "sp_help_job"
    SQLcmd.CommandType = CommandType.StoredProcedure
    SQLcmd.Parameters.Add("job_name", SqlDbType.VarChar, 50)
    SQLcmd.Parameters.Item("job_name").Value = "test"
    Connection = New SqlConnection("Data Source=
        localhost;Initial Catalog=msdb;Integrated
        Security=SSPI;")
    Using Connection
        Connection.Open()
        SQLcmd.Connection = Connection
        SQLda = New SqlDataAdapter(SQLcmd)
        Results = New DataSet()
        SQLda.Fill(Results)
    End Using
    'Do something with the results from the Results variable here.
```

```
        SQLcmd.Dispose()
         SQLda.Dispose()
       Results.Dispose()
       Connection.Close()
       Connection.Dispose()
    End Sub
```

Example 6.4: VB.NET code showing how to use parameters to safely call a stored procedure.

```
private void MySub()
   {
       SqlConnection Connection = new SqlConnection("Data
          Source=localhost;Initial Catalog=msdb;Integrated
          Security=SSPI;");
       DataSet Results = new DataSet();
       SqlCommand SQLcmd = new SqlCommand ();
       SQLcmd.CommandText = "sp_help_job";
       SQLcmd.CommandType = CommandType.StoredProcedure ;
       SqlParameter parm1 = new SqlParameter();
       parm1.ParameterName = "job_name";
       parm1.DbType = DbType.String;
       parm1.Precision = 255;
       parm1.Value = "test";
       SQLcmd.Parameters.Add(parm1);
       Connection.Open();
       SQLcmd.Connection = Connection;
       SqlDataAdapter SQLda = new SqlDataAdapter(SQLcmd);
       SQLda.Fill(Results);
       //Do something with the results from the Results variable
            here.
       SQLcmd.Dispose();
       SQLda.Dispose();
       Results.Dispose();
       Connection.Close();
     Connection.Dispose();
   }
```

Example 6.5: C# code showing how to use parameters to safely call a stored procedure.

As you can see in the above, .NET code using a parameter to pass in the value is easy to do, adding just a couple of extra lines of code. The same can be done with an inline dynamic SQL string, as shown in Example 6.6 and Example 6.7.

```
Private Sub MySub()
    Dim Connection As SqlConnection
    Dim Results As DataSet
    Dim SQLda As SqlDataAdapter
```

```
Dim SQLcmd As SqlCommand
SQLcmd = New SqlCommand
SQLcmd.CommandText = "SELECT * FROM dbo.sysjobs WHERE name=
    @job_name"
SQLcmd.Parameters.Add("job_name", SqlDbType.VarChar, 50)
SQLcmd.Parameters.Item("job_name").Value = "test"
SQLcmd.CommandType = CommandType.Text;
Connection = New SqlConnection("Data
    Source=localhost;Initial
    Catalog=msdb;Integrated Security=SSPI;")
Using Connection
    Connection.Open()
    SQLcmd.Connection = Connection
    SQLda = New SqlDataAdapter(SQLcmd)
    Results = New DataSet()
    SQLda.Fill(Results)
End Using
'Do something with the results from the Results variable here.
SQLcmd.Dispose()
SQLda.Dispose()
Results.Dispose()
Connection.Close()
Connection.Dispose()
End Sub
```

Example 6.6: VB.NET code showing how to use parameters to safely call an inline dynamic SQL String.

```
private void MySub()
    {
        SqlConnection Connection = new SqlConnection("Data-
            Source=localhost;Initial Catalog=msdb;Integrated
            Security=SSPI;");
        DataSet Results = new DataSet();
        SqlCommand SQLcmd = new SqlCommand ();
        SQLcmd.CommandText = "SELECT * FROM dbo.sysjobs WHERE
            name = @job_name";
        SQLcmd.CommandType = CommandType.Text;
        SqlParameter parm1 = new SqlParameter();
        parm1.ParameterName = "job_name";
        parm1.DbType = DbType.String;
        parm1.Precision = 255;
        parm1.Value = "test";
        SQLcmd.Parameters.Add(parm1);
        Connection.Open();
        SQLcmd.Connection = Connection;
        SqlDataAdapter SQLda = new SqlDataAdapter(SQLcmd);
        SQLda.Fill(Results);
        //Do something with the results from the Results variable
            here.
```

```
    SQLcmd.Dispose();
    SQLda.Dispose();
    Results.Dispose();
    Connection.Close();
  Connection.Dispose();
  }
```

Example 6.7: C# code showing how to use parameters to safely call an inline dynamic SQL String.

Once each parameter that is being passed into the database has been protected, the .NET code (or whatever language is being used to call the database) becomes safe. Any value that is passed from the client side to the database will be passed into the database as a value to the parameter. In the example code shown at the beginning of this chapter, the string value that has been passed into the application would then force an error to be returned from the client Microsoft SQL Server database as the value would be passed into a parameter with a numeric data type.

Note
Don't Trust Anything or Anyone!

The golden rule when dealing with SQL Injection is to not trust any input from the website or front-end application. This includes hidden fields and values from dropdown menus. Nothing should be passed from the front end to the database without being cleaned and properly formatted, as any value passed in from the front end could be compromised.

Hidden fields are probably the SQL Injection attacker's best friend. Because they are hidden from the end user's view and are only used by system processes, they are sometimes assumed to be safe values. However, changing the values that are passed in from a safe value to a dangerous value is a trivial matter for a script kitty, much less a skilled attacker.

When dealing with SQL Injection, the mantra to remember is never, ever, trust anything that is sent to the application tier from the end user, whether or not the end user knows that he submitted the value.

Using the sample query shown in the .NET sample code in Examples 6.6 and 6.7, if the user were to pass in similar attack code to what is shown in the SQL Server sample code in Example 6.2, the query that would be executed against the database would look like the one shown in Example 6.8. This resulting query is now safe to run as the result which is executed against the database engine contains all the attack code as a part of the value.

```
SELECT * FROM dbo.sysjobs WHERE name = 'test; delete from Orders';
```

Example 6.8: Sample T/SQL code showing the resulting T/SQL Code that would be executed against the database if an attacker were to put in an attack code against the prior sample .NET code.

In the sample code you can see that while the attack code has been passed to the engine, it has been passed as part of the value of the WHERE clause. However, because this is within the value of the parameter, it is safe because the parameter is not executable. If attackers were to pass in the same command with a single quote in front of it, in an attempt to code the parameter, and then execute their own code, the single quote would be automatically doubled by the .NET layer when it passed to the SQL Server database again, leaving a safe parameter value as shown in Example 6.9.

```
SELECT * FROM dbo.sysjobs WHERE name = 'test"; delete from Orders';
```

Example 6.9: The resulting T/SQL code that would be executed against the database when an attacker passes in an attack string with a single quote in an attempt to bypass the protection provided by the .NET application layer.

Protecting Dynamic SQL within Stored Procedures from SQL Injection Attack

When you have dynamic SQL within your stored procedures, you need to use a double protection technique to prevent the attack. The same procedure needs to be used to protect the application layer and prevent the attack from succeeding at that layer. However, if you use simple string concatenation within your stored procedure, then you will open your database back up to attack. Looking at a sample stored procedure and the resulting T/SQL that will be executed against the database by the stored procedure; we can see that by using the simple string concatenation, the database is still susceptible to the SQL Injection attack, as shown in Example 6.10.

```
CREATE PROCEDURE sel_OrdersByCustomer
    @LastName VARCHAR(50)
AS
DECLARE @cmd NVARCHAR(8000)
SET @cmd = 'SELECT *
FROM Orders
JOIN Customers ON Orders.CustomerId = Customers.CustomerId
WHERE Customers.LastName = '" + @LastName + '"
EXEC (@cmd)
GO
/*The command that will be executed when the attacker passed
    in '; DELETE FROM Orders.*/
SELECT *
FROM Orders
```

```
JOIN Customers ON Orders.CustomerId = Customers.CustomerId
WHERE Customers.LastName = 'Smith'; DELETE FROM Orders '
```

Example 6.10: T/SQL stored procedure that accepts a parameter from the application layer and concatenates the passed-in value to the static portion of the string, executing whatever attack code the attacker wishes against the database engine.

Because of the value attack, the value being passed into the SQL Server Engine is passed in through the application layer, and the SQL Server engine does as it is instructed to do, which is to run the query. However, if we parameterize the dynamic SQL within the stored procedure, then the execute SQL code will be rendered harmless just as it would be if the dynamic SQL was executed against the database by the application layer. This is done via the sp_executesql system stored procedure as shown in Example 6.11.

```
CREATE PROCEDURE sel_OrdersByCustomer
    @LastName VARCHAR(50)
AS
DECLARE @cmd NVARCHAR(8000)
SET @cmd = 'SELECT *
FROM Orders
JOIN Customers ON Orders.CustomerId = Customers.CustomerId
WHERE Customers.LastName = '" + @LastName + ""
EXEC sp_executesql @cmd, '@LastName VARCHAR(50)',
    @LastName=@LastName
GO
/*The command that will be executed when the attacker passed in';
    DELETE FROM Orders.*/
SELECT *
FROM Orders
JOIN Customers ON Orders.CustomerId = Customers.CustomerId
WHERE Customers.LastName = 'Smith"; DELETE FROM Orders '
```

Example 6.11: T/SQL stored procedure that accepts a parameter from the application layer and uses parameterization to safely execute the query passing whatever attack code the users input safely against the database as a simple string value.

Removing Extended Stored Procedures

In addition to running all code from the application layer as parameterized commands instead of dynamically generated T/SQL, you should also remove the system procedures that can be used to export data. The procedures in question that you'll want to remove are xp_cmdshell, xp_startmail, xp_sendmail, sp_makewebtask, and sp_send_dbmail. You may also want to remove the procedures that configure Database Mail such as sysmail_add_account_sp and sysmail_add_profileaccount_sp, so that attackers can't use these procedures to give themselves a way to e-mail out information from the database. Of course, you'll want to make sure that you aren't using these procedures in any released code and that you have Database Mail configured before removing your ability to configure it.

Of course, removing system stored procedures poses a risk of causing system upgrades to fail, so you'll want to keep copies of these objects handy so that you can put the objects back before database version upgrades.

Unfortunately, this isn't a surefire way to prevent an attacker from using these procedures. Crafty attackers can actually put these procedures back after they see that they have been removed. This is especially true of the extended stored procedures called DLLs (Dynamic Link Libraries), which must be left in their normal locations because other extended stored procedures that you don't want to remove are part of the same DLLs. The only saving grace is that you have to be a highly privileged user within the database engine to put an extended stored procedure into the SQL Server engine. Thus, the only way that an attacker could successfully put the extended stored procedures back would be to log into the database with a highly privileged account. If your application logs into the database engine using a highly privileged account, all bets are off as the attacker now has the rights needed to put the extended stored procedures back.

Not Using Best Practice Code Logic Can Hurt You

The application login process is probably the most important one that an attacker may want to take advantage of. Many times when developers are building a login process, the front-end developer will simply look for records in a record set, and if there are none will assume that the user didn't login correctly. If there are records in the record set, the developer will assume that the user logged in correctly and so will grab the first record and use that record to find the user's permissions. Attackers wishing to exploit this situation would be able to get past the login screen, probably being logged in with a high level of permissions. This is done by adding a small text string in the username field such as "user' OR 1=1 −". What this will do is change the code shown in Example 6.12 into the code shown in Example 6.13. Example 6.14 shows the T/SQL code that would be executed against the database engine.

```
SELECT * FROM dbo.Users WHERE UserName = 'user' AND Password =
   'password'
```

Example 6.12: The way a sample record set looks when validating a user account.

```
SELECT * FROM dbo.Users WHERE UserName = 'user' OR 1=1 - AND
   Password = 'password'
```

Example 6.13: The way the code looks when the attack code has been inserted.

```
SELECT * FROM dbo.Users WHERE UserName = 'user' OR 1=1
```

Example 6.14: The executable part of the code against the database engine from the prior sample code.

Because of the OR clause in the prior sample code, it doesn't matter if there is a record where the UserName column equals user because the $1 = 1$ section will tell the database to return every record in the database.

As you can see in the sample code above, the code that gets executed against the database engine would return the entire User table. Assuming that the front-end application simply takes the first record from the record set returned from the database, the attacker would then be logged into the application, probably with an administrative-level account. Preventing this sort of attack is easy; refer back to the beginning of this section of this chapter for the sample .NET code. Now that the user has been logged in, potentially with administrative rights, the user doesn't need to use any additional dynamic SQL to get access to your customer data, as he or she will now have full access through your normal administrative system.

What to Return to the End User

The next important thing to configure within the front-end application is what errors are returned to the end user. When the database throws an error, you should be sure to mask the error from the end user. The end user doesn't have any need to know the name of either the primary key or the foreign key that has been violated. You might want to return something that the end user can give to customer service or the help desk so that the actual error message can be looked up.

What this has to do with SQL injection is important. If the attacker is able to send in code that breaks the query and returns an error, the error may well contain the name of a table or other database object within the error message. For example, if the attacker sends in an attack string of "' Group by CustomerId –" to a query that looks like "SELECT * FROM Customers WHERE

UserName = 'UserName' AND Password = 'Password'" creating the query "SELECT * FROM Customers WHERE UserName = 'UserName' Group by CustomerId – AND Password = 'Password'". The default error message that SQL Server would return gives the attackers more information than they had before. It tells them the table name. The attacker can use this same technique to figure out which columns are in the table. Over all, Being able to see the actual SQL Server error message, even if the error doesn't give the attacker any database schema information it tells the attacker that the attack attempt was successful. By using the sp_MSforeachtable system stored procedure and the raiserror function, the attackers could easily return the list of every table in the database, giving them a wealth of information about the database schema, which could then be used in future attacks.

Note
Why Are SQL Injection Attacks Still So Possible?

One major reason why SQL Injection attacks are still possible today is that there is so much bad information circulating about how to protect yourself from an SQL injection attack. For example, an article published by Symantec at http://www. symantec.com/connect/articles/detection-sql-injection-and-cross-site-scripting-attacks says that all you need to protect yourself is to verify the inputs using a regular expression that searches for the single quote and the double dash, as well as the strings "sp" and "xp." As you can see throughout this chapter, SQL Injection attacks can occur without tripping these regular expressions, and considering the high number of false positives that looking for a single quote would give you (especially if you like doing business with people of Irish descent), the protection would be minimal at best. If you were to read this article and follow its instructions you would be leaving yourself open to SQL Injection attacks.

There is more useful information that an attacker could get thanks to the error message being returned. For example, if the users were to run a stored procedure in another database that they didn't have access to, the error message would return the username of the use—for example, if the attacker sends in an attack string "'; exec model.dbo.Working –". It doesn't matter if the procedure exists or not, for the attacker won't get that far. The error returned from this call is shown in Example 6.15.

```
Msg 916, Level 14, State 1, Line 1
The server principal "test" is not able to access the database
    "model" under the current security context.
```

Example 6.15: Error message returned by an attacker running a stored procedure that doesn't exist.

The model database is an excellent database to try this against, as typically no users have access to the model database. If the attacker gets an error message saying that the procedure doesn't exist, the attacker now knows that the login that the application is logging into the database has some high-level permissions, or the model database has some screwed-up permissions.

After finding the username, the attacker can easily enough find the name of the local database that the application is running within. This can be done by trying to create a table in the database. This is because the error message when creating a table includes the database name. For example, if the attack code "'; create table mytable (c1 int);–" is sent, the error message shown in Example 6.16 will be returned.

```
Msg 262, Level 14, State 1, Line 1
CREATE TABLE permission denied in database 'MyApplication
   Database'.
```

Example 6.16: Error message returned when creating a table when you don't have rights returning the name of the database to the attacker.

These various values can be used in later attacks to clear the database of its data or to export the data from the database.

Cleaning Up the Database After an SQL Injection Attack

There are a few different attacks that an attacker can perform against an SQL Server database. As shown so far in this chapter, delete commands can be passed into the SQL engine. However, other commands can be executed as well. Usually, attackers don't want to delete data or take a system offline; they instead want to use the SQL database to help launch other attacks. A simple method is to identify tables and columns that are used to display data on the website that uses the database as a backend. Then extra data is included in the columns of the database, which will allow attacking code to be executed against the database. This can be done using an update statement that puts an HTML iframe tag into each row of a table. This way when customers view the website, they get the iframe put into their web browser, which could be set to a height of 0 so that it isn't visible. This hidden iframe could then install viruses or spyware on the user's computer without their knowledge.

FAQ
IFRAME versus PopUp

Often people ask if a popup blocker would prevent this iframe attack from affecting the end user, and the answer is no, it wouldn't. An iframe doesn't show a web browser popup on the users screen. An iframe is an inline frame which shows within the displayed webpage. An iframe with a height of 0 would be totally invisible to the end user, but it could be requesting data from a webpage on another website, passing information from the user's computer back to this unknown website. The website that is called from the iframe could then exploit vulnerabilities in the end user's web browser to install key loggers or command and control software turning the end user's computer into a member of a bot-net.

Once this attack has occurred and viruses or spyware have been installed on the customer's computer, the most important thing now is to stop additional users' computers from being attacked. This means going through every record of every table looking for the attack code that is pushing the iframe to the customer's web browser. Obviously, you can go through each table manually looking for the records in question, or you can use the included sample code, shown in Example 6.17, which searches through each column in every table for the problem code and removes it. All you need to do is supply the variable with the attack code. The only columns that are not cleaned by this code are columns that use the TEXT or NTEXT data types. This is because the TEXT and NTEXT data types require special attention as they do not support the normal search functions.

```
DECLARE @injected_value NVARCHAR(1000)
SET @injected_value = 'Put the code which has been injected here.'
/*Change nothing below this line.*/
SET @injected_value = REPLACE(@injected_value, "", """)
CREATE TABLE #ms_ver (indexid INT, name sysname, internal_value
    INT, character_value VARCHAR(50))
INSERT INTO #ms_ver
EXEC xp_msver 'ProductVersion'
DECLARE @database_name sysname, @table_schema sysname,
    @table_name sysname, @column_name sysname, @cmd NVARCHAR
    (4000),
@internal_value INT
SELECT @internal_value = internal_value
FROM #ms_ver
```

```
DECLARE cur CURSOR FOR SELECT TABLE_CATALOG, TABLE_SCHEMA,
   TABLE_NAME, COLUMN_NAME
   FROM INFORMATION_SCHEMA.columns c
   JOIN systypes st ON c.DATA_TYPE = st.name
   WHERE xtype IN (97, 167, 175, 231, 239, 241)
OPEN cur
FETCH NEXT FROM cur INTO @database_name, @table_schema,
   @table_name, @column_name
WHILE @@FETCH_STATUS = 0
BEGIN
   SET @cmd = 'SELECT NULL
WHILE @@ROWCOUNT <> 0
BEGIN
'
   IF @internal_value > 530000
      SET @cmd = @cmd + ' SET ROWCOUNT 1000
   UPDATE'
   ELSE
      SET @cmd = @cmd + 'UPDATE TOP (1000)'
   SET @cmd = @cmd + '[' + @database_name + '].[' + @table_
         schema + '].[' + @table_name + ']
      SET [' + @column_name + '] = REPLACE([' + @column_name + '], '
         " + @injected_value + "', "")
   WHERE [' + @column_name + '] LIKE "%" + @injected_value + '%"
END'
   exec (@cmd)
   FETCH NEXT FROM cur INTO @database_name, @table_schema,
         @table_name, @column_name
END
CLOSE cur
DEALLOCATE cur
DROP TABLE #ms_ver
```

Example 6.17: T/SQL Code that will clean a database that has had its values updated to send unvalued code to users.

Note
Notes About Using This Sample Code

Before running the included T/SQL code, be sure to make a full backup of the database in case of accidental data modification. The larger the database that you run this against, the longer it will take. When running this sample code, it is recommended that you change the output type from the default output style of grid to text by pressing <cTRL>+T, in order to reduce the resources needed to run the query. The included code will execute against all versions of Microsoft SQL Server from version 7 to 2008 R2.

Note
SQL Injection is Serious Business

In case you hadn't guessed after reading this chapter, SQL Injection attacks are a very serious threat. Normally when an SQL Injection attack is launched, it isn't launched against a single website. An attacker will often write a problem that will check as many websites as possible before the attacker is taken off the Internet. The last successful large-scale attack on the Internet (as of the writing of this book) successfully changed the data in tens of thousands of separate databases that run tens of thousands of different websites. At the time of the attack, this was verified by searching on Google for the text of the code that was inserted into the attacked databases and looking at the number of domains that Google returned with matches.

Falling prey to these attacks puts users and customers at major risk, as these attacks often are trying to install viruses or Trojan horses on the end user's computer, so that confidential data such as credit card numbers, and banking usernames and passwords can be gathered by the attacker and used to commit future fraud against the users and customers of the attacked websites. This can lead to months or years of credit report problems and the like.

One final point to keep in mind: If you use your own company's websites or services, then the SQL Injection attacker is attempting to attack you as you are also a customer. So do yourself a favor and protect the database so that you don't get viruses or Trojan horses installed on your computer through your own company's website.

Summary

SQL Injection attacks pose some of the greatest dangers to the database and customers because they are typically used to directly affect the information that the customer sees and can be rather easily used to attempt to push malicious code to clients' computers. These attacks are very popular with attackers because they are a relatively easy way to exploit systems design. They are also popular because they are easy to reproduce once a site is found to be compromisable, as it usually takes a long time to correct all the potential attack points in a website. This length of time leaves the website and database open to attack for a long period of time as companies are usually unwilling to shut down their customer facing websites while the website design is being repaired.

Because of the way that the SQL Injection attacks work, the Database Administrator, Database Developer, Application Developer, and Systems Administrator all need to work together to ensure that they are correctly protecting the data within the database and the company network at large. As the database and application developers begin getting in the habit of writing code that isn't susceptible to SQL Injection attacks, the current project will become more secure, as will future projects that the team members work on.

SQL Azure is just as susceptible to an SQL Injection attack as any other SQL Instance. What the attacker can do within the instance is much less dangerous simply because there are many fewer features available. For example, protection against xp_cmdshell isn't a priority because xp_cmdshell isn't available on an SQL Azure instance. Neither are features such as database mail or SQL mail, so protecting against attackers that plan to use these vectors doesn't need to be done. As time goes on, and more features are added to SQL Azure, this may change; however, as of this writing, this information is accurate.

References

"Wall Street Journal, Others, Hit in Mass SQL attack—SC Magazine US." *IT Security News and Security Product Reviews—SC Magazine US*. N.p., n.d. Web. October 21, 2010.

7

DATABASE BACKUP SECURITY

INFORMATION IN THIS CHAPTER

- Overwriting Backups
- Media Set and Backup Set Passwords
- Backup Encryption
- Transparent Data Encryption
- Compression and Encryption
- Offsite Backups

All too often people spend all their time securing the database while it is active within the database engine, without providing protection for the database backups. Not securing the database backups provides an easy way for a data thief to get access to all the information stored within the database. This is because the database backups are by definition the least secure portion of the database. They are so insecure because they actually leave the building on a regular basis. This is because the database backups are typically put on tape and shipped offsite to another location, such as Iron Mountain or another secure facility. Where problems can occur is that the number of tapes that end up being lost is a lot higher than any of these offsite storage companies want to admit.

There are some key things you need to remember no matter which encryption solution you select for your backup. The first of these needs is to balance the encryption protection with the amount of time and CPU power that encryption solution will take to implement. While stronger encryption will better protect your data, it will also increase the load on the server that is processing the encryption. If the application that is using the database requires 24 x 7 uptime, you may not be able to implement the stronger levels of backup encryption because while the backups are running, the database engine may not be able to service requests quickly enough to maintain your service levels.

Tip
RAID != Backup

One of the biggest misconceptions is that if your SQL Server has a RAID array, then you are protected, and you don't need to worry about backing up your database. This is not the case at all. Without backups you are not protected from either data deletion problems or multiple disk failures. If you still don't think that backups are important, ask the folks over at JournalSpace.com what happens when you don't have backups. You can read about what happened to them in detail at http://bit.ly/JSpace and then a follow-up at http://bit.ly/JSpace2.

The short version of what happened to them is that they didn't have any backups being taken on their database server, and their systems administrator got disgruntled and deleted all the data from the database. Without any backups of the database being available, they ended up having to scrap the Google cache to get back as much data as they could.

Overwriting Backups

When setting up backup policies, it is very important to ensure that the backups don't simply overwrite the prior backup file each time a backup is taken. If the backups are done to the same file over and over, and the backup fails, there is no longer a useful backup that can be used to restore the database in the event the database fails. This rule applies to full backups, differential backups, as well as the transaction log backups.When you use the FORMAT key word within the BACKUP DATABASE command, this tells the database engine to remove any backups that exist within the backup media—either the file when backing up to disk or the tape when backing up to tape. If you do not use the FORMAT statement, the backup is appended to the backup media. When you do not include the FORMAT key word and you back up to disk, there is no way to remove the old backups from the backup media. Because of this behavior, writing each backup to its own backup file is highly recommended. When using the SQL Server Maintenance plan to manage backups, the Mainte-nance plan will use this behavior automatically. When writing custom T/SQL backup scripts using the BACKUP DATABASE and BACKUP LOG commands, this adjustment must be done manually. The easiest way to handle this is to declare a variable and set that variable to a date string and then use that date string as part of the backup file name as shown in Example 7.1.

```
DECLARE @FileName AS NVARCHAR(255)
SET @FileName = 'D:\backups\MyDatabase-' + CAST(DATEPART
  (yy, GETUTCDATE()) AS NVARCHAR(4))
```

```
   +CASE WHEN DATEPART(mm, GETUTCDATE()) BETWEEN 1 AND 9 THEN 'O'
      ELSE '' END + CAST(DATEPART(mm, GETUTCDATE()) AS NVARCHAR
      (2))
   +CASE WHEN DATEPART(dd, GETUTCDATE()) BETWEEN 1 AND 9 THEN 'O'
      ELSE '' END + CAST(DATEPART(dd,GETUTCDATE()) AS NVARCHAR
      (2))
   +CASE WHEN DATEPART(hh, GETUTCDATE()) BETWEEN 1 AND 9 THEN 'O'
      ELSE '' END + CAST(DATEPART(hh, GETUTCDATE()) AS NVARCHAR
      (2))
   +CASE WHEN DATEPART(mi, GETUTCDATE()) BETWEEN 0 AND 9 THEN 'O'
      ELSE '' END + CAST(DATEPART(mi, GETUTCDATE()) AS NVARCHAR
      (2))
   +CASE WHEN DATEPART(ss, GETUTCDATE()) BETWEEN 0 AND 9 THEN 'O'
      ELSE '' END + CAST(DATEPART(ss, GETUTCDATE()) AS NVARCHAR
      (2)) + '.bak'
BACKUP DATABASE MyDatabase TO DISK=@FileName
```

Example 7.1: T/SQL code showing how to back up the database to a different file each time the backup is taken.

The same technique that is shown in Example 7.1 to back up the full database can be done for a differential backup by adding the DIFFERENTIAL key word or for a transaction log backup by using the BACKUP LOG statement as shown in Example 7.2.

```
DECLARE @FileName AS NVARCHAR(255)
SET @FileName = 'D:\backups\MyDatabase-' + CAST(DATEPART(yy,
   GETUTCDATE()) AS NVARCHAR(4))
   +CASE WHEN DATEPART(mm, GETUTCDATE()) BETWEEN 1 AND 9 THEN 'O'
      ELSE '' END + CAST(DATEPART(mm, GETUTCDATE()) AS NVARCHAR
      (2))
   +CASE WHEN DATEPART(dd, GETUTCDATE()) BETWEEN 1 AND 9 THEN 'O'
      ELSE '' END + CAST(DATEPART(dd,GETUTCDATE()) AS NVARCHAR
      (2))
   +CASE WHEN DATEPART(hh, GETUTCDATE()) BETWEEN 1 AND 9 THEN 'O'
      ELSE '' END + CAST(DATEPART(hh, GETUTCDATE()) AS NVARCHAR
      (2))
   +CASE WHEN DATEPART(mi, GETUTCDATE()) BETWEEN 0 AND 9 THEN 'O'
      ELSE '' END + CAST(DATEPART(mi, GETUTCDATE()) AS NVARCHAR
      (2))
   +CASE WHEN DATEPART(ss, GETUTCDATE()) BETWEEN 0 AND 9 THEN 'O'
      ELSE '' END + CAST(DATEPART(ss, GETUTCDATE()) AS NVARCHAR
      (2)) + '.bak'
BACKUP LOG MyDatabase TO DISK=@FileName
```

Example 7.2: T/SQL code showing how to back up the log to a different file each time a log backup is taken.

The code shown in Examples 7.1 and 7.2 can be a little difficult to read at first glance. The code first creates the file name by getting the year, month, day, hour, minute, and second of the current time. The case statements look at the same number that is being outputted on that same line and putting a 0 before it if the value is a single-digit value. This padding of the values with 0s is done so that no matter the second, minute, hour, day, or month that the database is backed up, the length of the string is always the same. This uniformity doesn't have a technical reason for existing; rather, it is done to make it easier for humans to read the files names and identify the file or files they are looking for.

Deleting Old Backups

Once each of the backups is being done to a separate file, the older files will need to be deleted at some point. If the backups are not deleted, eventually the backups will fill the hard drive they are being written to, causing new backups to fail to function. If a database maintenance plan is being used to back up the databases, it can be configured to remove the database backups after a specified number of days. In the SQL Server 2000 maintenance plan, this can be done by checking the checkbox and setting the value to the required number of days as shown in Figure 7.1. In the SQL Server 2005 and above maintenance plan, this can be done by adding a "Maintenance Cleanup Task" to the maintenance plan and setting the path for the backup files as well as the file extension to be deleted as shown in Figure 7.2.

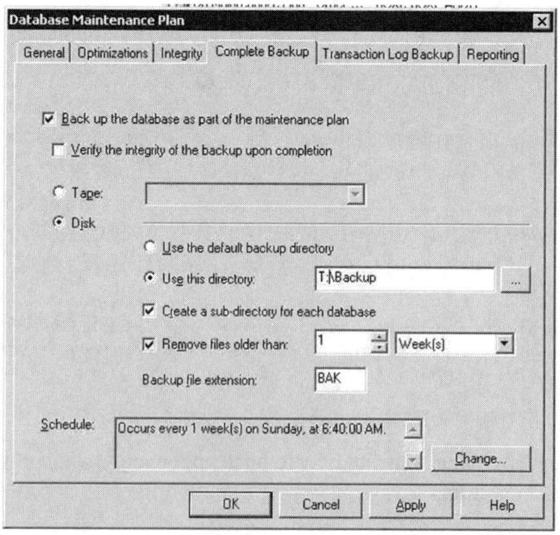

Figure 7.1 Showing the page of the SQL Server 2000 maintenance plan that controls the deletion of database backups.

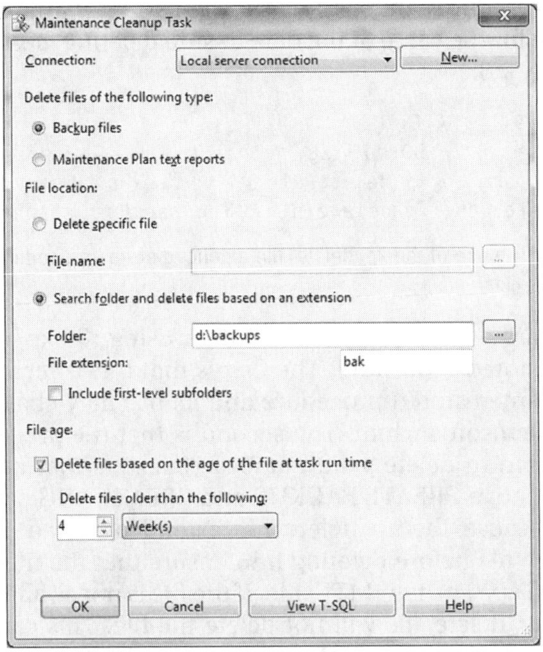

Figure 7.2 The page of the SQL Server 2005 and up maintenance plan that controls the deletion of database backups.

As shown in Figure 7.2, which presents the SQL Server 2005 and higher, the "Maintenance Cleanup Task" only supports cleaning up one file extension at a time. If transaction log backups are backed up with a different file extension, then a second "Maintenance Cleanup Task" will need to be added to the maintenance plan for the second file extension.

The "Maintenance Cleanup Task" in SQL Server 2005 and above isn't all that complex as a function, as can be seen by clicking the View T-SQL button at the bottom of the "Maintenance Cleanup Task" dialog. This operator simply calls the xp_delete_file extended stored procedure, which can be found in the master database. This procedure, when the correct parameters are passed to it, will automatically delete any backup files in the specified path, as well as subfolders. The extended stored procedure xp_delete_file accepts five parameters:

1. Reports or Backups = Uses a 1 for reports and 0 for backups;
2. Path = The path to the backup files;
3. Extension = The extension of the backups to process;
4. Date to delete to = The newest backup to keep;
5. Search subfolders = 0 only searches the specified folder, 1 searches the specified folder and the first level of subfolders.

This procedure can be easily called passing a variable into the procedure for the value of the date to stop deleting files, as shown in Example 7.3.

```
DECLARE @date DATETIME
SET @date = DATEADD(dd, -28, getdate())
EXEC master.dbo.xp_delete_file 0,N'd:\backups',N'bak',@date,1
EXEC master.dbo.xp_delete_file 0,N'd:\backups',N'trn',@date,1
```

Example 7.3: The use of the xp_delete_file extended stored procedure to delete older backup files.

There are a couple of catches when using the xp_delete_file extended stored procedure. The first is that this is technically an undocumented stored procedure and its use may change at any time at Microsoft's whim. The second is that the procedure can only be used to delete valid database backups that are created using the native CREATE BACKUP and CREATE LOG commands. This is because the xp_delete_file extended stored procedure opens each file before deleting it to ensure that the file is a valid Microsoft Tape Format (MTF) file. If the file is not a valid MTF file, then the xp_delete_file will not delete the file. This can become a problem when using one of the third-party backup utilities such as Quest's LiteSpeed for SQL Server, Red Gate SQL HyperBac, or Red Gate SQL Backup, as these backup utilities do not use the native MTF file format, and as such these backups are not recognized by xp_delete_file extended stored procedure. When using one of these third-party tools, a different technique needs to be used to manage these database backups.

One technique to do this is to use PowerShell to delete the backups that are older than the required amount of time to keep. A simple one-line PowerShell script will identify all the files that are more than four weeks old, sending that list to the remote-item applet that will remove each of the files as shown in Example 7.4. Example 7.3 shows how to process two different file extensions (or more) in a single command. To change the file extensions, simply change the values in the comma separated list within the -include parameter. If a single value needs to be passed into the -include parameter in the PowerShell script, the double quotes can be removed from around the -include parameter.

```
Get-ChildItem "d:\backups\" "-include *.BAK,*.trn" -recurse |
    where {((get-date)-$_.creationTime).weeks -ge 4} |
    remove-item -force —recurse
```

Example 7.4: PowerShell script that removes the database backups that do not need to be kept on hand.

Beyond the need to delete old backups to keep disk space free, there is a security implication to keeping database backups on disk for longer than is needed. The more files that are on disk, the more data that a data thief could walk away with. Any data breach, including the loss of encrypted backup files, should be taken seriously. The fewer files to maintain, the smaller the risk in keeping those files around. For those worried about having to restore the database from older files, the files should never be removed from the local disk until they have been archived to a tape backup system that would allow the backup files to be restored to disk and then restored to the SQL Server engine.

· Note

SQL Server Analysis Services Does Not Use MTF

Only two components of the SQL Server product suite require that backups be made of the data they keep: the SQL Server engine and the SQL Server Analysis Services engine. However, the SQL Server Analysis Services engine doesn't create its database backups using the MTF format. This means that, like the third-party SQL Server engine database backups, the SQL Server Analysis Services backups cannot be deleted by using the xp_delete_file extended stored procedure. A process such as the PowerShell script shown in Example 7.4 must be used to remove these older backups.

Media Set and Backup Set Passwords

When you back up your Microsoft SQL Server database, you have the option of specifying a backup set password as well as a media set password. These passwords provide a very basic level of protection of your database backups. The backup set password is designed to prevent accidental restore of the database, while the media set password is designed to prevent the media from being accidently overwritten. Even with this most basic level of security, these passwords will give you some level of protection, for, without the passwords, the backups cannot be restored to another SQL Server.

When you password protect the media, no additional backup sets can be created on that media without supplying the correct password, and no backup can be restored from the media without supplying the media password. You can password protect both the media and the backup set, or just one or the other. Obviously, the more passwords that are in place, the more secure the data within the backup is. However, because the format that is used to store these passwords within the backup and/or the media are well documented and have been around for decades, it is quite easy for someone to read the value, and reverse engineer the source password, or to simply write a new password into the media and then use this new password value to then restore the data from the backup.

While these passwords are not the most secure method available, for older versions of Microsoft SQL Server these passwords are your only native option for securing your database backups. The most common way to use these passwords would be within a T/SQL script so that the backup of the database can be scheduled. Password protected databases are backed up using the BACKUP DATABASE command like a normal database backup as shown in Example 7.5.

```
BACKUP DATABASE YourDB TO DISK='D:\YourDB.bak'
WITH MEDIANAME='YourMediaPassword',
    PASSWORD='YourBackupSetPassword',
    FORMAT
```

Example 7.5: T/SQL Script to back up a database with a backup set password and media password.

Note
Backup Set Passwords and Media Set Passwords Are Going, Going, Gone...

It should be noted that both the backup set password and the media set password are scheduled to be removed in the version of Microsoft SQL Server being released after SQL Server 2008 R2. Because of this scheduled removal, these passwords should not be used in new database instances that are configured, and they should be removed from current policies.

Backup Encryption

Encrypting your database backups is probably the most reliable way to secure your database backups from prying eyes. There are a few different ways to encrypt your database backup. You can use a third-party backup application such Quest Software's LiteSpeed for SQL Server, Red Gate Software's SQL HyperBac, or Red Gate Software's SQL Backup to encrypt your database backups as they are written to either disk or when they are written directly to tape. If you use a media library such as

CommVault, IBM's Tivoli, or another of the large Enterprise Class tape backup solutions where you back up the database directory from the database to the tape library, then these third-party tape backup options may not work for you. In these cases you'll need to look at encrypting your SQL Server backups using the native functions of your existing tape backup solution.

LiteSpeed for SQL Server

Using LiteSpeed to handle encryption is actually quite easy once you have the products installed and configured. If you are using LiteSpeed to back up your databases, you'll need to edit each database backup job that LiteSpeed has created, adding in the @encryptionkey or the @jobp parameter. The @encyrptionkey parameter allows you to provide a plain text password that Lite-Speed can then use to encrypt your backup, while the @jobp parameter allows you to pass in an encrypted value so that you don't have to store an unencrypted password in your backup scripts as shown in Example 7.6.

```
EXEC master.dbo.xp_backup_database @database='YourDatabase',
    @backupname='YourDatabase Backup', @encryptionkey=
    'YourKey', @file='D:\Backups\YourDatabase.bak';
```

Example 7.6: A sample SQL LiteSpeed job designed to encrypt a database backup.

In order to get the encrypted value for use with the @jobp parameter, use the extended stored procedure xp_encrypt_ backup_key that SQL LiteSpeed creates in the instance. The extended stored procedure accepts a single-input parameter of @key and returns a single value as a recordset. The value that is returned is the encrypted version of the password.

When restoring a database from a LiteSpeed for SQL Server encrypted backup, simply pass in the @encryptionkey or @jobp parameter so that LiteSpeed is able to read the database backup and write the data back to the SQL Server engine.

Red Gate SQL HyperBac

Using Red Gate SQL HyperBac (formerly "HyperBac for SQL Server") to handle your encryption is also quite simple. After configuring Red Gate SQL HyperBac for which folders to monitor on your SQL Server, you need to edit each SQL Server database backup job, changing the backup file extension from ".bak" or ".trn" to ".hbe" as shown in Example 7.7. This tells Red Gate SQL

HyperBac that you want it to encrypt (and/or compress) the backup as it is written to the hard drive.

```
BACKUP DATABASE MyDatabase
TO DISK='D:\Backups\MyDatabase.hbe';
```

Example 7.7: A sample Red Gate SQL HyperBac job designed to encrypt a database backup.

Restoring a Red Gate SQL HyperBac encrypted file is extremely easy. Simply place the file into a directory that Red Gate SQL HyperBac is configured to monitor, and the file will automatically be decrypted from Red Gate SQL HyperBac as the SQL Server requests the file to be restored.

Red Gate SQL Backup

Red Gate software has two backup products available that can handle encryption. Red Gate SQL Backup is configured and used very much like LiteSpeed for SQL Server Enterprise. Red Gate SQL Backup uses an extended stored procedure to run the backup process. Unlike LiteSpeed for SQL Server Enterprise where a parameter is passed to the extended stored procedure, Red Gate SQL Backup takes a single parameter with a variety of parameters passed within that single-text parameter.

To enable encryption of your backup, two values must be specified: KEYSIZE and PASSWORD. The KEYSIZE is the size of the encryption key that will be used. Red Gate SQL Backup supports either a 128-bit key or a 256-bit key. The PASSWORD is the key phrase that allows the encryption to be used as shown in Example 7.8.

As with other backup products, you can pass in an encrypted password or a plain text password. Like always, passing in an encrypted value is more secure as this doesn't require storing the password in plain text within the Red Gate SQL Backup Job.

```
EXECUTE master.dbo.sqlbackup '-SQL "BACKUP DATABASE [Adventure
    Works] TO DISK = "D:\Backup\<AUTO>.sqb" WITH PASSWORD =
    "<ENCRYPTEDPASSWORD>o1a5dA==</ENCRYPTEDPASSWORD>",
    DISKRETRYINTERVAL = 30, DISKRETRYCOUNT = 10, COMPRESSION =
    0, KEYSIZE = 256, THREADCOUNT = 2"';
EXECUTE master..sqlbackup '-SQL "BACKUP DATABASE [Adventure-
    Works] TO DISK = "D:\Backup\<AUTO>.sqb" WITH PASSWORD =
    "test", DISKRETRYINTERVAL = 30, DISKRETRYCOUNT = 10,
    COMPRESSION = 0, KEYSIZE = 256, THREADCOUNT = 2"';
```

Example 7.8: T/SQL code showing how to create a Red Gate SQL Backup Job using both an encrypted password and a plain text password.

When you encrypt your SQL Server databases (or any backups) using any technique, you'll need to take special care to protect the keys that you use when backing up the data. If the keys are lost or are unavailable when it comes time to restore the backups, then the backups are effectively useless as there will be no way to decrypt the backup and restore the data. A common practice is to place a copy of the key on a USB drive or other portable media such as a CD. This media should then be placed into a sealed envelope and stored in a secure location such as a safe in the Human Resources Department or the Legal Department. If possible, this location should be at a facility other than the primary facility that you are attempting to back up data from. The tapes should be stored at a second facility so that in the event of a major failure of the primary facility such as an earthquake, flood, or hurricane, which destroys the primary facility, the backup tapes are still available to restore the data and get the business back up and running.

Regardless of the encryption technique you use, there is a CPU overhead to process this encryption, and this overhead must be taken into account when you configure your backup encryption solution.

Third-Party Tape Backup Solutions

Dozens of enterprise-class tape backup solutions are available. Each one of these solutions has its own method of encrypting data. For the most part, they all work basically the same way. They use the SQL Server API to create a virtual backup tape device within the SQL Server, which sends the data to the application installed on the SQL Server. This then directs the data stream to the tape backup server, which then sends the data to be backed directly to tape (or written to disk, then moved later on to tape).

In these backup environments, there are typically a huge variety of encryption options. Before selecting your encryption options with these larger platforms, it is important to know where the encryption will take place. The documentation that came with your backup and recovery application (BURA) should be able to tell you at what layer the encryption is done. Typically, the encryption will be done in one of two locations; either within the backup application running on the SQL Server or within the service running on the tape backup control server.

The preference for performance of the SQL Server is to have the encryption handled at the tape backup server's level as this takes the CPU load of the encryption away from the SQL Server's CPU. However, the systems administrator will prefer to have the encryption done on the SQL Server because this distributes the encryption load back to each SQL Server instead of putting all that very expensive data encryption on the backup server. The problem of putting all the backup encryption on the backup server's CPUs can be offset by running various systems backups at various times of the day and night, instead of backing up all the databases at the same time.

Not all enterprise backup solutions support encryption within the backup solution. If the enterprise backup solution doesn't support encryption of data as it is written to the tapes, care must be taken to ensure that the enterprise backup solution does support having SQL Server back up the data in an encrypted form. If the backup solution cannot tell the SQL Server to back up the data with encryption (either using the native SQL 2008 and higher encryption or a third-party tool), then the backups should be first configured to back up to disk in an encrypted form, and then those backups should be moved from the disk to the tape backup array without the need to worry about encryption, as the database encryption has already been handled by the database engine.

For an extra layer of protection, if the tape backup solution does support encryption and it supports using either the native SQL Server 2008 and up or third-party encryption options, then the database can encrypt the data before it is sent to the tape backup solution, which can then encrypt the data again. This would provide an extra layer of protection, as for someone to read the backup tapes they would first need to break through the encryption on the backup tape itself, and then they would need to break the encryption that the SQL Server or third-party tool placed on the data. This double layer of encryption increases the complexity of the solution because now two different sets of keys will need to be maintained and safely stored. Nonetheless, this would be a more secure solution.

Transparent Data Encryption

Using Transparent Data Encryption (discussed in the "Encrypting Data at Rest" section of Chapter 2 of this book) protects not only your data at rest on the production server's hard drive, but also your SQL Server backups when taken with either the native backup process or one of the third-party backup tools that have been discussed in this chapter. Transparent Data Encryption does this by ensuring that each data page is encrypted as it is written on disk. Then when the data page is transferred to the backup file, the page is still encrypted.

Transparent Data Encryption is configured by creating a database master key in the master database. After creating the database master key, a Certificate is created in the master database. Then a database encryption key is created in the user database, and this database encryption key is secured using the certificate that was created within the master database. After the database encryption key has been created, the ENCRYPTION option on the user database can be enabled telling the Transparent Data Encryption engine to begin the background encrypting of data. Much more information on this topic is available in Chapter 2 of the present volume.

This means that in order to restore the backed up database to the same SQL Instance or to another SQL Instance you will first need to export the Certificate from the source instance's master database and then restore the key into the destination instance's master database. Without having this certificate restored, you will be unable to restore the database to the SQL Instance. Because of this, backing up these certificates is critical. Without backups of the certificates, you will NOT BE ABLE TO RESTORE YOUR DATABASE that is being encrypted.

FAQ
Certificate Management

Without proper backups of the certificates used to secure the database encryption key, a simple restore or rebuild of the master database will prevent you from accessing the user database, even on that same instance. Simply creating a new certificate in the master database with the same name and other settings of the original certificate will not be enough to allow the database to be restored, as the keys within that certificate will not match the original certificate.

Compression and Encryption

Two of the most important concepts in today's IT world are Encryption and Compression (or deduplication). Encryption stores the data in a safe and secure manor, while compression reduces the amount of physical data being stored. Unfortunately, however, these two concepts usually don't play well together. This is because compression of data requires lots of duplicates within your data, but encryption tends to make your data very unique.

Not all is lost, however: There is a way to make compression and encryption work together. The trick is to compress the data before the data is encrypted. This allows the duplicates to be removed, allowing for maximum compression, and then the data can be encrypted providing the needed protection.

The third-party tools that have been discussed all do an excellent job of compressing and encrypting within a single step. If you are using one of the larger enterprise solutions to back up to tape directly from the SQL Server, in order to do compressions and encryption the compression must be done before the data is sent to the tape library. This requires that when the tape library performs the BACKUP DATABASE operation against the SQL Server database it must know how to tell the SQL Server to compress the database backup. If the tape library doesn't know how to use the COMPRESSION option, it will attempt to do the decryption after the data has been encrypted and as it is written to tape. At this point it is too late, as the level of compression will drop to 1%–2% compression compared to the normal 40%+ compression that the native backup or the third-party software compression backups can provide.

Note
Working Together Gets the Best Results

Deciding at what level the compression and the encryption are going to be done will require working with the systems administrator in charge of the tape backup system. By working together on the solution design, you can get the best results out of the solution.

If the tape backup system takes an already encrypted backup and tries to compress it, the tape backup system won't get any acceptable level of compression, which will lead to wasted tape and wasted time and CPU power while attempting to compress the backup. However, if you can compress and encrypt the backup within the SQL Server (or use a third-party tool) and write that backup to disk and have the tape backup solution move the backups to tape without trying to compress, then time and CPU power will be saved.

If, however, the tape backup solution has to compress and encrypt, then your best bet may be to back up a nonencrypted database backup. This way the backup server can handle the entire compression and encryption process.

Offsite Backups

Offsite backups of your SQL Server backups are probably the biggest weakness in database backup security. This is because by the nature of the offsite backup, you are trusting another company and that company's employees to keep your backup data safe and secure. While these offsite backup companies are expected to keep the backup tapes, there have been many cases (both published in the news and heard about through word of

Story Time

I'm Sorry to Inform You of This, But We've Lost the Backup Tape with All Your Customer Information on It.

A quick search on Google, Bing, or your favorite search engine for "lost backup tapes" will give you a pretty clear idea of what can happen when backup tapes go missing.

In June 2005, CitiGroup, one of the largest financial companies in the world, reported that a backup tape was lost. This wasn't just any old set of backup tapes either; these specific tapes were being shipped via UPS from the financial giant to one of the credit bureaus in the United States. These tapes, which were most likely sent without any sort of encryption in place to protect the data, included customer information for about 3.9 million of CitiGroup's customers. The data on the tapes included the customer's name, Social Security number, account history, and loan information about current and former customers. Basically, they had just about everything a data thief would need to begin a massive amount of identity theft.

CitiGroup wasn't the only large company to lose tapes in 2005. In February of that same year, Bank of America reported that it lost backup tapes that contained personal information on 1.2 million credit card customers. Not to feel left out, Time Warner reported in May 2005 that it lost information (one can easily enough assume backup tapes)

with information relating to 600,000 current and former employees.

The companies that own the data and the tapes aren't the only ones that can lose backup tapes. In 2005 Iron Mountain, a company that specializes in storing backup tapes, reported that it "lost track" of four sets of customer backup tapes during the first four months of the year. While admitting that the tapes were lost, Iron Mountain says that it loses only a very small number of tapes as it ships more than 5M tapes annually.

More recently, in June 2010, the insurance broker Marsh and Mercer reported that in April of that year they lost tapes that were being shipped between their offices. Although the total number of people affected was not disclosed, the company reported to the New Hampshire Attorney General's office that information on 131 New Hampshire residents was on the tapes that were being transferred.

These few items are just a few of the articles that can be found with a couple of quick searches online. Considering the frequency with which tapes disappear during shipping and long-term storage, the issue of protecting data stored on tape becomes extremely important. The data should be encrypted and password protected at the very minimum.

mouth) where tapes have been lost or returned to the wrong company when recalled.

Because there is no guarantee that the tapes you send out won't be sent to another company, you need to ensure that when another company gets these tapes they are completely worthless to whoever receives them. Although one would hope that whatever company that receives your tapes would simply return them when they find that the tapes aren't theirs, there is no way to know that this company isn't a competitor who would love to have access to your company's proprietary information.

Tapes being returned to the wrong company is not the only thing that can go wrong. There have been stories about tapes literally falling off the truck between the customer's office and the remote storage facility. In this case you have no way of knowing who has your tapes or what their end goal of having the tapes might be. If your offsite storage facility is an employee's or manager's home, there is an even higher chance of tape loss. This is not due to any fault of the employees, but rather to the fact that cars get stolen and houses get broken into with much more frequency than happens with professional offsite service.

With all the potential problems that come with moving database backups offsite, still offsite backups are a necessary evil in order to meet the organization's disaster recovery and business continuity requirements. The key to taking your database backups offsite is to mitigate these risks by using database encryption best practices.

Note
Ditch the Tape

Another way that these risks can be mitigated is by using a virtual tape library (VTL) instead of a physical tape library. A VTL connects to a traditional enterprise backup solution, but instead of backing up to a tape drive the backup is written to a hard drive. The advantage of the virtual tape library is that the backups run much, much faster.

When using a VTL, a second virtual tape library can be placed in a second data center. The first virtual tape can then be configured to replicate data over the Wide Area Network (WAN) to the second virtual tape library. This gives the VTL the offsite backup capabilities that traditional tape libraries can provide by getting the backups out of the primary data center facility while continuing to use the existing backup server infrastructure.

Summary

Just because the data has left the SQL Server or even the office doesn't mean that the DBA's responsibilities have ended. Some of the primary responsibilities of any DBA, is to secure the data, while maintaining the ability to keep the system up and running, and having the ability to restore the data as needed so that the system can be restored quickly in the event of a failure. In order to accomplish this, security best practices need to be followed not just in the production environment but within your back solution as well.

As you work with older and older versions, you have much fewer options available to you. On the native function side, Microsoft began introducing compression in Microsoft SQL Server 2008, and native encryption with Transparent Data Encryption was introduced in Microsoft SQL Server 2008. When using older versions of Microsoft SQL Server, you will need to use a third-party solution to encrypt your backup solution. Check with your backup solution provider to see what options are available to you based on the version of Microsoft SQL Server.

As of this writing, SQL Azure doesn't support any sort of database backups, thus, the information in this chapter doesn't apply. This is because Microsoft doesn't expose the backup solution in place on the SQL Azure instances. As Microsoft takes care of all the database backups, the backup options that are discussed in this chapter are handled by Microsoft and not Microsoft's customer.

References

CNN. "Citigroup Division Tells 3.9M Customers Personal Info Lost—Jun. 6, 2005." *Business, financial, personal finance news—CNNMoney.com.* N.p., June 5, 2005. Web. September 25, 2010. http://money.cnn.com/2005/06/06/news/fortune500/security_citigroup.

"Marsh and Mercer Report Lost Backup Tape (update 1) | Office of Inadequate Security." *Office of Inadequate Security.* N.p., June 12, 2010. Web. September 25, 2010. "SQL Server tools, Oracle tools, .NET developer tools, Email archiving tools—Red Gate Software." *SQL Server tools, Oracle tools, .NET developer tools, Email archiving tools—Red Gate Software.* N.p., n.d. Web. September 25, 2010.

"Storage, Backup Compression, Encryption, Object Recovery by HyperBac." *Storage, Backup Compression, Encryption, Object Recovery by HyperBac:.* N.p., n.d. Web. September 24, 2010.

8

AUDITING FOR SECURITY

INFORMATION IN THIS CHAPTER

- Login Auditing
- Data Modification Auditing
- Data Querying Auditing
- Schema Change Auditing
- Using Policy-Based Management to Ensure Policy Compliance
- C2 Auditing
- Common Criteria Compliance

Setting security policies is a great start, but you need to ensure that the system remains secure. This is where auditing comes into play. Auditing by itself isn't good enough; someone needs to review the auditing information that has been collected in order to ensure that the system has remained as secure as expected. This includes monitoring the logins into the database, the data that has been changed, and any changes to the schema.

As you move from the newer versions of Microsoft SQL Server into older versions of the product, there are fewer and fewer auditing features available to you. Microsoft really began putting auditing features into the SQL Server product starting with Microsoft SQL Server 2008. Prior to SQL Server 2008, the auditing options are very limited and have to be mostly done through third-party products or homegrown systems.

Note
Auditing in SQL Azure

At the time of this writing, if you are working with an SQL Azure database, none of the auditing options discussed in this chapter are available to you. Hopefully, the SQL Azure team will be able to include auditing features into the product in the future.

Do keep in mind that in any book about SQL Azure, including this one, information about SQL Azure can get out of date very quickly as the SQL Azure product is a constantly moving target. This is because the SQL Azure team releases new versions of the database engine every few months so what you see here may not be relevant after the summer of 2010.

Login Auditing

Login auditing in SQL Server falls into two categories: SQL Server 2005 and prior and SQL Server 2008 and newer. SQL Server 2005 and older only provides very basic information, and that information is written to the SQL Server ERRORLOG file and to the Windows Application log. The only configuration option is to enable login failure logging, successful login logging, logging of both successful and failed logins, or logging of neither. SQL Server 2008 and newer allow for a much more granular level of auditing controlled through "Server Audit Specifications."

SQL Server 2005 and Older

In the older auditing version, a change was made between SQL Server 2000 and SQL Server 2005. While this was a relatively small change, it is a very important one. The change was to include the source IP Address that was attempting to log into the database engine. Before the change to the login auditing specification, the logged messages looked like that shown in Example 8.1, while the post-change audit message looks like that shown in Example 8.2.

```
2010-09-06 18:50:01.28 Logon Login succeeded for user 'DOMAIN
    \UserName'. Connection made using Windows authentication.
```

Example 8.1: Sample auditing information for a successful login into an SQL Server 2000 or order instance.

```
2010-09-06 18:50:01.28 Logon Login succeeded for user 'DOMAIN
    \UserName'. Connection made using Windows authentication.
    [CLIENT: 10.3.30.84]
```

Example 8.2: Sample auditing information for a successful login into an SQL Server 2005 or newer instance.

Changing the auditing level setting is most easily done through the Enterprise Manager or SQL Server Management Studio (depending on the version you are using) as the setting is controlled via a registry key. When using Enterprise Manager, connect to the server and right click on the server and select properties. When using SQL Server Management Studio, connect to the server in the object explorer and select properties. Regardless of which version is used, then select the Security tab. Next look for the "Login auditing" section in the dialog box. Here you can select from None, failed only, successful only, or both failed and successful, as shown in Figure 8.1. While the screenshot shown in Figure 8.1 is from Microsoft SQL Server 2008 R2s

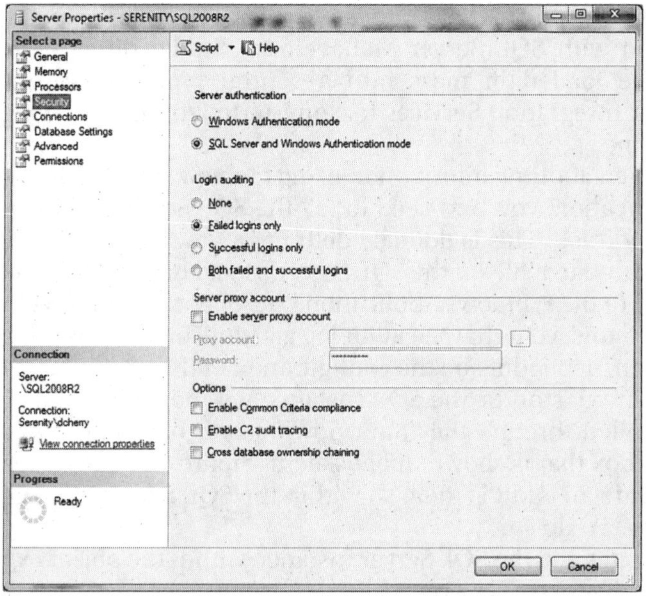

Figure 8.1 The security tab of the server properties dialog from the 2008 R2 version of the SQL Server Management Studio.

Management Studio, the dialog from SQL Server 7 and 2000s Enterprise Manager looks very similar to the one shown.

If you want to change this setting via T/SQL, you will need to use the xp_instance_regwrite system stored procedure to do this passing in an integer, which defines what the setting should be set to as shown in Example 8.3. A setting of 1 indicates that successful login only should be logged. A setting of 2 indicates that failed logins only should be logged. A setting of 3 indicates that both successful and failed logins should be logged. A setting of 0 indicates that neither failed nor successful logins should be logged.

No matter if you change this setting via T/SQL or the management tool, a restart of the SQL Instance is required before the setting change will take effect.

```
EXEC xp_instance_regwrite N'HKEY_LOCAL_MACHINE', N'Software
    \Microsoft\MSSQLServer\MSSQLServer', N'AuditLevel',
    REG_DWORD, 2
GO
```

Example 8.3: Sample T/SQL code: how to change the logging level.

SQL Server 2008 and Newer

Starting in SQL Server 2008, Microsoft introduced server side auditing, which allows the SQL Server to capture a wide variety of information into audit files. The files can then be viewed with SQL Server Management Studio directly, or they can be loaded in mass into a central repository using SQL Server Integration Services for long-term storage, querying, and trending.

When auditing information using the new server-side auditing specification, you first need to tell the SQL Server where to store the audit log. This is done by defining a new audit. An audit can be written to a file on the SQL Server's local hard drive, a network share, to the Windows Application Log, or to the Windows System Log. In the event that the audit log gets full, one of two things will happen; depending on the configuration of the audit, the auditing will simply stop or the SQL Instance will be shut down. This is controlled through the "Shut down server on audit log failure" checkbox that is shown unchecked in Figure 8.2. The easiest way to create an audit is to do so within the SQL Server Management Studio. To do so:

1. Connect to the SQL Server Instance within the object explorer.
2. Navigate to Security.
3. Navigate to the Audits folder under Security.
4. Right click on Audits and select "New Audit" from the context menu which pops up.

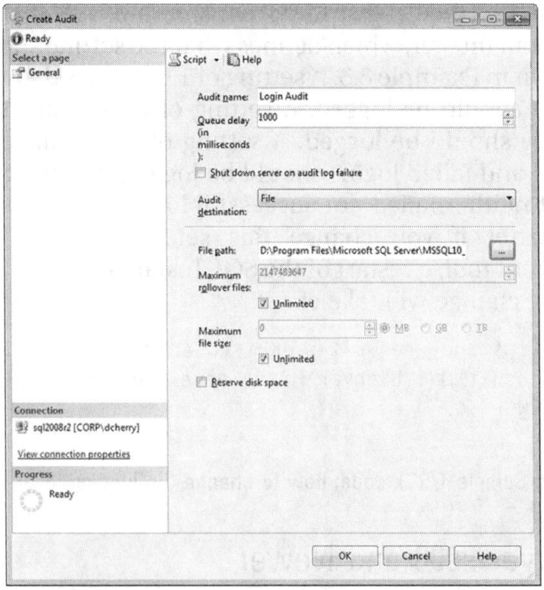

Figure 8.2 The filled-out Create Audit screen creating a new audit file in SQL Server 2008 and higher.

In the Create Audit screen that opens, give the audit a name, specify the queue delay in miliseconds, and select the audit destination as shown in Figure 8.2.

Like all new features with Microsoft SQL Server, you can also create an audit using T/SQL. This is done by using the CREATE SERVER AUDIT command. The command creates the same server audit destination that is created from within SQL Server Management Studio as shown in Example 8.4.

```
CREATE SERVER AUDIT [Login Audit]
TO FILE
(   FILEPATH = N'D:\Program Files\Microsoft SQL Server
    \MSSQL10_50.MSSQLSERVER\MSSQL\Log'
   'MAXSIZE = 0 MB
   'MAX_ROLLOVER_FILES = 2147483647
   'RESERVE_DISK_SPACE = OFF
)
WITH
(   QUEUE_DELAY = 1000
   'ON_FAILURE = CONTINUE
)
GO
```

Example 8.4: Creating a server audit using the CREATE SERVER AUDIT statement in T/SQL.

Weather you create the audit using SQL Server Management Studio or T/SQL, you need to enable the audit. You can do this either by right clicking on the Audit within the object explorer and selecting "Enable Audit" or by using the ALTER SERVER AUDIT statement in T/SQL as shown in Example 8.5.

```
ALTER SERVER AUDIT [Login Audit]
WITH (STATE = ON)
GO
```

Example 8.5: Enabling a server audit using the ALTER SERVER AUDIT statement.

After creating the audit destination using the CREATE SERVER AUDIT, you can create the Server Audit Specifications. The Server Audit Specifications tell the SQL Server exactly what instancewide actions to audit. In this example, we create a single audit specification that monitors for failed or successful logins and logs that information into the Login Audit file we just created. When creating a Server Audit Specification within SQL Server Management Studio, right click on "Server Audit Specifications" in the object explorer (found directly under the "Audits" folder in the object explorer) and select "New Server Audit Specification."

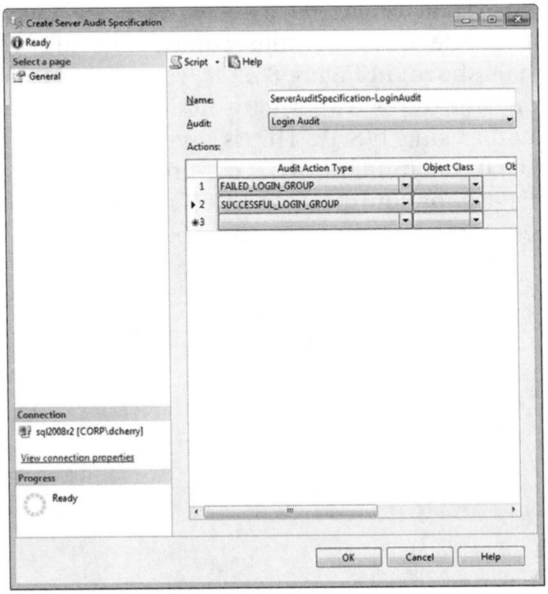

Figure 8.3 Create Server Audit Specification screen capturing both failed and successful logins and writing the data to the "Login Audit" audit file.

In the Create Server Audit Specification window that opens, name the audit and select the Audit to which the information should be saved, as well as the actions that should be audited in the Actions section. In the example presented in Figure 8.3 two different audit actions are shown. The first audit action captures failed logins, while the second audit action captures successful logins.

A server audit specification can also be created via the CREATE SERVER AUDIT SPECIFICATION statement in T/SQL as shown in Figure 8.6.

```
CREATE SERVER AUDIT SPECIFICATION
    [ServerAuditSpecification-LoginAudit]
FOR SERVER AUDIT [Login Audit]
ADD (FAILED_LOGIN_GROUP),
ADD (SUCCESSFUL_LOGIN_GROUP)
```

Example 8.6: Creating a Server Audit Specification using the CREATE SERVER AUDIT SPECIFICATION command in T/SQL.

Weather you create the specification using the SQL Server Management Studio or by using T/SQL, you will need to enable the Server Audit Specification. To enable the specification within SQL Server Management Studio, you can right click on the specification and select "Enable Server Audit Specification" from the context menu. To enable the specification using T/SQL, you can use the ALTER SERVER AUDIT SPECIFICATION statement as shown in Example 8.7.

```
ALTER SERVER AUDIT SPECIFICATION
   [ServerAuditSpecification-LoginAudit]
WITH (STATE=ON)
```

Example 8.7: Enabling a Server Audit Specification using T/SQL.

Once the Audit and the Server Audit Specification have been enabled and a user logs into the database, instance data will begin being logged into the Audit file. If the Server Audit Specification is enabled but the Audit is disabled, then no information will be collected; both the Server Audit Specification and the Audit need to be enabled for data collection to begin. To view the information within the file, locate the Audit within the object explorer. Then right click on the Audit and select "View Audit Logs" from the context menu that pops up. This will open the log file viewer reading the log file information into the grid for easy viewing, filtering, sorting, and searching, as shown in Figure 8.4.

You can also query the data using a T/SQL statement by using the fn_get_audit_file function as shown in Example 8.8. The guide shown in the file path can be found in the audit_guid column of

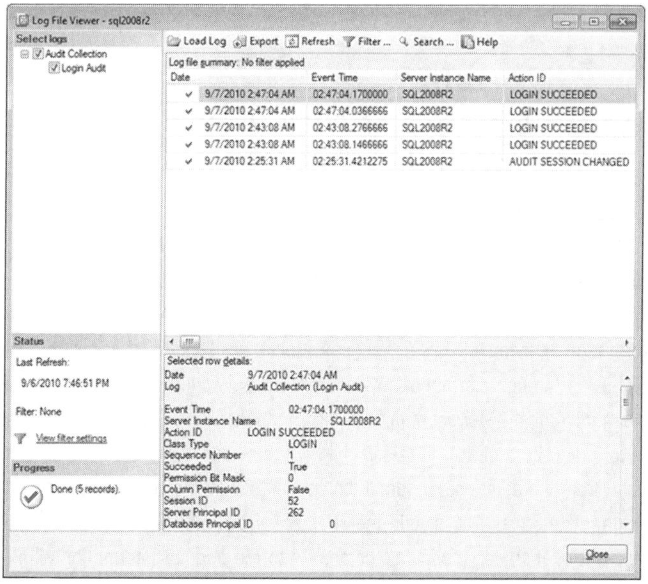

Figure 8.4 The Audit log for the Audit and Server Audit Specification shown in Figures 8.2 and 8.3.

the sys.server_audits system catalog view. The guide shown in your database will be different from that shown in Example 8.8.

```
select TOP(1000) *
from fn_get_audit_file('D:\Program Files\Microsoft SQL Server
    \MSSQL10_50.MSSQLSERVER\MSSQL\Log\*_3fb9ea26-29c9-408c-
    a7bb-eb27371ac3d8*',null,null)
order by event_time desc,sequence_number
```

Example 8.8: T/SQL code to view the audit information from the specified audit log.

When looking at the output from the fn_get_audit_file system function, the columns of importance are the succeed column, which tells you if the action (in this case a login attempt) was successful; the server_principal_name, which tells you the login name that was used to connect; and the additional_information column, which contains an XML document that has a variety of information in it including the IP Address from which the user was attempting to connect. If the login was not successful, the server_principal_name may be NULL depending on the cause of the login failure, as the login may not have been transmitted to the server.

In the case of login audit information, there will be two different values in the action_id column. These are LGIS and LGIF, where LGIS is for a successful login attempt and LGIF is for a failed login attempt.

Note
Ways to Gather Server Audit Data

As the Server Audit data is easily accessed through the fn_get_audit_file system function, the information can be collected into a central repository fairly easily, which would then allow for centralized reporting and management of the audit information. A side benefit of moving the audit information into a central repository is that the information can be more easily secured in this central repository and then it can be on the server's local hard drive. The reason for this is that in order for the SQL Server to write the audit files, it needs to modify access to the files in the folder which stores the files. Now someone who didn't want the audit information to be found could use xp_cmdshell to easily delete the files from the folder.

The data can be moved from the audit log through just about any method one would like. Among these methods is moving data through a linked server after a job gets the newest data from the audit log. Another technique could be to use SQL Server Integration Services (SSIS) to query the data from the source server and transfer it to the destination server, pulling out the needed information from the additional_information column. When moving auditing information to a central repository, it is extremely important to be sure to include the original values from the audit without making any modification. This way the extracted information can always be compared to the original information within the repository to verify that the information has not been modified.

After the Auditing Specifications have been created, they can be modified using either the user interface or the ALTER SERVER AUDIT SPECIFICATION T/SQL statement. In order to make changes to a Server Audit Specification, the Audit Specification must be disabled using the ALTER SERVER AUDIT SPECIFICA-TIO. Then the changes can be made, and the Server Audit Specification can be enabled, allowing it to begin capturing data again as shown in Example 8.9.

```
ALTER SERVER AUDIT SPECIFICATION
    [ServerAuditSpecification-LoginAudit]
WITH (STATE = OFF)
GO
ALTER SERVER AUDIT SPECIFICATION
    [ServerAuditSpecification-LoginAudit]
DROP (SUCCESSFUL_LOGIN_GROUP)
GO
ALTER SERVER AUDIT SPECIFICATION
    [ServerAuditSpecification-LoginAudit]
WITH (STATE = ON)
GO
```

Example 8.9: The T/SQL code to disable a Server Audit Specification, changing the specification, then enabling the specification, allowing it to begin capturing data.

One very important item that needs to be audited is any change to the auditing, in order to ensure that the auditing has not been disabled and to allow unaudited changes to be made to the data within the database. Without auditing the configuration of the Auditing, there is no way to guarantee that the auditing configuration today is the same as it was yesterday.

Note
Auditing the Auditing

When you audit your auditing configuration, the SQL Server will successfully audit the changes to all the auditing specifications on the server, with the exception of the auditing specification that is auditing the auditing. When the Audit Specification is disabled to allow a change, this will be the last line audited by the Audit Specification. When the specification is enabled, this will not be logged, nor will any of the changes made to the Audit Specification that is auditing changes to the Auditing.

Data Modification Auditing

Auditing of Data Modification in versions of Microsoft SQL Server 2008 and older is much harder to do because it all needs to be done manually. Microsoft SQL Server 2008 R2 introduced the Change Data Capture (CDC) feature to the product. Once configured, CDC is used to capture all insert, update, and delete activity that occurs on the tables in question.

Adding any auditing to the database will increase the CPU load by some extent as additional work is being performed by the database engine. To keep this increase to the minimum, only audit the information required so as to reduce the performance impact on the database engine. The amount of additional load that will be added to the database by enabling Change Data Capture will depend on a variety of things, including the number of transactions per second and the number of columns that are being changed within each transaction.

Change Data Capture Configuration

Before you can use Change Data Capture, it must be enabled on both the database that is to be monitored and the specific tables within the database that are to be tracked. CDC is enabled on a specific database using the sys.sp_cdc_enable_db system stored procedure as shown in Example 8.10. Change Data Capture is disabled by using the sys.sp_cdc_disable_db system stored procedure.

```
use MyDatabase
GO
EXEC sp_cdc_enable_db
GO
```

Example 8.10: Enabling Change Data Capture on the MyDatabase database.

When the sys.sp_cdc_enable_db system stored procedure is run, a new user will be created within the database with the name cdc, as will a new schema named cdc, which will hold the Change Data Capture tables. The tables that are created are as follows:

1. cdc.captured_columns, which contains one row for each column in each table that is being tracked.
2. cdc.change_tables, which contains one row for each table being tracked.
3. cdc.ddl_history, which contains the schema modification changes to the tables that are being tracked.
4. cdc.index_columns, which contains one row for each index column within the tables that are being tracked.
5. cdc.lsn_time_mapping, which contains one row for each transaction that has rows in a table being tracked. This is used to map the time transactions that are logged to the

specific log sequence number (LSN) that logged the change. There may be rows in this table when there are no changes, which allows for the completion of LSN processing in time periods of low or no user activity.

After Change Data Capture has been enabled for the database, it can then configure Change Data Capture for the specific tables that need to be tracked. This is done using the sys.sp_cdc_enable_table system stored procedure. The stored procedure sys.sp_cdc_enable_table has nine parameters, but only three of them are required. These required parameters are:

1. @source_schema, which is the schema of the table to be tracked.
2. @source_name, which is the object name (without the schema) of the table to be tracked.
3. @role_name, which is the name of a database security role that will be created if it doesn't already exist. This role can be ignored, or it can be used to assign permissions to users so that they can access the data that Change Data Capture has captured. Multiple captured tables can use the same role, but any user who is a member of this role will have access to read the captured data for all those tables.

Note
CDC Must be Enabled at the Database First

If you don't enable Change Data Capture at the database level before you attempt to enable it at the table level, SQL Server will throw error message 22901. This message informs you to enable CDC on the database before attempting to enable it on the table.

The six optional parameters for the sys.sp_cdc_enable_table system stored procedure are:

1. @capture_instance, which is the name that will be used to capture the change data for this specific table. If not specified, the system will auto generate a name based on the values of the @source_schema and @source_name parameters.
2. @supports_net_changes, which indicates whether the captured data should support querying for net changes in addition to row-level changes. If this parameter is set to 0, then the functions that support this querying are not created. If this parameter is set to 1, which is the default, then the functions that support this querying are created.

3. @index_name, which indicates the name of the unique index that can be used to uniquely identify the rows within the source table. If the @index_name value is included, the specified index takes precedence over the defined primary key columns as the unique identifier that Change Data Capture uses.

4. @captured_column_list, which indicates what columns within the specified table should be tracked. If not included, all columns are tracked. The column list is a comma-separated list of columns and can be quoted using double quotes ("") or square brackets ([]) as needed. If a column list is specified, then all columns that are included in the primary key (or the index specified by the @index_name parameter) must be specified.

5. @filegroup_name, which is the filegroup where the Change Data Capture tables should be created. If not specified or if a NULL value is passed in, then the default file group will be used.

6. @allow_partition_switch, which tells the SQL Server if the SWITCH PARTITION command of the ALTER TABLE statement can be executed against the monitored table. If the value is set to 0 (the default is 1) and the table is partitioned, data cannot be moved between partitions. This is done to ensure that CDC data matches the actual data in the table. The SWITCH PARTITION command of the ALTER TABLE statement will move data between partitions, but this change is not logged by Change Data Capture. Thus data captured will not match the source table data if data is moved from one partition to another.

Enabling Change Data Capture to capture all changes on all columns can be easily done using just the first three parameters—@source_schema, @source_name, and @role_name, as shown in Example 8.11.

```
exec sys.sp_cdc_enable_table @source_schema='dbo',
    @source_name='MyTable',
    @role_name='cdc_MyTable'
```

Example 8.11: Enabling Change Data Capture for the table dbo.MyTable with the role name cdc_MyTable.

Querying Changed Data

Querying data from the Change Data Capture tables is done through a system of table-valued functions. For each table being tracked by CDC, a function whose name starts with "cdc.fn_cdc_get_all_changes_" and ends with the name of the capture instance as specified by the @capture_instance parameter (or the @source_schema and @source_name parameters if the @capture_instance parameter is not specified) of the sys.sp_cdc_enable_table system stored procedure.

If the @supports_net_changes parameter of the sys.sp_cdc_enable_table system stored procedure was set to 1 (or true), then a table-valued function whose name starts with "cdc.fn_cdc_get_net_changes_" and ends with the name of the capture instance as specified by the @capture_instance parameter (or the @source_schema and @source_name parameters if the @capture_instance parameter is not specified) of the sys.sp_cdc_enable_table system stored procedure will also be created. This "cdc.fn_cdc_get_net_changes_" function allows the user to query for the net changes instead of the individual changes.

Querying these table-valued functions requires use of the cdc.lsn_time_mapping system table. This table will show the transaction log LSN and will map it to the system time that the LSN was logged. These LSNs must be used to pass into the table values functions as the first two parameters. Both table-valued functions require three parameters:

1. from_lsn is the first LSN to process.
2. to_lsn is the last LSN to process.
3. filter_option accepts one of two values "all," which returns all values within the LSNs, or "all update old," which returns both the old and new values for each row. The "all update old" value will return twice as many rows as the "all" option, as the "all update old" returns one row for the old value and one for the new value.

The easiest way to get the needed data from the cdc.lsn_time_mapping table is to use the system functions sys.fn_cdc_get_min_lsn and sys.fn_cdc_get_max_lsn. The min_lsn function accepts a single parameter, which is the name of the capture instance that is specified when creating the capture and the function returns the minimum stored LSN for that table. The max_lsn function doesn't accept any parameters and returns the most recent LSN for the database. These functions are used in conjunction with the cdc.fn_cdc_get_all_changes and cdc.fn_cdc_get_net_changes functions.

```
DECLARE @from_lsn binary(10), @to_lsn binary(10)
SET @from_lsn =
  sys.fn_cdc_get_min_lsn('dbo_MyTable')
SET @to_lsn = sys.fn_cdc_get_max_lsn()
SELECT * FROM cdc.fn_cdc_get_all_changes_dbo_MyTable
  (@from_lsn, @to_lsn, N'all');
GO
```

Example 8.12: Sample T/SQL code showing the usage of the Change Data Capture functions to return data.

Data Querying Auditing

Auditing when someone runs a query against database tables has historically been the hardest audit to perform, with the traditional answer being run start an SQL Trace against the engine looking for select statements and logging that information somewhere where it can be easily read. Starting with SQL Server 2008, Microsoft has had a solution for this auditing problem, and that is to use the Server Side Auditing, which was discussed earlier in this chapter, but instead of creating a Server Audit Specification create a Database Audit Specification.

Before you can configure a Database Audit Specification, however, you must create an audit to write the data to, unless you intend to write to an existing audit, as discussed earlier and shown in Figure 8.2 and Example 8.4.

To create a Database Audit Specification using the SQL Server Management Studio User Interface, follow these steps:

1. Connect to the database instance using the object explorer.
2. Navigate to the "Databases" folder.
3. Navigate to the Database you wish to create the Database Audit Specification in.
4. Navigate to the Security folder.
5. Navigate to the "Database Audit Specification" folder.
6. Right click on the "Database Audit Specification" folder and select "New Database Audit Specification."

A Database Audit Specification, which would be used to capture select statements, should have its "Audit Action Type" set to

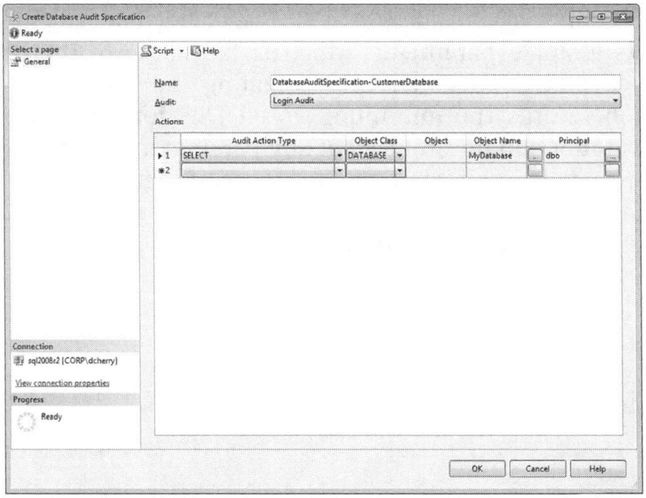

Figure 8.5 Creating a Database Audit Specification to monitor all select statements issues against the MyDatabase database.

"SELECT." When you create a Database Audit Specification, you can set the Object Class to Database, Schema, or Object, depending on how wide you want to set your audit. An audit that has the Object Class set to database will capture all the select statements that are executed against the specified database, as shown in Figure 8.5. An audit that has the Object Class set to Schema will capture all select statements that are executed against the specified schema. An audit that has the Object Class set to Object will capture all queries that are executed against the specified object.

Database Audit Specifications can also be created using the CREATE DATABASE AUDIT SPECIFICATION T/SQL statement as shown in Example 8.13.

```
CREATE DATABASE AUDIT SPECIFICATION
    [DatabaseAuditSpecification-CustomerDatabase]
FOR SERVER AUDIT [Login Audit]
ADD (SELECT ON DATABASE::[MyDatabase] BY [dbo])
    GO
```

Example 8.13: Creating a Database Audit Specification using T/SQL to monitor all select statements against the database MyDatabase.

As with the Server Audit Specifications, the Database Audit Specification must be enabled before it can be used. Enabling can be done by right clicking on the Database Audit Specification in the object explorer and selecting the "Enable Database Audit Specification" or by using the ALTER DATABASE AUDIT SPECI-FICATION statement as shown in Example 8.14.

```
ALTER DATABASE AUDIT SPECIFICATION
    [DatabaseAuditSpecification-CustomerDatabase]
WITH (STATE=ON)
```

Example 8.14: T/SQL code enabling a Database Audit Specification using the ALTER DATABASE AUDIT SPECIFICATION statement.

Once the Database Audit Specification has been enabled, data will be captured to the Audit specified when the Database Audit Specification was created, and it can be viewed using the log explorer discussed earlier in this chapter.

After the Database Auditing Specifications have been created, they can then be modified using either the user interface or the ALTER DATABASE AUDIT SPECIFICATION T/SQL statement. In order to make changes to a Database Audit Specification, the Audit Specification must be disabled using the ALTER DATABASE AUDIT SPECIFICATION. Then the changes can be made, and the Database Audit Specification can be enabled, allowing it to begin capturing data again as shown in Example 8.15.

```
ALTER DATABASE AUDIT SPECIFICATION [Server-
   AuditSpecification-LoginAudit]
WITH (STATE = OFF)
GO
ALTER DATABASE AUDIT SPECIFICATION
   [ServerAuditSpecification-LoginAudit]
DROP (SUCCESSFUL_LOGIN_GROUP)
GO
ALTER DATABASE AUDIT SPECIFICATION
   [ServerAuditSpecification-LoginAudit]
WITH (STATE = ON)
GO
```

Example 8.15: The T/SQL code to disable a Server Audit Specification, changing the specification, then enabling the specification, allowing it to begin capturing data.

Schema Change Auditing

Like auditing select statements, auditing schema changes have traditionally been difficult to make without running a server-side trace. Like auditing select statements, this problem has been solved starting in SQL Server 2008, as have auditing schema changes, by using the Database Audit Specifications.

To audit schema changes, there is a specific Audit Action Type that will track all schema changes; this is the SCHEMA_OBJECT_CHANGE_GROUP, as shown in Figure 8.6. This will then log all schema changes to the specified Audit destination.

Like the other Database Audit Specifications, you can also create a schema audit in T/SQL, as shown in Example 8.16.

```
CREATE DATABASE AUDIT SPECIFICATION [Object_Changes]
FOR SERVER AUDIT [Login Audit]
ADD (SCHEMA_OBJECT_CHANGE_GROUP)
```

Example 8.16: T/SQL Code to create the schema change audit shown in Figure 8.6.

Like the other Database Audit Specifications, the schema audit specification would need to be enabled using the ALTER DATABASE AUDIT SPECIFICATION T/SQL statement or by using the object explorer.

Using Policy-Based Management to Ensure Policy Compliance

Policy-Based Management, which was introduced in Microsoft SQL Server 2008, can be used to audit the servers

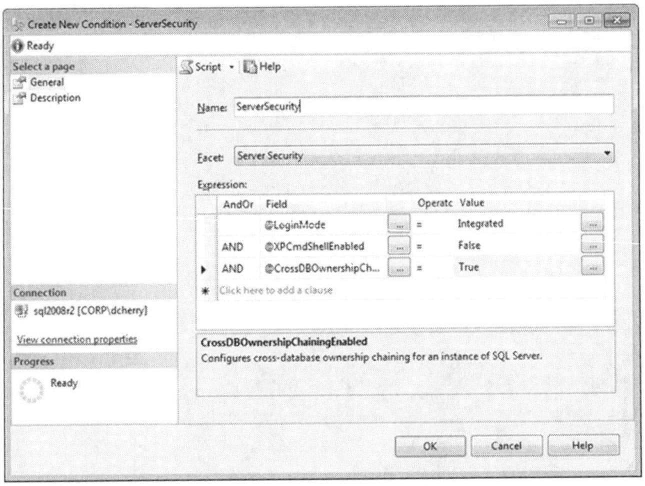

Figure 8.6 Creating a new condition that evaluates three instance wide settings.

automatically on a regular basis either when the server starts or on a regular schedule, such as daily or monthly. Policy-Based Management can be used to audit a wide variety of security-related settings to ensure on a regular basis that the settings are set correctly. Once the Policies and Conditions are set (these are defined more fully in Chapter 4 in the section entitled "Using Policies to Secure Your Instance") and the policies are configured to check automatically, the results are easily available for viewing by using the Log viewer by right clicking on the Policy Management folder and selecting "View History."

Policy-Based Management can be accessed in the object explorer within SQL Server Management Studio by:

1. Navigating to Management
2. Navigating to Policy Management

Conditions can be created with multiple expressions in them, as long as the expressions are all within the same Facet. In the Facet shown in Figure 8.6, three expressions are being monitored, which all must pass in order for the condition to be successfully evaluated.

After creating the conditions that you wish to evaluate, policies need to be created, such as those in Figure 8.7, to evaluate the condition and run it on a schedule. Additional information about the conditions that are monitored by the policy can be entered on the Description page, including a link to a webpage that can be set up with more information.

If you manually evaluate a policy such as the ones created in Figure 8.7 by right clicking on the Policy and select evaluate on

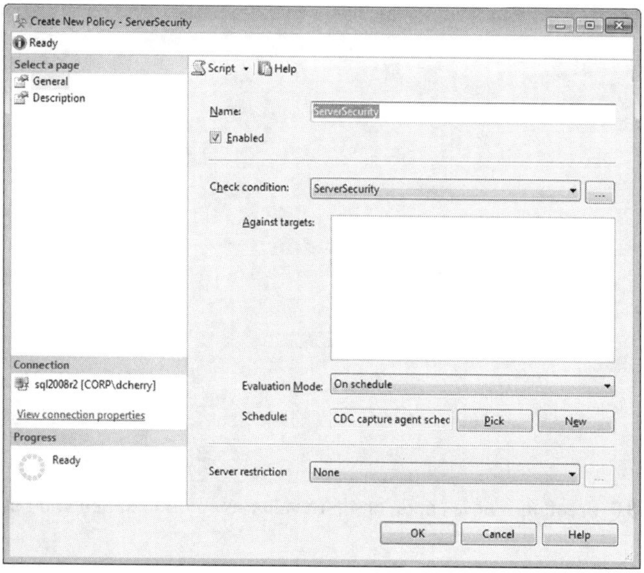

Figure 8.7 Creating a policy to monitor the Server Security condition shown in Figure 8.6.

the context menu, a screen will pop up with the results of the evaluation, as shown in Figure 8.8.

Clicking on the "View…" link in the "Target details" section of the "Evaluate Policies" window shown in Figure 8.7 will bring up the window shown in Figure 8.8, which shows exactly which expressions were evaluated and the results of each expression.

When policies are evaluated on a schedule there is a way to see if those policies were evaluated successfully or not. Within the SQL Server Management Studio this evaluation can be done by right clicking on the Policies folder under the "Policy Management" folder and selecting "View History" from the context menu (you can also right click on a Policy and select "View History"). This will bring up the Log File Viewer, which will be configured to view the policy history. When a policy has failed, you can drill down into the entry of the evaluation, which will give you a Details link, shown in Figure 8.10, which, when clicked, will present the same screen shown in Figure 8.9.

Using SQL Server Management Studio is great when you have only a couple of policies on a couple of servers. However, if you have dozens or hundreds of servers, you could easily have thousands or tens of thousands of policies whose results you would have to check. In this case your best bet would be to create a central repository and use either an SQL Agent job or an SQL

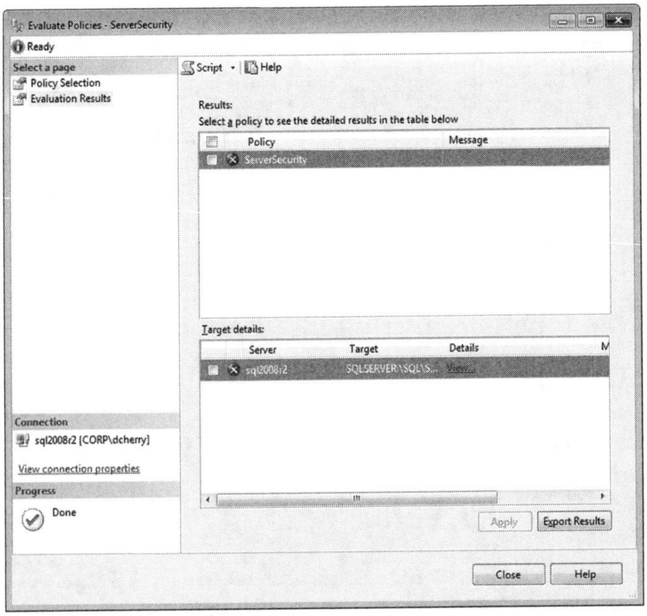

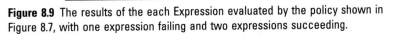

Figure 8.8 Evaluation of the ServerSecurity policy shown in Figure 8.7.

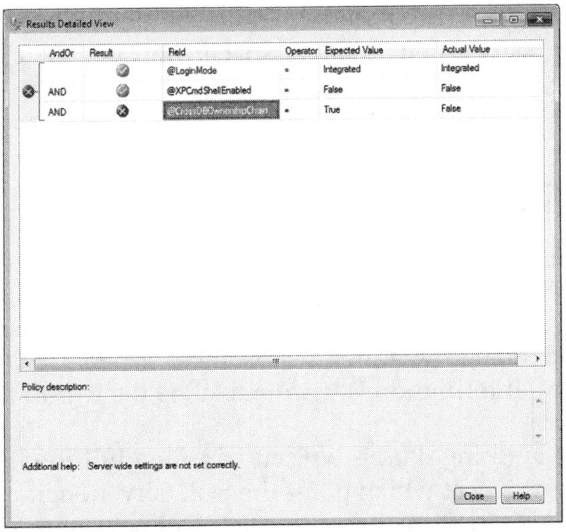

Figure 8.9 The results of the each Expression evaluated by the policy shown in Figure 8.7, with one expression failing and two expressions succeeding.

Server Integration Services (SSIS) package to query for the policy evaluation history from the msdb.dbo.syspolicy_policy_ execution_history table and the msdb.dbo.syspolicy_policies table. To get the details of which Expression succeeded or failed,

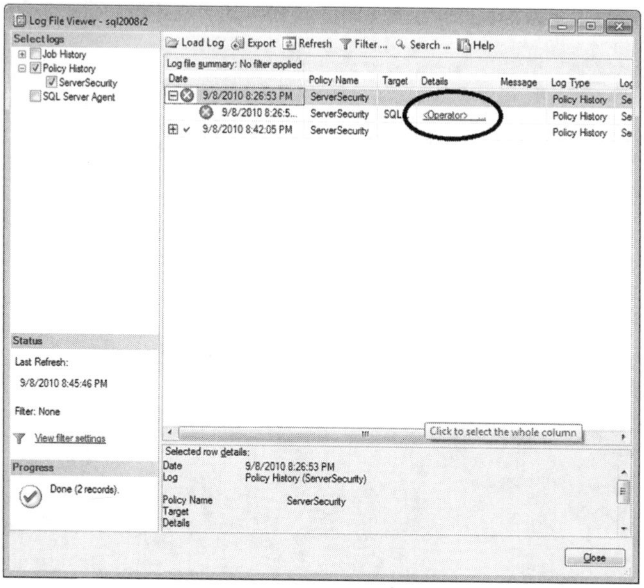

Figure 8.10 The Log File Viewer showing Policy History.

that information is located in msdb.dbo.syspolicy_policy_execution_history_details table, specifically in the result_detail column.

C2 Auditing

C2 auditing is probably the oldest form of auditing within Microsoft SQL Server. C2 auditing is an option that will configure the SQL Server instance to record all attempts to access statements and objects within the instance. When C2 auditing is enabled, the information is written to a log file within the default log folder.

The C2 auditing data is written to a file until the file reaches 200 Megs in size, at which point the SQL Server engine will close the file and begin writing to a new file. This will continue until C2 auditing is disabled or until the hard drive fills, at which point the database engine will shut itself down and it will not be able to be restarted until space has been made available.

C2 auditing can be enabled in two ways: by using SQL Server Management Studio as shown in Figure 8.11 (or SQL Enterprise Manager for SQL 2000 and older) or by using the sp_configure system stored procedure.

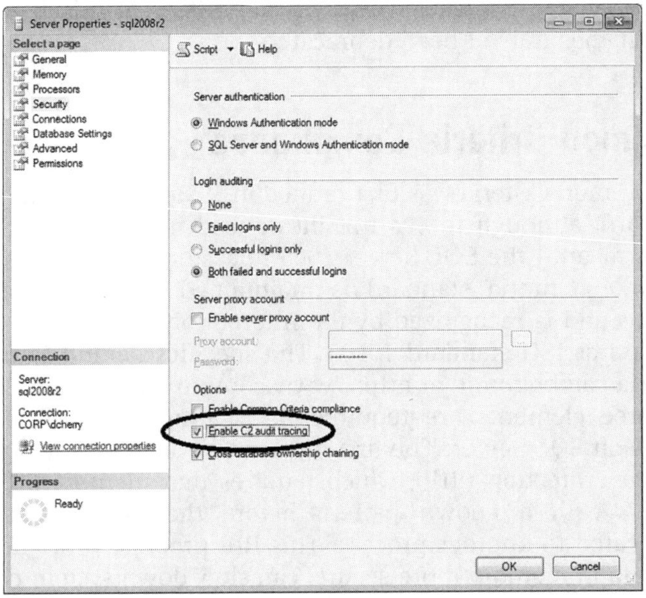

Figure 8.11 Where to enable C2 auditing on the Security Tab of the instance properties in SQL Server Management Studio.

In order to enable C2 auditing using T/SQL, the sp_configure procedure is used. Before C2 auditing can be enabled, the advanced options setting must also be enabled using the sp_configure procedure, as shown in Example 8.17.

```
EXEC sys.sp_configure N'show advanced options', N'1' RECONFIGURE
  WITH OVERRIDE
GO
EXEC sys.sp_configure N'c2 audit mode', N'1'
GO
RECONFIGURE WITH OVERRIDE
GO
EXEC sys.sp_configure N'show advanced options', N'0' RECONFIGURE
  WITH OVERRIDE
GO
```

Example 8.17: T/SQL code used to enable C2 auditing.

In either case using SQL Server Management Studio or sp_configure to change the C2 auditing setting, there is no restart of the database engine to begin the C2 auditing. With either configuration method the auditing change will begin immediately.

When using sp_configure on an SQL 2000 server or older, change the schema from sys to dbo. C2 auditing has been superseded by "Common Criteria Compliance" starting in

Microsoft SQL Server 2008. As of the writing of this book, C2 auditing has not yet been deprecated.

Common Criteria Compliance

Common Criteria was first ratified in 1999 as an international standard, although it was not introduced into the SQL Server platform until the SQL Server 2005 release of the product. The Common Criteria standard is maintained by more than 20 nations and is recognized by the International Standards Organization as ISO standard 15408. The specifics behind Common Criteria can be found at http://www.commoncriteriaportal.org/.

Three elements are required for Common Criteria within Microsoft SQL Server. The first element is called Residual Information Protection (RIP), which requires that memory be overwritten with a known pattern before the memory can be reallocated to another process. This RIP process, while making the data in memory more secure, can slow down system performance because of the memory rewriting. The second element involves turning on login auditing. This login auditing is exposed within the SQL Server by including the load successful login time, the last unsuccessful login time, and the number of attempts between the last successful and current login times within the sys.dm_exec_sessions dynamic management view. The third element is that column-level GRANTs do not overwrite table-level DENY privileges.

Common Criteria can be enabled via SQL Server Management Studio by viewing the properties of the instance and by viewing the security tab as shown in Figure 8.12 or by using the sp_configure system stored procedure as shown in Example 8.18.

Like enabling C2 auditing, Common Criteria is an advanced option that must be made visible by turning on advanced options using sp_configure as shown in Example 8.18.

```
EXEC sys.sp_configure N'show advanced options', N'1'
    RECONFIGURE WITH OVERRIDE
GO
EXEC sys.sp_configure N'common criteria compliance enabled', N'1'
GO
RECONFIGURE WITH OVERRIDE
GO
EXEC sys.sp_configure N'show advanced options', N'0'
    RECONFIGURE WITH OVERRIDE
GO
```

Example 8.18: Enabling Common Criteria using sp_configure.

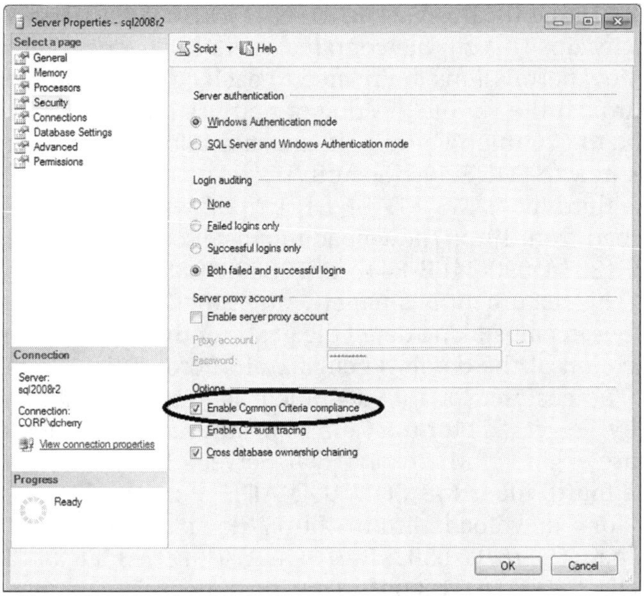

Figure 8.12 Enabling Common Criteria using the SQL Server Management Studio.

Common Criteria is a feature available only in the Enterprise, Evaluation, and Developer editions of Microsoft SQL Server 2005 and 2008, as well as the same editions of SQL Server 2008 R2, in addition to the Data Center edition.

If you are using Microsoft SQL Server 2008 and you wish to use Common Criteria, some extra steps need to be performed. First, you need to run a script called SQL_Server2008_EAL1_trace.sql, which can be downloaded from Microsoft at http://download. microsoft.com/download/9/5/F/95FDD106-4E98-47B4-B676- 7FDB9A403AF0/SQL_Server2008_EAL1_trace.sql. This script cre- ates a stored procedure that starts a server-side trace and then marks the stored procedure as a startup stored procedure.

Some other downloads are available to assist in implementing Common Criteria, the first of which is integritycheck_SQL 2008_EE.zip, which is available for download from http:// download.microsoft.com/download/1/B/1/1B18883E-BDBF-4A58- 861B-C6A551A172DA/integritycheck_SQL2008_EE.zip. This zip file contains a batch file and an XML document that will ensure that the files making up the SQL Server 2008 binaries are unchanged. It does this by comparing the files on the server's hard drive against the known MD5 hashes for each of the files.

The second file is permission_hierarchy.zip, which is available for download from http://download.microsoft.com/download/B/

F/8/BF81F5DE-8CD5-4531-87A1-F57D9ED09E0D/permission_hierarchy.zip. This zip file contains a set of PDF documents that show how permissions are related to each other at various levels and through the various nesting of permissions. While this isn't specific to Common Criteria, it is useful information to anyone who is new to SQL Server Security.

The third file is MS_KEAL1_ST_1.2.pdf, which is available for download from http://download.microsoft.com/download/E/1/2/E12F1277-D096-44FB-8442-EC77B3790C88/MS_KEAL1_ST_1.2.pdf. This document is a paper written by Roger French, and it describes in painstaking detail the goals for the Common Criteria certification of the database engine of Microsoft® SQL Server® 2008. The abstract for this document is "This document is the Security Target (ST) for the Common Criteria certification of the database engine of Microsoft® SQL Server® 2008."

The fourth file is MS_SQL_AGD_ADD_1.3.pdf, which is available for download from http://download.microsoft.com/download/C/7/6/C763829F-6F3C-4A70-9D97-37F8482FF2E1/MS_SQL_AGD_ADD_1.3.pdf. This document is a paper, also written by Roger French, that builds on the information in the MS_KEAL1_ST_1.2.pdf. The abstract for this document is "This document is the Guidance Addendum for the Common Criteria certification of the database engine of Microsoft® SQL Server® 2008."

Summary

A wide variety of auditing options are found within Microsoft SQL Server. As applications are moved from older versions of Microsoft SQL Server to the newer versions, more and more auditing features are made available. As future versions of the product are released, even more auditing options will surely be made available.

References

French, Roger. "MS_KEAL1_ST_1.2.pdf." *MS_KEAL1_ST_1.2.pdf.* Microsoft, January 23, 2009. Web. September 25, 2010. download.microsoft.com/download/E/1/2/E12F1277-D096-44FB-8442-EC77B3790C88/MS_KEAL1_ST_1.2.pdf. Copied the abstract and referenced the file for download by the user.

French, Roger. "MS_SQL_AGD_ADD_1.3.pdf." *MS_SQL_AGD_ADD_1.3.pdf.* Version 1.3. Microsoft, January 30, 2009. Web. September 25, 2010. download.microsoft.com/download/C/7/6/C763829F-6F3C-4A70–9D97-37F8482FF2E1/MS_SQL_AGD_ADD_1.3.pdf. Copied the abstract and referenced the file for download by the user.

9

SERVER RIGHTS

INFORMATION IN THIS CHAPTER

- OS Rights Needed by the SQL Server Service
- OS Rights Needed by the DBA
- OS Rights Needed to Install Service Packs
- OS Rights Needed to Access SSIS Remotely
- Console Apps Must Die
- Default Sysadmin Rights
- Vendor's and the Sysadmin Fixed-Server Role

When working with Microsoft's SQL Azure, as of the writing of this book the only section of this chapter that applies to you is the last, "Console Apps Must Die." The remaining sections don't apply to Microsoft's SQL Azure as Microsoft handles the installation of the database engine and the installations of the SQL Azure service packs and hotfixes. The SSIS pieces don't currently apply as SQL Azure doesn't offer SSIS as part of the SQL Azure product.

OS Rights Needed by the SQL Server Service

The Microsoft SQL Server service needs specific rights in order to function correctly. Older versions of Microsoft SQL Server required extremely high-level permissions at the Windows operating system (OS) to function, usually requiring being a member of the local administrators group. Starting in Microsoft SQL Server 2000, the Windows account that runs the SQL Server no longer needs to be a member of the local administrators group. The SQL Service needs just a few permissions granted to it. When installing Microsoft SQL Server 2000 or newer, the installer will automatically grant the Windows account, which will run the Microsoft SQL Server service, the correct rights, if it doesn't already have these rights.

Windows System Rights

The rights that are required to be granted to run the SQL are:

- Log on as a service
- Replace a process-level token
- Adjust memory quotas for a process

If it becomes necessary to change the Windows account that the SQL Server runs under, then the new account that will be running the service will need to be granted these rights. If the "SQL Server Configuration Manager" is used to change the Windows service account, when using Microsoft SQL Server 2005 or newer these changes are made automatically for you. When using Microsoft SQL Server 2000, the permissions changes need to be made manually. If when using Microsoft SQL Server 2005 or higher the change is made using some method other than the "SQL Server Configuration Manager," then these changes would also need to be made manually. The easiest way to make these changes is to add the new account to the local Windows group, which was created during installation. This group is named "SQLServerMSSQLUser$*ServerName*$*InstanceName*," where the *ServerName* and *InstanceName* values are the name of the server and the SQL Server instance, respectively. When the instance is the default instance, the *InstanceName* value will be MSSQL SERVER instead of default.

When changing the Windows account that the Microsoft SQL Server Agent is running under, similar changes need to be made to the local group "SQLServerSQLAgentUser$*ServerName* $*InstanceName*," again where the *ServerName* and *InstanceName* values are the name of the server and the SQL Server instance, respectively. This local group has the same security rights as the groups starting with SQLServerMSSQLUser. In addition, this group grants the Windows user that will be running the Microsoft SQL Server Agent service the "Replace a process token level" and the "Bypass traverse checking" rights. These additional rights are needed in order for the various impersonations the SQL Server Agent will do to function.

When changing the Windows account that the SQL Server Integration Services (SSIS) runs under, similar changes need to be made to the local group "SQLServerDTSUser$*ServerName*" where the *ServerName* value is the name of the server.

It is highly recommended that the SQL Server not be run under the local system account as the local system account grants the SQL Server more rights to the operating system than are actually needed. By granting the SQL Server more rights than it needs, either by giving the Windows account more rights than it needs or by having the services run under the local service account, an attacker can obtain local Administrator rights on the server.

The SQL Server should never, ever be run under a domain account that is a member of the "Domain Admins" group. The "Domain Admins" group is a domain group that is created in all windows domains, and gives all members of the group administrative rights to all computers within the Windows Domain. There are few, if any, valid reasons to run the SQL Server under a domain admin account. When an SQL Server is run under a domain admin account if attackers were to get into the SQL Server database and get access to the operating system via the SQL Server database, they would then have domain administrator rights and they would have the ability to create or delete accounts for users or computers, as well as make changes to any server within the company.

SQL Server's NTFS Permissions

When first installing SQL Server, the installer will modify the permissions on the folders where the database files are installed in an attempt to limit access to the database files. When the Microsoft SQL Server service is not running under an account that has local administrator rights, additional NTFS permissions need to be accounted for. As one example, the SQL Server service will not be able to create databases at the root of a hard drive or mount a point when the Windows operating system is running Windows 2008 or higher. This is because the NTFS and UAC permissions do not allow users who do not have administrative access to create files at the root level of the hard drive.

Another feature, which many find to be an annoyance, is as follows: When using Microsoft SQL Server 2005 or higher and a database is detached, the NTFS permissions for all the database files that make up the database are changed, removing the NTFS permissions for all users except for that of the user issued the database detach command. In Microsoft SQL Server 2008 and higher, the Windows account that is running the SQL Server database will also be left as having NTFS permissions on the files that make up the detached database. On SQL Server 2008 and higher, the database can be reattached right away, as needed. On SQL Server 2005, before the database can be attached, the NTFS permissions must be changed to allow the SQL Server engine to have rights to the database files. This must be done for all the database files that make up the Microsoft SQL Server database.

OS Rights Needed by the DBA

Technically a database administrator (DBA) doesn't need many rights to the SQL Servers operating system. This is because the DBA should not be managing the operating system that runs the Microsoft SQL Server Service. The management and patching of the base operating system should be handled by the members of the systems administration team and not by the DBA team.

The DBA may, however, from time to time need rights to the Windows OS, which will allow viewing performance metrics. If the company has a performance monitoring solution such as Microsoft Operations Manager (MOM), the DBAs can grant the Microsoft Operations Manager rights to view the captured performance data. However, at times the DBAs may need the ability to collect real-time performance data directly from the performance monitor. The right to use a performance monitor remotely can be granted by adding the DBAs to the "Profile system performance" local system right. This local system right grants users that have the right the ability to connect to the system remotely and gather performance monitor data.

Many of these performance metrics can be accessed via the "sys.dm_os_performance_counters" dynamic management view from within the SQL Server instance. This allows the DBA to access the performance monitor data and to log it into a table or simply view the record set by querying the needed information from the dynamic management view without having any special operating system level permissions.

Dual Accounts

When the DBA need access to the server's console, it is recommended that a second account be set up and used to access the servers console. This is recommended for a couple of reasons. First, this allows the systems administrators to selectively allow the DBA to have access to the SQL Server's console as needed. Second, it will prevent the DBA's roaming profile from being loaded onto the server's system drive. This does add a layer of complexity to the system as the DBA now needs to keep track of two usernames and passwords and the DBA will need to ensure that this admin account has the needed rights to both the database and the server so that the needed operations can be performed.

OS Rights Needed to Install Service Packs

While DBAs do not typically need rights to the Windows operating system, there are times when they do. Specifically, this is the case when a Microsoft SQL Server Service Pack or Microsoft SQL Server Hotfix needs to be installed on the Microsoft SQL

Server Instance. The system administrators should not be installing these service packs and hotfixes against the Microsoft SQL Server instance as the systems administrator should not have rights within the Microsoft SQL Server instance in order to complete the service pack or hotfix instance.

When the Microsoft SQL Server service pack or hotfix needs to be installed, the DBA will need to be granted administrative rights to the Microsoft SQL Server's operating system to complete the service pack and hotfix installation. This level of permissions is needed so that the service pack or hotfix can update the Microsoft SQL Server binaries within the "C:\Program Files\Microsoft SQL Server\" folder (or wherever the binaries are installed to).

OS Rights Needed to Access SSIS Remotely

By default, only members of the local administrators group have the ability to connect to the SQL Server Integration Services (SSIS). This can prevent developers from accessing the SSIS in the development environment, as well as preventing the SQL Server service from connecting to the SSIS.

Fortunately, correcting these rights is a fairly easy process to complete without granting the users rights to the SSIS without making the user a member of the local administrators group. The needed change involves granting the user or users additional rights to the MsDtsServer DCOM object (or the MsDtsServer object that has a number such as 100 after it) within the Windows operating system. This change is easily done in a few easy steps:

1. Click Start.
2. Click Administrative Tools.
3. Click Component Services.
4. When the Component Services application opens, open the "Component Services" tree menu.
5. Open the Computers tree menu.
6. Open the "My Computer" tree menu.
7. Select the "DCOM Config" tree menu.
8. Locate the MsDtsServer object in the window on the right. When using SQL Server 2005, the object will be called MsDtsServer. When using SQL Server 2008 (either the R1 or R2 release), the object will be called MsDtsServer100. Future versions may have a different name with a higher number.
9. Right click on the correct object and select properties from the context menu that opens.
10. Select the security tab on the properties page that opens.

11. Under the "Launch and Activations Permissions" section, select the Customize radio button and select the Edit button.
12. Select or add the Windows user or Windows group (using groups is recommended to keep management simple) that needs the rights to connect and grant them the "Remote Launch" and "Remote Activation" rights or the "Local Launch" and "Local Activation" rights (or all four rights), depending on what rights are needed as shown in Figure 9.1.
13. Click OK to close this screen.
14. Under the "Access Permissions" section, select the Customize radio button and select the Edit button.
15. Select or add the Windows user or Windows group (using groups is recommended to keep management simple) that needs the rights to connect and grant them the "Remote Access" and/or "Local Access" permissions as shown in Figure 9.2.
16. Click OK on each screen and close the Component Services.

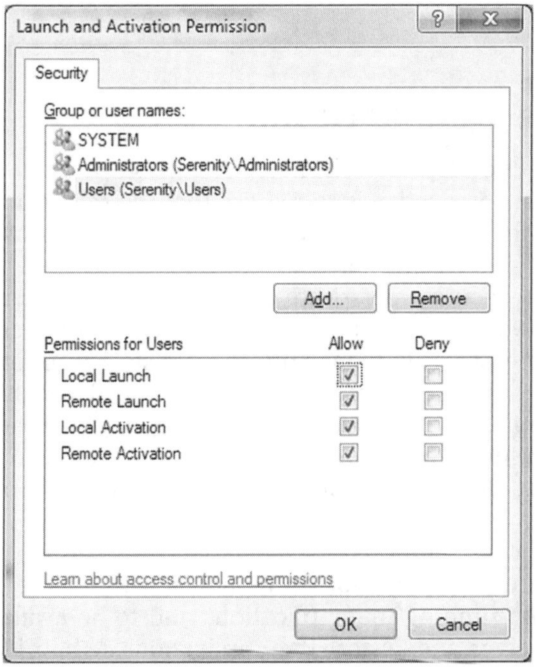

Figure 9.1 Granting addition launch and activation permissions to all members of the local Users group.

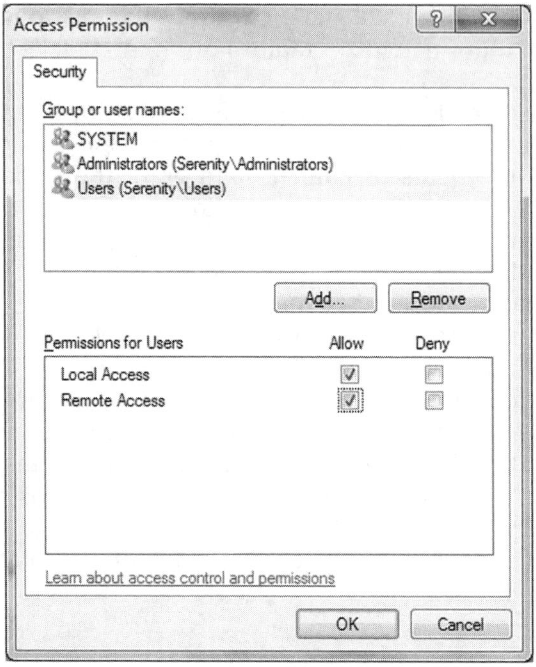

Figure 9.2 Granting Remote Access to the members of the local Users group for the SSIS.

Console Apps Must Die

One of the biggest nightmares from both a security and an operational perspective is to require that the server be logged in either on the console or on a remote session by a user so that console-based applications can be run.

From a security perspective, this is a problem because if a virus or worm were to be installed on the server, then either or both could easily be launched under that user's account. This also requires that the person who needs to be logged into the server to run the applications have access to log into the server. This person is usually the developer who wrote the application, which means that the developer needs to have access to the production server.

From an operational perspective this creates problems because the server cannot be rebooted without the user, who needs to be running the applications and to be available to log into the server and restart the applications. When it comes to patching, this is a major problem since the system cannot be kept up to date with the needed security patches.

This problem can be fixed by ensuring that the application is written to be used as a Windows service. There is little difference between writing a Console application and a Windows service. The biggest difference is that the Windows service does not have a console output to write debugging information like the Console Application does. This change, however, is minor compared to the security and operational issues this solves.

Applications that cannot be converted to a Windows service application can usually be configured to run as a Windows service by using the svrany.exe and instsrv.exe applications, which is provided as part of the Windows Resource Kit. Using these applications any application can be configured to run as a Windows service. The syntax for these applications is shown in Example 9.1.

```
instsrv.exe MyServiceName c:\reskit\srvany.exe
```

Example 9.1: Syntax used by instsrv.exe and srvany.exe to create a custom service.

After creating a custom Windows service, you can verify that the service was created correctly by looking in the Windows registry under HKEY_LOCAL_MACHINE\SYSTEM\CurrentControlSet\Services\MyServiceName. If the key exists, then the Windows service was created correctly. After verifying that the key was created, a couple of changes will need to be created under the folder. The first key that needs to be created is a key named "Parameters" with the class left blank. If the application requires no parameters, then leave the value blank; otherwise set the value to the parameters that the application needs. The second key which needs to be created is one named "Application", which is of the class of REG_SZ. The value of the Application string should be the full path to the application as well as the application name and extension such as "c:\windows\system32\calc.exe."

Once these changes have been made, the registry editor can be closed and the service can be started. If the service needs to be run under a domain account, it can be set up using the Services application from within the Administrative Tools folder in the Control panel. The service should not be configured to run under the developer's account; it should instead be configured to run under a new domain account that is set up for the sole purpose of running these Windows services.

Default Sysadmin Rights

When installing a new SQL Server, special attention needs to be paid to who becomes a member of the sysadmin fixed server role. The sysadmin fixed-server role grants all members of the role full rights to the entire database engine. Anyone who is a member of the sysadmin fixed-server role can do anything they want, and there is no way to stop them.

When installing Microsoft SQL Server 2000 or older, anyone who is a member of the Administrators group will automatically be made a member of the sysadmin fixed-server role. This includes any domain administrators or any other users who are members of the Administrators group. This group is shown within the Microsoft SQL Server engine as the BUILTIN\Administrators login. Best security practices dictate that this group should be removed from the sysadmin fixed-server role. Before removing this group from the sysadmin fixed-server role, the DBAs should be added to the sysadmin fixed-server role. Otherwise, there may not be any members of the sysadmin fixed-server role to administrate the system, especially if the instance is running in Windows only authentication mode.

When using Microsoft SQL Server 2005 or later, the local Administrators group is not made a member of the sysadmin fixed-server role by default. During installation of the Microsoft SQL Server 2005 and higher database engine, the installer asks for the groups or logins that should be made members of the sysadmin fixed-server role. If no one is added to this list, then only the sa account will be a member of the sysadmin fixed-server role. This is fine if this is the intended installation. However, if the server is installed using the Windows Authentication only mode, then there are no members of the sysadmin fixed-server role on the instance and no one can manage the database instance. For this reason during the installation the DBAs need to be added to the sysadmin fixed-server role so that the DBAs can manage the instance. When going through the installer, no error message is displayed if there are no Windows logins or groups that are assigned to the sysadmin fixed-server role. This can make it very easy to install the Microsoft SQL Server instance without any members of the sysadmin fixed-server role.

Vendor's and the Sysadmin Fixed-Server Role

All too often when installing a vendor's application, the vendor says that the login to the SQL Server instance needs to be a member of the sysadmin fixed-server role. And all too often the vendor is lying and doesn't actually need to be a member of the sysadmin fixed-server role. Vendors typically say that they need the greatest permissions possible because it is simply the easiest way to ensure that their application will have the rights needed to run. For the bulk of vendor installation processes, only the login that is used to install the application needs to be a member of the sysadmin fixed-server role. The login that runs the vendor application typically only needs to be a member of the dbo fixed database role. However, the login may need additional rights beyond this to function, such as the ability to create jobs or to create databases depending on the application design.

Note
Some Vendors Actually Know What They Are Talking About

When installing applications such as the Blackberry server, RIM (Research In Motion) actually knows what they need. They recommend that the account the Blackberry will connect to the database be a member of the sysadmin fixed-user role. Later in the documentation, however, they actually state that they only need to be a member of the dbcreator fixed-server role and the securityadmin fixed-server role. While these are still broad permissions, they are a much lower-level set of permissions than that which would be granted by the sysadmin fixed-server role.

Getting a vendor to say what server-wide rights the application actually needs can be difficult at best, especially if the application has already been purchased. If the DBA can get involved in the purchase process early on, the DBA will have a better chance of getting the information needed from the vendor. When possible, applications that require being members of the sysadmin fixed-server role should be avoided. When preventing the purchase of the application that needs to be a member of the sysadmin fixed-server role isn't possible—which is probably 99.9% of the time—the application should be placed on its own instance or its own virtual machine. In that way, the impact of having the application being a member of the sysadmin fixed-server role can be mitigated, and the application doesn't have the ability to impact any other applications or databases within the enterprise environment. This placement of the application on its own instance or virtual machine may have additional licensing costs and should be explored beforehand and possibly billed back to the business unit purchasing the application.

Summary

Some specific permissions can be easily granted so that people only have the rights that are necessary to get done what they need to get done, without having full rights to the operating system. When security is taken to the extreme, employees will quickly find ways to work around it in order to get things done, bypassing the security that is designed to protect the data and the systems and the company.

A

EXTERNAL AUDIT CHECKLISTS

INFORMATION IN THIS CHAPTER

- PCI DSS
- Sarbanes—Oxley
- HIPPA

The information in this appendix is meant to be a guide. Each audit has a different set of criteria that must be met to be passed, and each auditing company and each individual auditor has a different interpretation of the specification that defines each audit. The information provided here should be used as a guideline to give you the best possible chance of passing the audit on the first try.

Note
Make no Assumptions...

When working with an auditor, always answer the question being asked, and only the question being asked. The auditor will hopefully be answering specific questions, which should require specific answers. If an auditor asks a question that is very broad, there is nothing wrong with asking for clarification of the question. Don't assume that you know what question the auditor is asking because if the audit is asking one thing, and you assume the opposite, your wrong assumption could cause the company to fail the audit.

PCI DSS

PCI compliance is designed to ensure that a company is providing a secure platform for the use and transmission of credit card information and customer account information. The PCI DSS (Data Security Standard) was designed by the founding members of the PCI council. These founding members include American Express, Discover Financial Services, JCB International, MasterCard Worldwide and Visa, Inc.

The goal of the PCI DSS specification was to lay out standards that cover network security, corporate policies and procedures, network architecture, and application design among other critical measures. The PCI council continues to enhance the requirements of the PCI DSS specification to ensure that the PCI DSS specification remains a relevant specification in today's ever changing technology world.

PCI Checklist

- Install and maintain a firewall designed to protect customer card information.
- Replace all default system passwords with user-defined passwords.
- Encrypt all customer data.
- Encrypt all data being transmitted over the network using IPSec and/or SSL.
- Install antivirus software on all servers that host, transmit, or receive customer information.
- Keep antivirus software on servers up to date.
- Restrict access to view customer information to those that require access.
- Shared logins should be disabled.
- All users should have a unique logins to all systems.
- Restrict physical access to the data center to systems administrators and network administrators only.
- Audit all access and changes to customer information.
- Test security access to network resources on a weekly or monthly basis.
- Your Credit Card Processing company is PCI DSS compliant.
- Electronic copies of customer credit card numbers are not stored.
- Management has approved the removal of all tapes to offsite storage.
- Drives that contain customer data are totally destroyed before being disposed of.
- Have a written policy in place with regard to employee access to customer data.
- Firewalls must prevent direct access from the Internet to systems that contain customer data.
- Default SMNP community strings have been changed.
- Default vendor-supplied passwords are changed before the device or computer is attached to the company network.
- Unneeded vendor-provided accounts have been removed or disabled.
- WiFi access point passwords have been changed.
- No unencrypted WiFi connections are available on the company network.

- All remote access to systems that contain account data is done over an encrypted connection?
- Never store all data from any one track stored on the credit card.
  - Cardholders Name
  - Primary Account Number
  - Expiration Date
  - Service Code
- Card Validation Code or Value are not stored.
- PIN Number is not stored.
- Application shows no more than first 6 digits and last 4 digits of credit card number unless for specific reasons.
- Use SSLTLS or IPSEC when transmitting data over the public Internet.
- Have written policies in place to prevent sending credit card information via e-mail, instant message, chat, etc.
- All systems are patched with all current patches.
- All critical security patches are installed with one month of patch release.
- Is cardholder data only accessible by those requiring such access to complete their job duties.
- Vendor accounts are enabled only when needed by vendors.
- Printouts with cardholder data are stored in secure, locked cabinets.
- Tape backups that hold customer data should be marked as classified and secured from unauthorized personal.
- All media that leaves the secured facility must be transported by secured courier.
- All hard copies of customer data must be shredded with a cross-cut shredder, incinerated, or pulped.
- Wireless Access Points should be tested quarterly to ensure that only authorized devices can gain access.
- Wireless Access Points should audit the devices that connect to them.
- Network scans must be run quarterly against all Internet facing systems. Scan must be run by a PCI SSC Approved Scanner Vendor.
- Network scans should be run any time there is a significant network change. Scan must be run by a PCI SSC Approved Scanner Vendor.
- Written security policy must be established, published, maintained, and disseminated to all IT employees. Policy must be reviewed and updated annually and as needed.
- Acceptable usage polices must be written and cover the use of all technologies such as remote access, VPN, WiFi, PDA, e-mail, and Internet access.

- Ensure that security policies clearly define information security policies for all employees and contractors.
- Ensure that security policies clearly define security incident, response, and escalation procedures to ensure effective handling of all security incidents.
- Create a security awareness program to ensure that all employees are aware of the importance of cardholder security.
- Ensure that all service providers and partners have policies in place to ensure cardholder data security is maintained.
- An up-to-date list of all service providers and partners with which cardholder data is shared is maintained.
- Service Providers PCI DSS compliance is audited annually.
- A change control process is in place for all network changes.
- A network diagram is maintained which documents all partner and service provider connections.
- Firewalls exist between public networks and all company networks.
- Firewalls exist between all DMZ (demilitarized zone) networks and internal networks.
- All network ports and protocols that are allowed through firewalls must have a business justification and must be documented.
- Firewall and router rule sets must be reviewed every 6 months.
- Firewalls to and from networks that contain cardholder information must block all network traffic that is not critical to the business at hand.
- Network access from WiFi networks to networks that hold cardholder data should be blocked.
- Restrict outbound network access from servers holding cardholder data to other networks, including the public Internet.
- The database must be on a server on the internal network, separate from the DMZ.
- NAT or PAT must be used to mask internal IP addresses from the Internet.
- Computers with remote access, including computers personally owned by employees, who have direct account to cardholder data have personal firewalls installed.
- WiFi networks are configured to use strong encryption for all network access.
- Each server fulfills only one function.
- Unnecessary services and protocols are disabled on each server.
- All unnecessary functionally is removed from each server.

- Cardholder data that is retained is only kept for the minimum amount of time as required by business processes and regulatory requirements.
- Primary Account Number is stored using one-way hash, truncated value, index token, or strong encryption technique.
- Encryption keys should be accessible by the minimum number of employees and contractors as possible.
- Encryption keys should be stored in the minimum number of locations as possible.
- Encryption keys must be rekeyed annually.
- Encryption keys that have become compromised must be retired and removed.
- Employees that have access to encryption keys must sign a document stating that they understand the responsibilities that go with this access.
- As of June 30, 2010 no WiFi network uses WEP (Wired Equivalent Privacy) for encryption and authentication
- All viewing and changing of customer account information must be logged within the application.
- All input from customers must be validated for cross-site scripting, SQL Injection attacks, malicious file execution, etc.
- All error handling must be tested prior to each deployment.
- All secure cryptographic storage must be tested prior to each deployment.
- All secure communication must be tested prior to each deployment.
- Role-based access controls must be used within the application.
- Development, QA (Quality Assurance), and production environments must be separated.
- Separation of personal duties between development, QA, and production environments.
- Production Primary Account Numbers are not used within development and testing (QA) environments.
- All accounts used for development and/or testing must be removed prior to releasing application to production.
- All changes to application code must be reviewed prior to changes being released to production.
- Change control procedures are followed for all changes to all system components, including scope of change, impact of change, management approval, and rollback procedures.
- All web-based applications are coded based on secure guidelines such as the Open Web Application Security Project Guide.

- Public facing web applications must be reviewed annually, as well as after each release, to ensure the application successfully prevents all known threats and vulnerabilities.
- Access to customer data should follow the minimum rights to complete the job specified for all application users.
- If rights are not specifically defined as granting access to information, the default right should be to deny access.
- Management must approve all access changes for a group or single employee.
- All user accounts must have a password or two-factor authentication in place before granting any system access.
- Two-factor authentication must be used for all VPN or remote access.
- All passwords must be transmitted in an encrypted form between end user and application.
- User identity must be verified before password resets are completed.
- First-time passwords must be set to a unique value for each new password, and passwords must be reset after first use.
- Access for terminated users must be terminated immediately.
- Passwords must be changed every 90 days.
- Passwords must be at least 7 characters.
- Passwords must contain both characters and numbers.
- Once a password has been used, it cannot be used again for at least four additional passwords.
- After failing to enter a password correctly six times, the user account must be locked out for at least 30 minutes.
- If the user's terminal (desktop, application, etc) has been idle for 15 minutes, then the user must specify username and password to reactivate the session (unlock the computer).
- No anonymous access to databases that contain customer data.
- Video cameras must monitor data center access, and recordings must be kept for at least 3 months unless prohibited by law.
- Video camera footage must be monitored.
- Physical access to network switches must be restricted.
- Employee badges must be visible in order to more easily identify unauthorized personal in the data center.
- All data center visitors must be logged and escorted.
- Offsite backup site security must be reviewed at least annually.
- Backup media inventory must be performed annually at least.
- The following information must be audited
  - All user accesses to cardholder data
  - All actions taken by persons with administrative rights

- All accesses to audit information
- All login attempts
- All changes to system auditing
- Creation and deletion of system objects
- Auditing must include
  - User triggering the event
  - Type of event
  - Date and time of event
  - Success or failure
  - Origination of event
  - Identity of affected data, component, or resource
- All system clocks are in sync.
- Auditing information is secured and cannot be altered.
- Audit trail files are protected from unauthorized viewing and modification.
- Audit trail files are backed up to a centralized log server or media, making it difficult or impossible to modify the audit information.
- Changes to existing log data should trigger an alert to security personal (alert should not be triggered for adding new audit information).
- All logs for intrusion detection systems (IDS), and authentication, authorization and accounting protocol (AAA) servers must be reviewed daily either manually or via an automated process.
- All auditing information must be kept for at least 1 year, with at least 3 months being available for immediate inspection.
- Network layer penetration testing must be performed annually.
- Application layer penetration testing must be performed annually.
- Intrusion detection systems must monitor all network traffic into cardholder systems and alert security personal to suspected compromises.
- File integrity solutions must monitor critical system files, configuration files, and notify personal of unauthorized changes.
- Technology that can compromise security (laptops, WiFi network access, etc) must be approved by company management.
- Copying of cardholder data to local hard drives and removable media is prohibited.
- Employees should review security policies annually.
- All potential employees should be screened prior to hire to minimize risks.

- Policies need to be in place to document personal responses to a security breach. This policy must be tested annually.

Sarbanes—Oxley

The Sarbanes—Oxley Act of 2002 officially known as the Public Company Accounting Reform and Investor Protection Act within the U.S. Senate and the Corporate and Auditing Accountability and Responsibility Act within the U.S. House of Representatives and known as Sarbanes-Oxley, SarBox, or SOX is probably one of the biggest headaches that IT professionals have to deal with today. This legislation was written and passed as a reaction after a number of corporate accounting scandals, including Enron, Tyco International, Adelphia, Peregrine Systems, and WorldCom. The Sarbanes-Oxley act contains 11 titles that range from various responsibilities for corporate executives to criminal penalties for violations. Implementation of the act falls onto the Securities and Exchange Commission (SEC). The SEC adopted dozens of rules in order to implement the Sarbanes-Oxley Act, including the creation of a new semipublic agency called the Public Company Accounting Oversight Board (PCAOB). The PCAOB is tasked with overseeing, regulating, inspecting, and disciplining the accounting firms that fulfill the role of auditors of the public companies that must follow the Sarbanes-Oxley Act.

The overall usefulness of the Sarbanes-Oxley Act has been a nagging question since the first drafts of the act were written. This debate comes from the overall complexity of the act and the cost of implementing the auditing which is required to be in compliance.

The section of the Sarbanes-Oxley Act that is of greatest importance to IT professionals is Section 404, labeled as Assessment of Internal Control, which basically means that management must produce an internal control report annually that documents "the responsibility of management for establishing and maintaining an adequate internal control structure and procedures for financial reporting" as per Title 15, Section 7262, of the United States Code. This report must also "contain an assessment, as of the end of the most recent fiscal year of the Company, of the effectiveness of the internal control structure and procedures of the issuer for financial reporting."

The end result of a Sarbanes-Oxley audit allows for the Chief Executive Officer (CEO) and Chief Financial Officer (CFO) to be able to report to the financial community that the financial systems that store and report on the company's financial data are accurate. In the IT space this accuracy is maintained through proper controls and procedures that ensure that modifications to the systems are made only by trained, approved personal. This includes having proper procedures in place in the event of a systems or location failure so that proper reporting can continue.

Sarbanes-Oxley Checklist

- Is there a Disaster Recovery (DR) plan for each datacenter?
- Is there a Disaster Recovery (DR) plan for each line of business application?
- Are their controls in place preventing users from accessing application data that they shouldn't have access to?
- Ensure that regular audits are in place confirming that physical systems inventory matches purchased inventory.
- All users must have a distinct username that allows them to be identified in all auditing methods. This username must be used to allow any computer system access.
- Ensure that only members of the sysadmin fixed-server role are able to make changes to the accounting or finance databases without using the specified application.
- Ensure that no users are members of the dbo fixed database role on the accounting or finance databases.
- Ensure that no users are members of the sysadmin fixed-server role on the accounting or finance database instances.
- Ensure that all viewing of data is audited within accounting and that finance applications are audited.
- Ensure that all data changes to data within accounting and finance applications are audited.
- Use extended protection between finance and account users and the database servers and application servers to ensure that man-in-the-middle attacks are not successful.
- Ensure that all data change audit information is stored securely and cannot be easily changed.
- Ensure that all data change audit information is reviewed regularly to ensure that only authorized personnel are making changes to the financial systems.
- Ensure that all auditing is fully audited to ensure that changes to auditing specifications are logged with the name of the person who changed the audit and what changes were made.
- Application developers should have no access to production systems using either the line of business application or the database management tools. Any rights granted to developers for troubleshooting purposes should be revoked as soon as the troubleshooting has been completed.

- Development, QA, and Staging databases must not contain customer data, as other employees within the company will have access to these environments. Any customer data that is loaded from production financial or accounting systems must be masked to prevent personnel with access to these systems from gaining access to customer data they should not have access to.
- Database backups of financial and accounting databases must be encrypted before being taken offsite.
- A change control committee must be established with membership of IT management, as well as business stakeholders, to review and approve all changes made to all financial and accounting applications, or any systems solution that affects the financial and accounting applications.
- No changes to any accounting or financial system may be made without management approval as well as approval by a change control committee.
- All changes to financial and accounting systems have been tracked.
- All changes to sysadmin fixed-server role on servers have been approved by management.
- All changes to the Domain Admins domain group have been approved by management.
- All changes to Windows domain groups within sysadmin fixed-server role have been approved by management.
- Members of the Domain Admins domain group should go through background checks prior to employment or promotion.
- Members of the sysadmin fixed-server role or the domain groups that are members of the sysadmin fixed server role should go through background checks prior to employment or promotion.
- Ensure that a high-availability solution has been defined for financial and accounting systems to prevent system outages in the event of system failures.
- Ensure that feeds from line-of-business applications to financial and accounting systems can survive database restores without duplicating data within the financial and accounting systems.
- Personnel who administer development and/or QA systems should not have administrative access to production systems.
- Ensure that changes to the system passwords, including the sa login, are logged via an approved change control processes. The password itself should not be included within the change

control; only the fact that the password has been changed should be included.

- All system passwords should be kept in a secure environment so that should all personell who know the password leave the company at once a member of management can retrieve the passwords if needed. Ideally, they should be written down sealed in a tamperproof envelope that is signed and dated over the seal and placed in a safe or other secure location outside the control of the IT staff. A safe under the control of the Director of Human Resources or the Legal department is a typical location.

Note
So what does all this Really Mean?

The key thing to remember about mechanisms like Sarbanes-Oxley is that the Act isn't so much about dictating specific controls to put into place, but about having plans in place that relate to those controls. The Sarbanes-Oxley Act is about ensuring that the C-level executives (CEO, CIO, COO, etc.) are able to stand up and say that, yes, these numbers are correct, and that the company has policies and procedures established to ensure that these numbers will always be correct.

Those policies and procedures are totally up to the company, as long as the C-level folks feel that they are good enough to keep the company running and keep the financial reports accurate. While these policies and procedures will probably be very long and very complex (they are written by lawyers for lawyers for the most part), the policies and procedures can be very simple. If the official approved company policy is that systems can be changed at will with no documentation, then that's fine, as long as it is the company policy. If the DR policy is that all members of upper management throw their hands into the air and run around like fools singing Ave Maria, then so be it. As long as the executive team feels that they can still say with certainty that the financial reports are accurate, then that is good enough.

Now the odds are that the executive team isn't going to accept upper management throwing their hands into the air and running around like fools singing Ave Maria as an acceptable DR plan. When the executives state that the financial reports are correct, they are doing so under the penalty of federal prison time if it turns out that the reports they certified were incorrect, especially if they knew that the measures that the company took were insufficient to create correct reports. Based on the desire of most, if not all, executives to remain out of federal prison, you probably won't be hearing Ave Maria sung around the office any time soon. If, however, you do, please for the love of god video tape it and post it on YouTube for the rest of us to watch.

HIPPA

The Health Insurance Portability and Accountability Act of 1996 Privacy and Security Rules, also known as HIPPA, was passed in order to ensure that patient medical data is stored in a secure manor and is only accessed by the patient's medical provider for medically relevant reasons. Unlike PCI, which has a clearly defined set of policies, and SOX, which has a loosely defined set of policies, HIPPA is an even looser set of policies. HIPPA provides some very basic guidelines that must be interpreted by the auditor and the administrator of the system in order to determine whether the system meets the privacy requirements of the act.

HIPPA Checklist

- Audit all data reads no matter how data is read, within the application or within the database engine directly.
- Audit all data changes no matter how changes are made.
- All users must have a distinct username that allows them to be identified in all auditing methods. This username must be used to allow any computer system access.
- Ensure that only members of the sysadmin fixed-server role are able to make changes to the patient data without using the specified application.
- Ensure that no users are members of the dbo fixed database role of the patient data databases.
- Ensure that no users are members of the sysadmin fixed-server role of the patient data instances.
- Ensure that employee work areas are set up in such a way as to prevent people from standing behind the employee viewing patient data without authorization.
- All paper records should be secured, preventing unauthorized access to records.
- All paper records that contain patient data set to be discarded must be shredded using a cross-cut shredder or pulped allowing for the total destruction of all data.
- Database backup patient data databases must be encrypted before being taken offsite.
- Ensure that all auditing is fully audited to ensure that changes to auditing specifications are logged with the name of the person who changed the audit, and what changes were made.
- Application developers should have no access to production systems using either the line of business application or the database management tools. Any rights granted to developers for troubleshooting purposes should be revoked as soon as the troubleshooting has been completed.
- Development, QA, and Staging databases must not contain customer data, as other employees within the company will

have access to these environments. Any customer data that is loaded from production systems must be masked to prevent personnel with access to these systems from gaining access to customer data they should not have access to. This includes randomly masking patient identifiers, names, diagnoses information, etc.

- Any patient data transmitted over an insecure network, such as the Internet, must be encrypted before transmission over the insecure network.
- All changes to sysadmin fixed-server role on servers have been approved by management.
- All changes to Domain Admins domain group have been approved by management.
- All changes to Windows domain groups within sysadmin fixed-server role have been approved by management.
- Members of the Domain Admins domain group should go through background checks prior to employment or promotion.
- Members of the sysadmin fixed-server role or the domain groups which are members of the sysadmin fixed-server role should go through background checks prior to employment or promotion.
- Ensure that changes to the system passwords including the sa login are logged via an approved change control processes. The password itself should not be included within the change control; only the fact that the password has been changed should be included.
- All system passwords should be kept in a secure environment so that should all personnel who know the password leave the company at once a member of management can retrieve the passwords if needed. Ideally, they should be written down sealed in a tamperproof envelope that is signed and dated over the seal and placed in a safe or other secure location outside the control of the IT staff. A safe under the control of the Director of Human Resources or the Legal Department is a typical location.

The Health Insurance Portability and Accountability Act of 1996 Privacy and Security Rules isn't supposed to secure systems, but it is designed to protect patient medical data from people who aren't authorized to view that data. Much of HIPPA is about training personnel to ensure that they follow the procedures so that they don't violate the act, which should be followed up with technical procedures that can be used to audit that the act is being followed.

Story Time
HIPPA Means Business

In March 2008 several medical professionals lost their jobs and probably ended their careers in the process when they took it upon themselves to access the medical records of Britney Spears. In January 2008 Ms. Spears was put on a 72-hour psychiatric hold at UCLA Medical Center in Los Angeles after she was deemed to be threat to herself or others as defined under Section 5150 of the California Welfare and Institutions Code.

Apparently, at some point after Ms. Spears was admitted at least 19 hospital personnel accessed her medical records without a medical need. UCLA reported that 13 of these people had their employment with the facility terminated and 6 others were suspended. Fortunately for UCLA and unfortunately for the medical professionals, UCLA's IT systems were designed to track this access and report on potential problems. The termination of these employees shows the seriousness with which HIPPA violations should be taken by employees and the people who design these systems.

Summary

Although the checklists in this appendix aren't perfect, they will get you past most auditors. Every auditor has a different checklist when performing a compliance audit; this is one of the reasons that these audits can be so difficult to deal with. In putting together these checklists, a great deal of research was done to give companies the greatest chance of passing these audits the first time instead of having to be re-audited. Typically, these audits are very expensive to conduct, and being able to avoid a re-audit can save much more than it would cost to go through this checklist in advance.

References

Carr, Jim. "Breach of Britney Spears patient data reported—SC Magazine US." *IT Security News and Security Product Reviews—SC Magazine US.* N.p., March 19, 2008. Web. October 9, 2010. http://www.scmagazineus.com/breach-of-britney-spears-patient-data-reported/article/108141.

INDEX